Modern Rhythmic Gymnastics

Andrea Bodo Schmid
Olympic Gold Medalist

Professor of Physical Education
California State University, San Francisco

Mayfield Publishing Company

Copyright © 1976 by Andrea Bodo Schmid
First edition 1976

All rights reserved. No portion of this book may be reproduced in any form or by any means without written permission of the publisher.

Library of Congress Catalog Card Number: 75-21074
International Standard Book Number: 0-87484-280-8

Manufactured in the United States of America
Mayfield Publishing Company
285 Hamilton Avenue, Palo Alto, California 94301

This book was set in Souvenir Light by Computer Typesetting Services and was printed and bound by the George Banta Company. Sponsoring editor was C. Lansing Hays, Carole Norton supervised editing, Sandra Sailer was manuscript editor, and Michelle Hogan supervised production. Book design was by Nancy Sears and illustrations were by Lynn C. Thomson. Cover design was by Ireta Cooper.

Contents

Introduction ix

1 History of Modern Rhythmic Gymnastics   1

    Competitive Modern Rhythmic Gymnastics   5
    Modern Rhythmic Gymnastics in the United States   8

2 The Basics: Accompaniment for Exercises, Exercises Without Hand Apparatus   10

    Accompaniment for Exercises   11
    Preparatory Exercises   14

        Movements for Arms   15
        Movements for Legs   21
        Movements for the Trunk   26
        Movements for Relaxing   32

Dance Movements   33

      Fundamental Locomotor Movements   33
      Dance Steps   35
      Jumps and Leaps   37
      Balances   43
      Turns   45
      Rolls   49

Teaching Suggestions   51
Competitive Rules   52

      Examples of Difficulties   53

Composition   54

---

3 Balls   57

Equipment   57
Techniques   58
Movements   60

      Throwing and Catching Movements   60
      Bouncing Movements   69
      Rolling Movements   79
      Swinging Movements   87
      Balancing Movements   93
      Movements with Two Balls   95

Teaching Suggestions   98
Competitive Rules   99

      Examples of Difficulties   100

Composition   101
Group Exercises   103

      Floor Pattern Examples   103
      Exchange Examples   104
      Suggested Group Assignment   105

4 Ropes   108

Equipment 109
Techniques 109
Movements 110

    Jumping Movements 110
    Swinging Movements 127
    Wrapping Movements 137
    Balancing Movements 139
    Tossing and Catching Movements 141

Teaching Suggestions 145
Competitive Rules 147

    Examples of Difficulties 147

Composition 148
Group Exercises 152

    Floor Pattern Examples 153
    Exchange Examples 154
    Suggested Group Assignment 155

5 Hoops   158

Equipment 158
Techniques 159
Movements 162

    Swinging Movements 163
    Turning Movements 172
    Circling Movements 176
    Throwing and Catching Movements 184
    Rolling Movements 191
    Jumping Movements 197

Teaching Suggestions 201

Competitive Rules   201

    Examples of Difficulties   202

Composition   203
Group Exercises   207

    Floor Pattern Examples   207
    Exchange Examples   209
    Suggested Group Assignment   209

---

6 Ribbons   213

Equipment   213
    How to Make Ribbons   214
Techniques   215
Movements   216

    Swinging Movements   217
    Circling Movements   221
    Figure-Eight Movements   225
    Serpentine Movements   228
    Spiral Movements   230
    Throwing and Catching Movements   234

Teaching Suggestions   237
Competitive Rules   238

    Examples of Difficulties   239

Composition   240
Group Exercises   245

    Floor Pattern Examples   245
    Exchange Examples   247
    Suggested Group Assignment   248

---

7 Clubs   252

Equipment   253
Techniques   254

Movements   256

    Swinging Movements   257
    Circling Movements   269
    Throwing and Catching Movements   281
    Clapping Movements   284
    Dropping and Kipping Movements   288

Teaching Suggestions   291
Competitive Rules   292

    Examples of Difficulties   293

Composition   294
Group Exercises   298

    Floor Pattern Examples   299
    Exchange Examples   300
    Suggested Group Assignment   301

---

8 Wands, Flags, and Scarves   305

Wands   305

    Swinging Movements   306
    Circling Movements   311
    Throwing and Catching Movements   311
    Turning Movements   315
    Jumping Movements   318
    Combination   320

Flags   321

    Swinging Movements   322
    Circling Movements   325
    Throwing and Catching Movements   326
    Combination   328

Scarves   331

    Swinging Movements   331
    Serpentine Movements   334
    Throwing and Catching Movements   335

Combination 338
Suggested Group Assignment for Scarves 341

9 Guidelines for Planning an MRG Unit — 344

Factors to Consider When Planning a Unit 344
Teaching Methods 347

10 Modern Rhythmic Gymnastic Competition — 357

Rules for Competition 357
Organizing an MRG Meet 361

Glossary — 372

Bibliography — 376

Introduction

Modern rhythmic gymnastics is a challenging and exciting feminine sport. It is rapidly gaining popularity with both spectators and participants. This sport offers total physical exercise, grace and beauty of movement, creativity, and self expression. It teaches appreciation of an art form of physical movement and provides enjoyment and aesthetic satisfaction.

This book has been written to be used by teachers, coaches, and students interested in modern rhythmic gymnastics, from the novice to the most advanced competitor. It includes basic dance movements and skills and movement combinations with all hand apparatus. The combinations help show the need for continuity and movement flow so necessary in this sport. Sequence illustrations are used to depict nearly every movement. The drawings show the perfect technique, style, and amplitude which should be the aim of every gymnast.

Each of the movement chapters has sections on technique, teaching suggestions, individual and group compositions, and competitive rules and offers suggestions for problem-solving group assignments. Each group assignment is accompanied by sheet music arranged especially for that assignment. Chapter 1 presents a short historical overview, chapters 9 and 10 offer guidelines for program planning, meet organization, and general judging procedures.

The author hopes that this book will be of valuable assistance to the development of modern rhythmic gymnastics in this country.

History of Modern Rhythmic Gymnastics

Chapter 1

Modern competitive rhythmic gymnastics developed from rhythmic gymnastics and dance gymnastics, which in turn emerged from natural gymnastics. Many individuals and schools have influenced the evolution of competitive modern rhythmic gymnastics. It would be impossible to refer to all of them in this brief historical sketch. Therefore, only the most influential persons and schools will be mentioned.

Natural gymnastics arose in the eighteenth century from an attempt to formulate a system of gymnastic exercises based on natural body movements. This form of gymnastics was greatly influenced by French philosopher Jean Jacques Rousseau's (1712–1778) theories of natural child development. Germany was the first country to put Rousseau's naturalistic philosophy into practice. This was done at Dessau in the Philanthropinum founded by Johann Basedow (1723–1790) in 1774. In Basedow's school, physical education emphasized a back-to-nature approach.

The Schnepfenthal Educational Institute, established in 1785 by Christian Salzmann (1744–1811), was modeled on Basedow's Philanthropinum. Johann Guts Muths (1759–1839), who is known as the grandfather of gymnastics, taught in this institute for over fifty years. Guts Muths, whose influence on the development of gymnastics was far reaching, was the first physical educator to write several books on gymnastics. His books were translated and used in many countries. In his books he emphasized that gymnastics should be enjoyable and that the exercises should develop the whole individual.

At the beginning of the nineteenth

century the great Swiss educational reformer Johann Heinrich Pestalozzi (1746-1827), who was deeply influenced both by Rousseau's writings and by the educational theories of ancient Greece, stressed that education is a method that encourages natural individual development through experiences—that the aim of education is to help the individual to develop all capacities of his mind and body into a well proportioned and harmonious personality.

Both Rousseau's and Pestalozzi's theories tremendously influenced the ideas of education and hence the development of natural movements in gymnastics. Natural education recognized individual differences and stressed that learning must be individualized.

Per Henrik Ling (1776-1839), the founder of Swedish gymnastics, classified exercises according to their functions, namely: pedagogical, military, medical, and aesthetic. However, he never cultivated aesthetic gymnastics; this was left to be developed by more modern educators.

In the second quarter of the nineteenth century François Delsarte (1811-1871) developed a system of gymnastics in France for the purpose of helping actors develop natural poses and expressive gestures to use in acting. The Delsarte system of gestures was never meant to be a system of gymnastics. Nevertheless, his system became a very popular form of women's gymnastics in the late nineteenth century because it emphasized grace and poise, and did much to develop a healthy body. The Delsarte system brought two new qualities into gymnastic movements, namely: aesthetic and expressive. This system was introduced to the United States by Delsarte's American student, Geneviève Stebbins, who opened the Geneviève Stebbins' School of Expression in New York City. Mrs. Stebbins believed that natural expression is the highest form of gymnastics. She created her own system of gymnastics by combining the Delsarte system with the Swedish Ling exercises. Her aim was to train the body as an effective instrument able to be used for graceful artistic expression. Although her system lost its appeal in the United States in the early twentieth century, in Europe, through the work of her pupils, the Stebbins method had a strong influence on the development of modern feminine gymnastics and modern dance.

Meanwhile, eurhythmics, described as a system of muscular and musical instruction that later became known as rhythmic gymnastics, was devised by the Swiss educator, Jacques Dalcroze (1865-1950), who was a professor of Harmony at the Geneva Conservatory of Music. He created his varied exercises to develop the musical sensitivity of the student through natural body movement. He opened two training schools for eurhythmics teachers—the first in 1911 in Germany, and a few years later another in Geneva, Switzerland. Many of those who laid foundations for modern rhythmic gymnastics studied in his schools and have been greatly influenced by his famous system of eurhythmics or rhythmic gymnastics.

Rudolf Bode (1881–1970) of Germany was a pioneer of rhythmic gymnastics. Bode, who was a teacher of music and a graduate of the Dalcroze Eurhythmic Institute, is well known for his creative work in dance and for his expressionistic gymnastics. In Munich in 1911 he established a school for teachers of gymnastics, music, and dance.

Bode derived many of his ideas from Dalcroze, although he disagreed with Dalcroze's belief that rhythm related only to music. Bode believed that human movement has a rhythm of its own and stressed that the principle of moving to a rhythm is found in natural rhythms within the body such as the pulse rate and the respiratory rate. The way of moving would then correspond to the body's own rhythm in which there is a forceful tension (contraction) phase followed by a relaxation phase. Thus, a rhythmic type of movement is one which is performed with the least amount of tension and surges throughout the entire body as alternating contraction and relaxation occur. The aim of this movement training was to develop a natural total-body movement.

Bode was also inspired by the ideas of Pestalozzi, who believed that free, natural movements develop the whole individual. Pestalozzi considered rhythmic gymnastics to be an art of natural expression of the entire man—body, mind, and soul.

Hinrich Medau (1890–) was another student of the Dalcroze system. Medau is a teacher of music and physical education and a graduate of the Bode School of Gymnastics. In 1929 he opened a school in Berlin and after the second World War he moved his famous Medau Schule to Coburg where it is still in operation today. Medau devised a system of gymnastics for girls and women which he claims produces health, good posture, and grace. Medau emphasizes natural total-body movement in his work. He believes that rhythmic gymnastics can offer an increased awareness of joy and aesthetics in movement.

Medau is also well known for his work with balls, hoops, and clubs in rhythmic gymnastics. He found that the student's concentration on using hand apparatus makes her less self-conscious and allows her movements to be more relaxed and natural. Because Medau believes that music is a very important factor in developing rhythm and expression in movement, he uses music in both training and in public performances.

Influenced by developments in movement education in Germany, Miss Elli Björksten (1870–1947), a teacher of gymnastics at Helsinki University, was the first Scandinavian to develop a new gymnastics program for girls and women. She believed that the Ling system of gymnastics was dull, rigid, and formal. She also felt that purely mechanical gymnastics exercises do not affect the whole person and cannot release people from their inhibitions. Her aim in gymnastics was to do more than merely provide exercises for health; her system was designed to free people's minds, bodies, and spirits from tensions and inhibitions —to create "harmonious" individuals. Björksten's work had a great influence in other Scandinavian countries.

In Sweden, Elin Falk (1872–1942) and Maja Carlquist (1884–1968) sought a new approach to Ling's principles of gymnastic exercises. They developed a freer, more natural type of gymnastics. In addition to free exercise movements (calisthenics), rhythmic gymnastics with hand apparatus has also been highly developed in all Scandinavian countries, where partner and group rhythm work is emphasized.

Most gymnastics leaders in Scandinavia promoted their work through team performances abroad. The most famous exhibition teams are the "Sofia girls," the "Idla girls," and the "Malmo girls," all from Sweden. These teams are renowned for their excellent work in rhythmic gymnastics with and without hand apparatus. Their ball gymnastics is probably the most refined. The Swedish girls showed their superiority in ball gymnastics at the 1952 Olympic Games, where their harmonized total-body movements and the high level of skill displayed in intricate techniques with the ball won the team a gold medal. The Malmo girls with their unique ball routine were unofficially named the best group at the Gymnaestrada in Vienna in 1965.

Concurrently with the development of rhythmic gymnastics a movement for natural dancing gained momentum under the creative efforts of Isadora Duncan, Rudolf Laban, and Mary Wigman.

Isadora Duncan (1878–1927), a famous American dancer who achieved world-wide acclaim during the late nineteenth and early twentieth centuries, rejected the artificial conventional methods of ballet. She believed that movement should be natural. Experimenting with body movements she concluded that all exercises were derived from natural movements such as running, skipping, and jumping. Her theories of dance were influenced by the ideas of Rousseau, Delsarte, and Dalcroze. She created a new style of free and natural movement for personal expression.

Rudolf Laban (1879–1958), a German dance teacher, advocated "absolute" dance to the extent of discarding all musical accompaniment. He believed that since movement is the substance of dance, dance should be movement alone. He developed a system of movement writing called Labanotation, which helps the dancer understand the rhythmical aspects of movement. Laban also made many other contributions to the development of natural dance.

Mary Wigman (1886–1973), a leading dance teacher in Germany who has had immeasurable influence on contemporary dance, was a student of Dalcroze and Laban. She created her own system of dance technique. She believed in simplicity, naturalness, and artistry in movement education. Her school became internationally well known for her technique of movement training.

Although the teaching methods and techniques of the above-mentioned pioneer teachers varied, they all shared a belief in the value of natural, total-body movement and the rhythmic flow of motion and fought against artificial movements.

COMPETITIVE MODERN RHYTHMIC GYMNASTICS

Modern rhythmic gymnastics developed from rhythmic gymnastics and dance. The name *modern* was given to this new sport to show that, although it had been invented, developed, and adapted from various sources, it is new and it has its own characteristics.

Group rhythmic gymnastics with hand apparatus has been used in team competition by women in the Olympic Games and the World Championships. The members of the group, however, were required to compete in apparatus gymnastics also, namely: uneven bars, balance beam, vaulting, and floor exercise. In 1956, the Federation of International Gymnastics (F.I.G.) decided to exclude group rhythmic routines from international competition. After the 1956 Olympic Games, Berthe Villancher of France, Valérie Nagy Herpich of Hungary, and other leaders of women's gymnastics, believed that this area of gymnastics is very important and that it should be developed into an internationally recognized competitive sport.

Modern rhythmic gymnastics started as an independent competitive feminine sport in Russia in the early 1950s. This new sport, which developed grace, poise, and femininity in the performer, gained popularity in Eastern European countries where it was called "Artistic Gymnastics" because it was considered an art of self expression through movements. Each year in the U.S.S.R., during the "Artistic Weeks" in Riga, Latvia, they include an international modern rhythmic gymnastics competition entitled "Artistic Rhythms." The competitors, instead of receiving medals, are awarded with paintings, statues, and ceramics, previously shown in the exhibit. In addition, the participating artists in the "Artistic Weeks" select a "Miss Rhythm." The title *Miss Rhythm* is awarded to the girl whom these artists judge moves the most harmoniously, aesthetically, and artistically and not necessarily to the winner of the meet. For example, in 1972 Mária Patocska of Hungary, who has competed in all of the World Championships and has been consistently able to hold her place among the best, was elected as "Miss Rhythm" but placed only fourth in the all around competition.

Modern rhythmic gymnastics became recognized as an independent sport by the Federation of International Gymnastics during its 41st congress held in Prague in June 1962. The first test of this new competitive sport was the first World Championships held in Budapest, Hungary, in 1963. Twenty-eight contestants from ten European countries participated in the meet. Each nation was allowed to enter three individuals. Many different styles were represented in this meet: Laban, Bode, ballet, and others. No rules had been developed and the judges mostly followed the rules of apparatus or Olympic gymnastics which is now called artistic gymnastics. In addition to all these initial problems, the F.I.G. christened this new international sport "Modern Gymnastics" and decided that every two years they would sponsor a world championship.

The second World Championships were conducted in 1965 in Prague, Czechoslovakia. In order to unify opinions and ideas as to how to evaluate the routines, an international judge's clinic was called by the F.I.G. three months before the Championships. The F.I.G. Committee of Women at this meeting set the direction of this new sport: Modern Gymnastics is neither ballet nor modern dance; it has a style of its own. It is a sport based on natural body movement and self expression. Only individuals competed in the second World Championships. Thirty-two contestants from twelve countries participated in four events which consisted of one compulsory exercise without hand apparatus and three optional exercises—rope, ball, and without hand apparatus. The compulsory exercise without hand apparatus was intended to indicate the direction and style Modern Gymnastics should take. It also provided a common basis of exercises for all contestants. The Czechoslovakian women at this time had successfully combined total body movement with ballet technique in their flowing rhythmical routines. Their success in this meet (first, third, and fourth places) indicated that this would be the direction modern gymnastics would go.

The third World Championships were held in Copenhagen, Denmark, in November, 1967. Thirty-nine competitors from fourteen countries participated. In addition to individual competition, team competition was included for the first time. Eleven groups competed. The individual and team competitions were held separately. An individual could enter either individual or team competition, or both. Thus, each nation could enter three individuals each of whom did four routines: one compulsory rope exercise and three optional exercises—with rope, hoop, and without hand apparatus. In addition each nation could also enter a six-girl team with a hoop routine.

After the third World Championship a Commission for Modern Gymnastics was formed within the F.I.G. The commission, which started its work in 1968, established the international competitive and judging rules for modern gymnastics. The commission approved three hand apparatus exercises—ball, hoop, and rope—for international competition, and clarified the difficulties of and specific techniques for each of these hand apparatus exercises. They drew up penalties for possible faults and listed the elements necessary for composition.

The fourth World Championships were held in Varna, Bulgaria, in 1969. Fifteen groups participated with a ball routine and forty-four gymnasts represented seventeen countries. This was the last meet in which exercises without hand apparatus were included because they had become too theatrical. This was the first time that the United States sent a delegate to observe the meet and participate in the judge's training sessions. After the meet, the F.I.G. Modern Gymnastics Commission convened and further developed judging rules and the list of difficulties. The International Gymnastics Federation then published the Commission's deliberations in the 1970 Code of Points—Modern Gymnastics.

In the fifth World Championships in Havana, Cuba, in 1971, a new hand apparatus was introduced with the compulsory ribbon routine. In addition, the gymnasts participated in three optional routines—ball, hoop, and rope. The team competition was conducted with three balls and three hoops. In this meet, participation decreased due to the geographical location of Cuba—because of the distance, many countries could not afford to send gymnasts. Three countries, however, participated in these World Championships for the first time: Canada, Mexico, and New Zealand.

In 1972, the F.I.G. changed the name of this new sport from Modern Gymnastics to Modern Rhythmic Gymnastics and submitted a request to the International Olympic Committee (I.O.C.) for the admission of modern rhythmic gymnastics to the program of the Olympic Games. At that time the I.O.C. refused to accept modern rhythmic gymnastics as an Olympic discipline. It is expected, however, to be included in the program of the 1980 Olympic Games in Moscow because many influential people on the I.O.C. attended the 1973 World Championships and saw for themselves the true value of this sport and the beauty and sportive character of the competition.

The sixth Championships took place in Rotterdam, Holland, in 1973. For the first time the United States was represented—by two gymnasts. Clubs, another new hand apparatus, were introduced with a compulsory routine. In addition the gymnasts had to demonstrate three optional routines with the ball, hoop, and ribbon. The six-girl team competition was conducted with the rope. This championship meet had the largest number of participants: eighteen teams and sixty-three girls in the four-event competition.

In 1975 the Commission for Modern Rhythmic Gymnastics became an independent committee. The members agreed unanimously that the name "Modern Rhythmic Gymnastics" would be changed to "Rhythmic

Sportive Gymnastics" in order to better stress the competitive character of the sport.

The seventh championship was held in Spain in 1975. The Committee for Modern Rhythmic Gymnastics decided not to add more apparatus to the international program of modern rhythmic gymnastics. They also decided not to use compulsory routines since the style has been established. Therefore, the 1975 World Championships included group exercises for six gymnasts with three balls and three ropes, as well as individual competition with ball, hoop, ribbon, and clubs.

Competitive modern rhythmic gymnastics have progressed very favorably in two essential respects: (1) at the technical level and (2) with regard to the number of participants. More and more nations have initiated programs for girls in modern rhythmic gymnastics and have begun to participate in the international competitions. The technique of handling hand apparatus has become more demanding with each World Championship.

MODERN RHYTHMIC GYMNASTICS IN THE UNITED STATES

Under the leadership of Mrs. Mildred Prchal, chairman of the Modern Rhythmic Gymnastics Committee of the United States Gymnastics Federation (U.S.G.F.), this new competitive sport was introduced in the United States. She prepared compulsory routines for beginning students which were published by the U.S.G.F. in 1969. She held the first Modern Gymnastics Workshop at Sokol Woodlands, Barryville, New York, in the summer of 1970. The workshop was designed to provide training in and knowledge about the field of modern gymnastics for women physical education teachers in colleges, high schools, gymnastics clubs, and organizations. Approximately thirty instructors from throughout the United States spent a week in a workshop learning the basic elements of performing and teaching this new sport, the compulsory routines to be used in the United States, and the construction and evaluation of optional exercises. The participants in this workshop became the leaders in the development of modern gymnastics throughout the nation.

The First National Modern Rhythmic Gymnastics Competition was held at George Williams College, Downers Grove, Illinois, in May 1973. This meet was conducted for the purpose of selecting individuals to represent the United States in the sixth World Championships in Holland. Seventeen gymnasts entered the meet which included three optional routines—ribbon, hoop, and exercise without hand apparatus.

In the 1974 National Championship a total of twenty-one gymnasts entered the competition in Chicago. Gymnasts from California, Nevada, New York, New Jersey, and Illinois participated in the meet. The competition included, for the first time, group exercises with rope and individual routines with ball, ribbon, and rope. The skill of the competitors in the second national meet far exceeded those who participated in the first competition.

Before the second National Championship the first modern rhythmic gymnastics judging clinic was sponsored by the United States Gymnastics Federation, under the leadership of Mildred Prchal, in order to develop judges in this sport. The three-day clinic was conducted by Mme. Kveta Cerna of Czechoslovakia, a member of the F.I.G. Modern Rhythmic Gymnastics Commission. Several participants in the clinic qualified to become judges for modern rhythmic gymnastics and were chosen to serve as judges in the second national competition with Mme. Cerna acting as a referee.

Compulsory routines in modern rhythmic gymnastics for beginning, intermediate, and advanced gymnasts, compiled by Mildred Prchal, were published in 1974. The beginning exercises are basic and short enough to be presented during regular physical education classes. They provide a foundation for competitive modern rhythmic gymnastics. The intermediate compulsory exercises build upon the beginning routines and are a little more demanding. The advanced exercises are patterned after the current international style so that talented gymnasts are exposed to the latest competitive movements and combinations. These compulsory routines are designed to develop competitive modern rhythmic gymnastics at all levels in the United States.

The television coverage of the Expo '74 (Spokane, Washington) gymnastics program included modern rhythmic gymnastics. The performers were the Russian modern rhythmic gymnastics team members including the 1973 World Champion, Miss Shugurova. This program introduced this beautiful new sport to many Americans.

The United States Gymnastics Federation sponsored a Russian Gymnastics Tour throughout the country in the fall of 1974. The best Olympic champions, such as Olga Korbut, and many top modern rhythmic gymnasts participated in the performances. As a result of these exhibitions many people have begun to appreciate this new competitive sport which develops total body movement, grace, poise, femininity, and self expression in the woman performer. Hopefully, the visits of the Russian team and the United States' participation in the 1973 and 1975 World Championships will help this new sport continue to grow in the United States.

The Basics: Accompaniment for Exercises, Exercises Without Hand Apparatus

Chapter **2**

Exercises without hand apparatus are the fundamentals of modern rhythmic gymnastics. The committee for Modern Rhythmic Gymnastics of the International Federation of Gymnastics (F.I.G.) recognized this and included this event in the developmental stages of this sport. In the first four Modern Rhythmic Gymnastics World Championships it was a part of the program either as a compulsory or optional exercise. After the fourth World Championship, exercises without hand apparatus were omitted from the International Modern Rhythmic Gymnastics competitions because of their susceptibility to dramatic or theatrical expression. Modern rhythmic gymnastics is a sport in which neither a story nor an idea should be expressed through physical movements. It should be expressive only insofar as to show satisfaction in the movement itself and understanding of the melody or music.

Many nations, including the United States, still include exercises without hand apparatus in their developmental modern gymnastics program because they serve as preparation for routines with hand apparatus. These exercises teach the gymnast how to move naturally, gracefully and harmoniously to music. There should be a close relationship between the gymnast's movements and the music. The melody and dynamics of the music should determine the form of the gymnast's movements.

Exercises without hand apparatus should develop good posture, strength, flexibility, balance, and coordination. They should also develop a knowledge and appreciation of the fundamentals of music such as meter and accent, as they relate to movement. They should help the gymnast to move with freedom. In other words, the exercises should develop the whole body, increase limberness and flexibility in all joints, and improve the gymnast's sense of movement and feeling of rhythm.

The exercises without hand apparatus might be called choreographed dances. Dance plays an important part in modern rhythmic gymnastics. Ballet is the foundation of good leg techniques. Modern dance background is also desirable for the understanding of total body movement and for learning the correct use of one's hips and trunk. However, the general style of the exercise in modern rhythmic gymnastics should neither be ballet nor modern dance. As a result none of the existing dance training methods suits the modern gymnast's need perfectly. Therefore, the gymnastics instructor must select the right exercises from ballet and modern dance to develop a dance training system for the gymnasts.

It is not the purpose of this book to include all of the ballet and modern dance skills that can be used in modern rhythmic gymnastics, but rather to give a few illustrations so that the reader can see the relationship between ballet, modern dance, and rhythmic gymnastics.

ACCOMPANIMENT FOR EXERCISES

Because modern rhythmic gymnastics exercises demand accompaniment of some type, gymnasts must work with music from the beginning of their training. The music should be light and lively music that the gymnast enjoys moving to. A teacher who has a good pianist is lucky because it is most enjoyable to work with live piano accompaniment. Unfortunately, very few clubs or schools in the United States have a pianist.

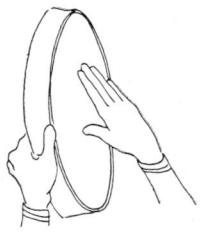

There are, however, many good records available for modern rhythmic gymnastics and for dance and rhythmic activities. Some of these records include an instruction booklet for specific activities, such as rope jumping, while others contain short selections marked with the type of movement for which the music was designed. In addition the teacher may use folk dance records such as schottisches, polkas, and czardas as well as other music selections with good rhythm.

A hand drum is also very suitable for establishing rhythm for modern rhythmic gymnastic movements. It may be struck with the fingers, with the lower part of the thumb or with a drumstick. The drumstick should be held lightly with the thumb, index, and middle fingers, with the other two fingers just resting on the stick. If the drumhead can be adjusted,

it should be tightened before the lesson and loosened after. Experiment with the drum to find what tones can be produced by striking it in different areas. Beat both the head and the trim either with the wool felt head or with the stick. Practice with both hands. You must learn to strike the drumhead with a steady beat. Your drumming proficiency will improve with practice.

To be able to accompany rhythmic exercises you should feel the rhythmic pattern of the movements. For example, strike the drum in an even tempo at a moderate speed for walking and twice as fast for running. You must, however, use an uneven tempo of long-short beats for skipping and galloping. You may play twice as slowly or twice as fast as the metric beat. You may play the accents only or play the other beats only, omitting the accents.

In order to be a good accompanist with the drum or to be able to select proper music for modern gymnastics you must be able to understand musical notation and some amount of music terminology. You must also understand music with respect to rhythm, accent, tempo, phrasing, and dynamics. Here a few of the basic musical concepts will be explained which should help you to understand music better. Acquaint your students with these musical concepts so they will be able to respond accurately in movement to the music.

In analyzing the structure of music you can find a series of grouped pulsations or *beats*. The beat may be even or uneven and may be fast or slow. Each recurring group of beats is called a *measure* or *bar*. The measures are separated from each other in musical notation by vertical lines or bars. A *double bar* is used to mark the end of a composition or of an important part of it. A *phrase* is a group of measures which expresses an idea. Thus, phrases are simply musical sentences. Each piece of music is divided by melodic and rhythmic punctuations, like a poem. Usually phrases contain four, six, or sixteen measures.

The number of beats in a measure is called the *meter*. There are two important types of meters: duple (with two beats to each measure) and triple (with three beats). Almost all other meters are multiples or combinations of these. For example, a four-beat group (quadruple meter) consists of two groups of two beats. A meter may contain:

Note value	Note symbol	Rest symbol
whole note = 4 beats	𝅝	𝄻
half note = 2 beats	𝅗𝅥	𝄼
quarter note = 1 beat	♩	𝄽
eighth note = ½ beat	♪	𝄾
sixteenth note = ¼ beat	𝅘𝅥𝅯	𝄿

13

*The Basics:
Accompaniment
for Exercises,
Exercises Without
Hand Apparatus*

A whole note represents a single continuous sound which lasts four beats. A half note is only half as long as a whole note. A quarter note is half as long as a half note. This sound lasts only one beat. When we sound eighth notes there are two sounds for each beat. Two sixteenth notes fill the same amount of time as one eighth note.

The *dot* symbol in music shows the rhythmic combination of a note tied to half its own value. For example, a half note can be tied to a quarter note this way: ♩ ♩ . In writing this combination, musicians often shorten the symbol by substituting a dot after the first note. Thus ♩ ♩ becomes ♩. .

When several eighth or sixteenth notes are grouped together musicians make one big hook, called a *beam*, to be shared by all stems. This is easier to write and more legible. For example: instead of writing ♪ ♪ ♪ ♪ , musicians write ♫♫ .

The *time signature* shows the metric division of a measure. The top number of the time signature indicates the number of underlying beats contained in the measure and the bottom number indicates the value of each beat. For example, a time signature of 3/4 means that each measure will have three beats and that each beat will be a quarter note. A piece of music in 3/4 meter need not have the same rhythm of three quarter notes in every measure but the notes in each measure must add up to a value of three quarter notes. For example:

Most dance steps are accented on the first beat. *Accent* can be described as additional force placed on certain beats in a measure. Accent may be shown by a louder tone on the drum.

Tempo refers to the speed of the music. It may vary from fast to slow.

Intensity applies to the force of the music. It may vary from loud to soft.

In written music the composer indicates or marks both the tempo and the intensity of the music by various words. Some words indicating tempo are:

vivace—lively
allegro—fast
moderato—moderate

andante—medium slow
lento—slow

Words indicating the magnitude of the force of the music are:

fortissimo (ff)—very loud
forte (f)—loud
mezzo forte (mf)—medium loud
piano—soft

pianissimo—very soft
crescendo (cresc.)—growing louder
decrescendo (decres.)—growing softer

Very often instead of the word *crescendo*, the sign ⟨ is used and instead of the word *decrescendo*, the mark ⟩ is used to show that the music is gradually increased or decreased in volume.

To increase your musical knowledge, listen to different types of music. Try to feel the beat, perceive the accented beats, identify the phrases, and recognize the variations in style, mood, tempo, and dynamics. This will help you get the feel of the music. It will also help you select the proper music for modern rhythmic gymnastics.

Music chosen for accompaniment of a competitive routine should meet certain requirements. It should be limited to a single musical instrument and should be the required length. Music must also have variety. All types of music may be used but it must be suitable for modern rhythmic gymnastics and should complement the individual style of the gymnast. The music need not be a single composition. A gymnast may use small selections of a larger composition or she may select parts of two or more pieces and combine them tastefully. The musical accompaniment should have a beginning, middle, and end, and should finish in a logical fashion with the end of the exercise. Whenever possible, the music should be composed to fit the temperament and movement of the gymnast.

PREPARATORY EXERCISES

The purpose of these preparatory exercises are: (1) the well balanced development of the muscles and (2) the improvement of flexibility in all joints.

When performing these exercises be sure to stress good posture and form in each movement. In addition, the whole body should be involved in every exercise. The movement should pass through the whole body as if it were a wave flowing from one part of the body to another. The exercises should be performed to music. It is easier to understand the exercise and do it correctly when one follows a rhythm.

The exercises have been divided into movements for the arms, the legs, the trunk, and for relaxation.

MOVEMENTS FOR ARMS

The ability of the gymnast to move her arms with grace is one of the best ways to show elegance in a routine. The arms should move in an aesthetically pleasing way. Unnecessary movements of the hands and arms are very distracting. Therefore, the discipline of balletic arm exercises is very helpful for the gymnast.

Five basic arm positions are used in ballet. Although many ballet schools suggest different positions for the arms, the more commonly used arm positions are those of the French school, and because this system seems to fit best with gymnastic movements, they are included here. In all of the balletic arm positions, the arms should be slightly curved; however, in modern gymnastics the arms may be held slightly curved or straight. The hands and the fingers should be relaxed with the thumb and middle finger brought close together.

In the beginning, arm movements should be practiced separately while standing in a simple ballet position; later, they can be combined with leg movements in order to develop coordination. After the gymnast has learned to control her arm movements she should experiment with various arm styles. Since the arms should move freely from the shoulders, movements that increase flexibility in this area should be included in the program. Also, flexibility exercises for the elbows and wrists will help develop graceful arm movements.

1. Exercises for the Shoulders

This series of exercises should help to develop shoulder flexibility. Sit tailor fashion with arms relaxed.

a) Shrug (lift) the shoulders as high as possible and let them fall relaxed. Repeat.

b) Lift the shoulders high, then forcibly push them downward, holding the arms straight.

c) Circle shoulders forward. Repeat, circling backwards.

d) Keep the left shoulder still and circle the right shoulder forward, then backward. Repeat this exercise with the left shoulder.

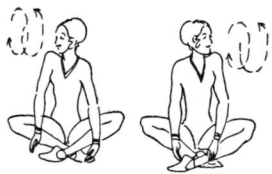

2. Exercises for the Elbows
This series improves elbow flexibility. Sit on the right buttock with both legs bent to the left side, the right arm extended to the side, and the left arm relaxed.

a) Keep the right upper arm still and make circles inward with your lower arm.

b) Do the same as in (a) but circle the lower arm outward.

c) Repeat (a) and (b) with your left arm.

3. Exercises for the Wrists
This series develops wrist flexibility. Stand with arms extended to the side.

a) Do wrist circles forward.

b) Perform wrist circles backward.

c) Raise and lower the wrists. Repeat this several times. Do this exercise in a relaxed rhythmical manner. Do not raise the shoulders.

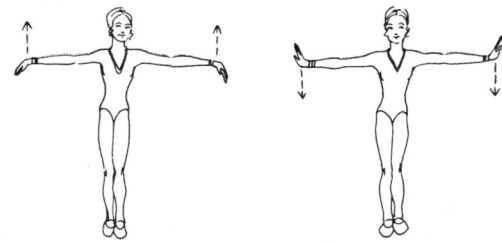

d) Move the wrists in opposite directions—the right goes upward as the left goes downward. Repeat several times.

4. Preliminary Exercise for Curved Arm
Sit on the right hip with both legs bent to the left side and the arms relaxed. Place the right hand on the floor at the right side. Stabilize the hand and shoulder while you move the elbow first outward and then back inward to the original position. This exercise should help you curve your arm gently from the shoulder to the hand. Practice with the left arm also.

5. Five Arm Positions from Ballet
Preparatory position: the arms are slightly rounded and held at the sides with the fingertips just touching the thighs.

First position: the arms form a circle in front of the body about waist high.

side view

18
Modern Rhythmic Gymnastics

Second position: the arms are extended to the sides with a soft line from the shoulders through the fingers.

Third position: one arm is curved above the head while the other is extended to the side.

Fourth position: one arm is curved over the head while the other is curved in front.

side view

Fifth position: both arms are curved around the head slightly in front of the body.

When the arms are raised from one position to another, they must pass through first position. When moving from a high position to a low one, the arms are generally lowered through second position. Transition of arms from one position to another constitutes a *port de bras*. Port de bras exercises can be varied infinitely. Two simple examples are the following:

a) Start in first position, raise the arms chest high and open the arms to the side to second position, turn the palms of the hands down and lower the arms to first position with the wrists leading.

b) Start in first position, raise the arms up to fifth position, carry them out sideways, with the palms of the hands up, to second position, then turn the palms forward and downward and lower the arms back to first position.

6. Arm Swings and Circles
The arms may be swung in frontal, sagittal, diagonal, or horizontal planes. All swings and circles are initiated from the shoulders and should be performed with the arms straight. Both arms may be swung together or they may be swung alternately. Or one arm may be swung at a time. Since clubs, because of their weight, serve as an excellent aid in teaching natural swinging and circling movements, these exercises are described under swinging movements in the chapter on clubs.

7. Arm Waves *(up and down)*
Stand with the arms at the sides. Initiating the movement in the shoulder region, raise the upper arms, the lower arms, and the hands successively sideward and upward; then lower them in a successive motion. Lead the movement with the elbows. Repeat this wavy motion

several times. There should be steady pulsations moving through the arms.

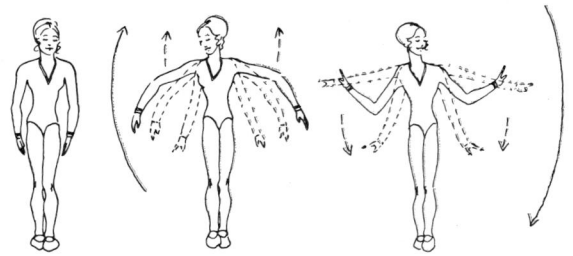

Variations:
a) Do the same exercise but move the arms forward and upward instead of sideward.

b) Start with small arm waves and increase them gradually.

c) Move the arms in opposite directions—one moves upward as the other moves downward.

8. Arm Waves *(in and out)*
Stand with the arms at the sides. Turn the shoulders inward and outward as the arms execute a waving motion. The hands will sketch small figure eights at the sides of the body.

Variations:
a) Do the same movement with the arms extended horizontally forward.

b) Move the arms in opposite directions—one moves outward as the other moves inward.

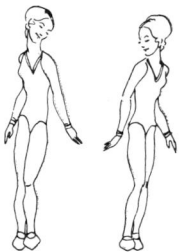

9. Spiral Arm
Stand with the arms extended to the sides. Swing the right arm in front of the body, then bend the right elbow and make a horizontal circle toward the body with the lower arm. Straighten the arm and execute a circle above the head, then return to the starting position. This should

be a continuous spiral movement. Repeat this exercise with the left arm.

Variations:
a) Perform a reverse spiral by reversing the movement described above.
b) Execute a spiral with both arms simultaneously.

MOVEMENTS FOR LEGS

Leg exercises should develop strength for jumps and leaps; flexibility for amplitude in leaps, kicks, and the like; and control for balance. The following ballet movements are the basis for mastery of good leg techniques. In gymnastics it is not necessary to strive for a complete turn out of the legs and feet. Therefore many gymnasts modify the five ballet positions by turning the legs out to a 90° angle. Most of these exercises may be performed either at the barre or in lying or sitting positions. Repeat the exercises four to eight times.

1. Five Leg Positions from Ballet

The footprints of the five ideal ballet positions are illustrated and described below:

First position: the heels are together and the toes are turned outward.

Second position: the heels are separated about one foot, weight distributed equally between the two feet.

Third position: one foot is in front of the other with the heel of the front foot against the instep of the back foot.

Fourth position: one foot is about twelve inches in front of the other.

Fifth position: one foot is in front of the other and the heel of the front foot is against the toes of the back foot.

Transitions from one position to the next are as follows (right side to the barre, right hand on the barre for support, left arm in second position).

First to second: Shift the weight to the right foot and slide the pointed left foot to the side into second position.

Second to third: Shift the weight to the right foot and slide the pointed left foot into third position.

Third to fourth: Shift the weight to the right foot and slide the left toes forward into fourth position.

Fourth to fifth: Shift the weight to the back foot and draw the front foot back into fifth position.

In moving through the five positions it is important to tuck the hips under, pull in the abdomen, keep the buttock muscles tight, lift the rib cage, lower the shoulders, hold the chin erect, and keep the arms relaxed. The weight of the body must be evenly distributed on three points of each foot: the big toe, the little toe, and the heel.

2. Pliés

A *plié* is the bending of the knee or knees. There are two kinds of pliés: *demi-plié* or half bending of the knees and *grand-plié* or full bending of the knees. All demi-pliés are done without lifting the heels from the ground. In grand-pliés the heels rise off the ground in the first, third, and fifth positions. In the second and fourth position the heels remain on the floor. In all pliés the weight of the body must be evenly distributed on both feet. Pliés are important to the gymnast since they are used before and after all jumps and leaps. Pliés enable a gymnast to obtain greater elevation in her jumps. They also help her to work with ease and lightness. Do pliés in all five ballet positions. Also practice them in lying and sitting positions.

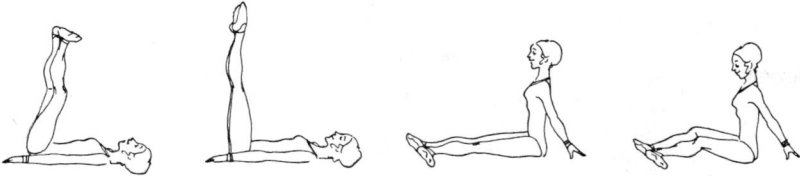

3. Relevé

Rising to the ball of the foot is called a *relevé*. Relevés are important to the gymnast because they will enable her to develop that good balance on her toes which is so important in the execution of turns.

A relevé may be done on two feet or on one foot only. But in all relevés the knees must be kept straight and the buttocks muscles tight. Weight should be on the ball of the foot between the big toe and the third toe—never toward the little toe.

As an exercise in combination with pliés, the relevé serves as a preparation for jumps. The following combination is an example. With the feet in first position, demi-plié (keeping the heels on the floor). Then straighten the knees as you lift the heels and rise to the toes. Lower the heels by bending the knees. Repeat.

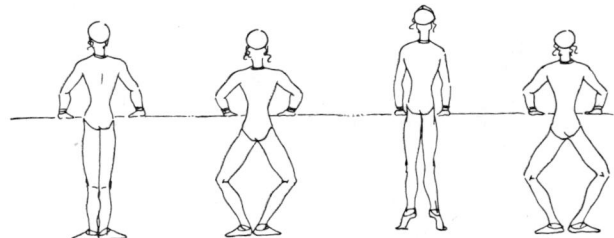

Practice this exercise in the other ballet positions also.

4. Battement Tendu

Battement means kicking of the leg; *tendu* means stretched. The battement tendu assists in developing the entire leg, a good point, and an arch. There are many types of battements, but the most fundamental is the battement tendu. When practicing a battement tendu keep both knees straight at all times, turn the legs out from the hips, and keep the toes on the floor. This may be practiced in first, third, or fifth position.

Stand in fifth position, with the right foot in front. Slide the right foot forward on the floor, then snap it briskly back into the starting position, extend the right leg sideward and close it in back of the left in fifth position; then extend the right leg backward and return to fifth position; slide the leg sideward again and close it in front of the left leg in fifth position. Usually battement tendu is practiced in this way. Repeat this with the left leg.

5. Battement Tendu Jeté

The *battement tendu jeté* is similar to the battement tendu but is done twice as fast and the foot is kicked briskly from the floor to a point forming a 45° angle with the floor. If done correctly, this will develop speed in pointing the feet. Practice this in all three directions: forward, sideward, and backward.

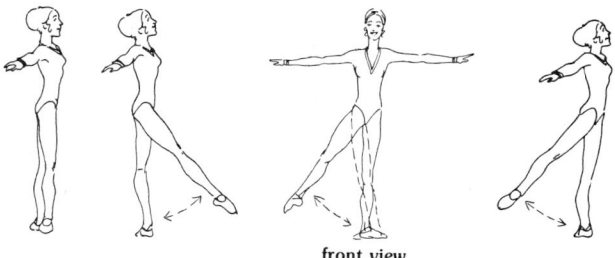

front view

6 Grand Battement

The *grand battement* is a continuation of the battement tendu jeté. Instead of lifting the leg 45°, kick it 90° or higher. The grand battement strengthens and stretches the upper leg muscles, allowing for the greater extension and amplitude which is so important for the gymnast. Follow all the basic rules of the battement tendu jeté when performing the grand battement. Keep both legs straight and rotate them outward from the hip. Keep the torso stationary except during the grand battement in back when you may lean slightly forward. Remember that the foot must arch before it leaves the floor and that the toes touch the floor first and then the heel when the leg comes back to fifth position. Practice grand battements in all three directions: forward, sideward, and backward.

front view

7. Battement Lying on the Back

Lie on the back with the arms raised overhead. Lift the right leg up to 45° a couple of times. Repeat with the left leg. Then try to kick the legs up higher to 90°, 135°, or to an aerial split. Don't be discouraged if this is difficult. Very few gymnasts are able to lift a leg up to 180°. Follow all the basic rules discussed under battement tendu. Lift and lower the straight leg without arching the back.

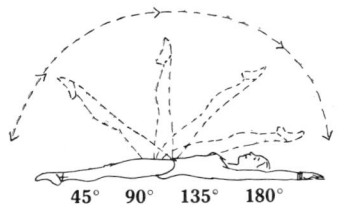
45° 90° 135° 180°

8. Battement Lying on the Side

Do the same exercise as described in exercise 7 above but kick the leg sideward. Rotate the leg outward so that the knee is toward the ceiling.

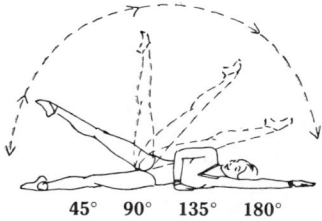
45° 90° 135° 180°

9. Battement Lying Facedown
Lift the left leg directly rearward. Don't turn your hip. Get the feeling of pushing down on the hip to keep it in the correct position. First practice lifting your leg 45°. Only when you can do this, keeping your hip in the correct position, should you try to lift your leg higher. Raise and lower your left leg four to eight times, then repeat with the right leg.

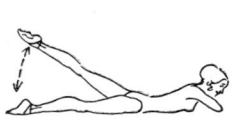

10. Sauté en Première
Sauté en première means jump in first position. Demi-plié in first position, spring into the air, and then land in a demi-plié in first position. Remember, the tips of the toes should touch the floor first, then the sole of the foot followed by the heel. When jumping, the toes leave the floor last.

This exercise will help you to get added lift in your jumps and leaps.

MOVEMENTS FOR THE TRUNK

Modern gymnastics combines ballet with central body movements. A competitive routine must include trunk bending movements and different kinds of body waves. The following exercises will help the gymnast learn these movements. Repeat these exercises four to eight times.

1. Trunk Bending Forward *(in sitting position)*
These exercises should help to develop trunk flexibility forward. Perform the exercises in a slow continuous fashion. Don't bounce up and down.

a) Sit with the legs straight and the arms stretched overhead. Bend forward over the legs. Try to touch the head to the knees.

b) Sit with the legs as far apart as you can, holding the knees straight and the back erect. Lean forward as far as you can, trying to touch the floor with your chest.

c) Sit with the legs spread far apart. Bend forward over the right leg and return to erect position. Then bend forward over the left leg and return to the starting position.

d) Combine the above exercises (a, b, c) into a series.

side view

e) Do all of the above exercises in standing position.

2. Backbend *(in kneeling position)*
Kneel with knees about 10–12 inches apart and hands on hips. Bend backward (starting with head) and try to touch your feet with your head. Return to starting position with the hip, chest, and head following in succession.

Variation:
Do the same exercise with the arms stretched overhead. Start the backbend from the upper back. Try to touch the floor near the toes with the fingers.

3. Backbend *(from standing position)*
Stand with legs apart and the arms stretched overhead. Bend backward, starting with the head. The shoulders, chest, and pelvis follow in

succession. Try to touch the floor with the fingers. Returning to starting position the body should move in a reverse order: pelvis, chest, shoulders, and head.

28
Modern Rhythmic Gymnastics

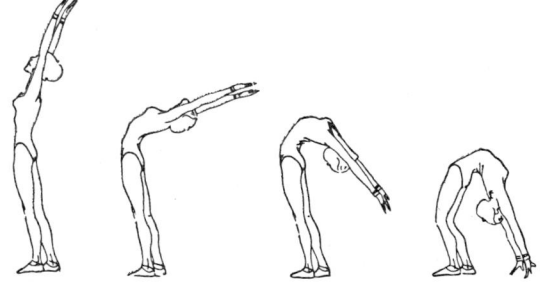

4. Sidebend *(from standing position)*
Stand with right arm stretched overhead, the left arm at the side. Bend to the left side by pushing the pelvis to the right. Repeat this four times and then reverse sides.

5. Sidebend *(in kneeling position)*
Kneel on left knee with the right leg extended to the side and the arms in second position. Bend the trunk to the right side over the right leg as the arms stretch overhead. Then bend the trunk to the left as the right knee bends and weight is placed on the right toe. Arms move to the fourth position with the right arm curved overhead. Repeat, alternating sides.

6. Trunk Circling

Trunk circling is a combination of ways of bending the trunk. Bend the trunk forward, to the right side, backward, and then to the left side. Complete circling of the trunk should be performed continuously and at the same level in all four directions. Trunk bending may be slight (45°) or deep (90-135°).

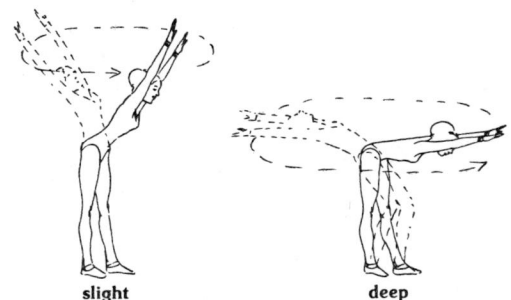
slight   deep

7. Trunk Twisting *(from standing position)*

Stand with the feet apart and the arms extended to the sides. Twist the trunk and bend forward, placing the left hand on the floor in front of you. Come to an upright position and perform the exercise, twisting to the opposite direction.

8. Trunk Twisting *(in sitting position)*

Sit with legs apart and arms extended to the sides. Twist and bend toward the right toe as you raise your arms overhead. Try to touch the floor with the right elbow. Return to starting position and repeat the exercise to the opposite side.

9. Trunk Waves

Trunk waves can be best learned in a kneeling position. Kneel and sit on heels, legs about 8 inches apart and the hands grasping the heels. First push the thighs and the hips forward and upward and then the chest. Then bend the head backward. As the head bends backward, simultaneously push the hip back and sit on the heels, tilting the body forward with a hollow back (the chest leading). Then round the lower back, upper back, and neck in succession. As the head bends forward, simultaneously start to push the hips forward to initiate another trunk wave. Raising, arching, lowering, and curving the trunk should be done in a smooth wave-like manner. This can be achieved only if the vertebrae follow each other one by one from the bottom to the last one in the neck. This exercise is very important when learning to do body waves.

10. Body Wave Backward

Stand with the left foot forward, the right side to the barre, the right hand on the barre for support, and the left hand overhead. Bend the knees slightly, round the back, and bend the head forward to a relaxed starting position. Then push the knees and hips forward and upward, and bend the chest and head backward as the left arm swings down, backward, and up. The knees should bend and straighten at the same time as the spine. Move the knees, hips, chest, and head in a successive wave-like manner.

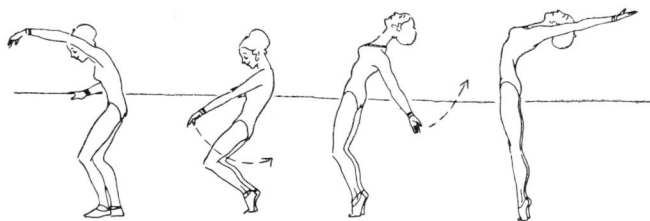

Variations:

a) Do the same exercise without support.

b) Do the same exercise with both arms swinging downward, backward, and up at the sides of the body.

11. Body Wave Forward

Stand with left foot forward and the arms stretched overhead. Tilt the upper back backward while arching the lower back. Return to the starting position by curving and straightening the body as the arms move backward, downward, and upward. Perform the movement in a wave-like manner, with the wave moving through the entire body.

The best way to learn this movement is to start by using only one arm at the barre.

12. Body Wave Sideward

Stand with feet slightly apart and the arms at the sides. Bend the knees to the right, then push the hips sideward and up to the right also. Continue the wave by bending the upper body and the head slightly to the left. Straighten the body as the right arm moves overhead. Practice this to the left side also.

Variations:
a) Do the same movement with the feet together.

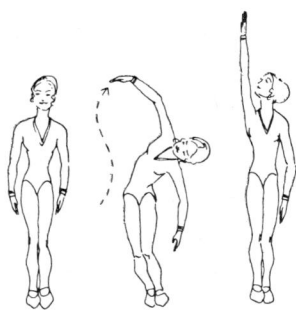

b) Do side body waves alternating sides.

MOVEMENTS FOR RELAXING

Relaxation exercises help the gymnast get rid of undue tensions that restrict freedom of movement. They also help develop an awareness of the natural movements of the body. Two types of relaxation exercises are used in modern rhythmic gymnastics: tension-relaxation and swinging. One example for each will be given.

1. Tension and Relaxation Exercise
Stand with the arms at the sides. Extend the arms overhead, straining all muscles. Then relax the body, letting it fall forward. The arms, head, and shoulders should be completely relaxed. To check whether or not they are relaxed, watch your arms when they fall. They should swing like pendulums with their movements gradually getting smaller and finally stopping.

2. Swinging Exercise
The purpose of this exercise is to develop freedom of the body in a relaxed, swinging type of movement. To achieve this, aim for a free, relaxed movement when performing it. You can tell that there is tension if the hands fail to pass close to the body as they swing.

Stand with the feet parallel and the arms stretched overhead. Swing the arms downward as the legs bend and the trunk falls forward. Continue the arm swing to the rear as the knees straighten. Swing the arms forward to a complete extension of the body (with the arms stretched overhead). Swing the arms freely, using them to help the trunk drop downward and swing upward. The trunk and knees should bend and stretch, conforming to the motion. Repeat the exercise several times in a uniform rhythm.

DANCE MOVEMENTS

The Basics: Accompaniment for Exercises, Exercises Without Hand Apparatus

The following are a few of the more common dance movements used in modern rhythmic gymnastics. Apply to these dance movements the basics learned through the preparatory exercises. For example, when you do a turn think about the relevé learned at the barre and remember to rise to the balls of your feet, keeping the legs straight, the buttocks tight, the back straight, and the hips over the feet. Incorporate many of these dance movements into every modern rhythmic gymnastics class.

FUNDAMENTAL LOCOMOTOR MOVEMENTS

1. Walking Step
Step from one foot to the other with the toes pointed and the feet slightly turned outward. Swing the arms freely from the shoulders in opposition to the feet. Keep the body erect and focus straight ahead at eye level. Practice walking in various directions.

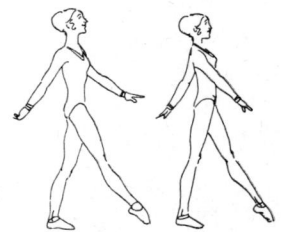

2. Running Step
The running step is similar to the walking step but is done faster and both feet are momentarily off the floor. There are many different running steps used in gymnastics. One may run with large steps; one may run bending the legs to the rear; and so on. Combine different arm movements with running steps.

3. Hopping
The hopping step is a spring from one foot landing on the same foot.

4. Skipping

The *skip* is a series of fast step-hops taken with alternate feet. It has an uneven rhythm. The hop has one-half or one-third the time value of the step.

5. Slide

The *slide* in gymnastics is referred to as a glissade or chassé. They all have the same movement principle: one leg chases the other out of its position. They also have the same rhythmic pattern which is identical to that of the skip.

The glissade is done close to the floor and is usually used to link other steps. For example: glissade, tour jeté.

The chassé is usually performed with a slight spring.

Both of these movements can be executed in all directions.

6. Gallop

The gallop is an exaggerated slide. It is a series of step-close-steps forward with the same foot leading. Keep the legs straight and the toes pointed at the height of the jump. Practice with one foot in front, then the other.

Variations:
a) Change the leading foot after each two gallops.

b) Gallop sideways. Step with the left foot to the side, bring right foot to the left in the air, land on the right foot, and kick left foot out to the side.

DANCE STEPS

1. Step-Hop *(2/4 time)*
As its name indicates, the step-hop is a step followed by a hop on the same foot. The rhythm is even. That is, each movement has the same duration. Successive step-hops are taken on alternate feet. The positions of the arms and the free leg may vary. Practice the step-hop in various directions with the leg either extended or bent forward, backward, or sideways. In the illustration the free leg is extended backward and the arms are in second position.

step   hop   step   hop

2. Schottische Step *(4/4 time)*

The schottische step consists of three walking or running steps and a hop. On the hop the free foot is swung forward. It may be done forward or backward. Arm positions may vary.

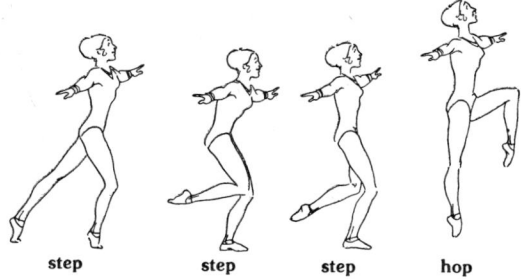

step   step   step   hop

3. Polka Step *(2/4 time)*

The polka step consists of two gallop steps forward with a quick little hop in between to change feet.

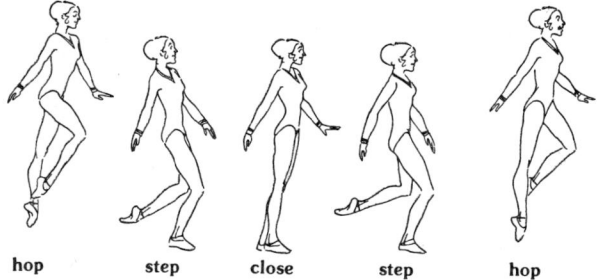

hop   step   close   step   hop

4. Waltz *(3/4 time)*

The waltz step may be performed in a variety of styles, in any direction or while turning. In gymnastics the walking or running waltz step is used most often. This is performed with a deep plié on count one and a rise to half-toes on counts two and three. It is helpful if you tell yourself down, up, up, while you perform in order to get the proper rhythm.

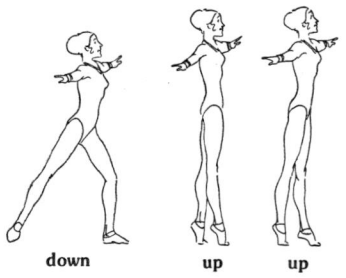

down   up   up

5. Grapevine Step

The grapevine step is a sideways movement. When moving to the left, start by standing on the straight left leg with the right leg extended to the side. Cross the right foot in front of the left, stepping on a slightly bent leg; step to the side onto a straight left leg, with the weight on the ball of the foot; cross right foot behind left, stepping onto a bent right leg; and so on. Emphasize the down-up rhythm.

6. Balance (3/4 time)

The balancé is a rocking step. It may be performed with a slide along the floor or with a small jump. Stand in fifth position with the right foot in front. Demi-plié and slide the left foot to the left side and step on it. Bring the right foot directly behind the left foot and shift weight for a second onto the ball of the right foot as you slightly lift the left foot off the floor. Immediately shift the weight back to the left foot as the right foot rests in back of the left ankle. Reverse to the opposite side. This may be done forward or backward also.

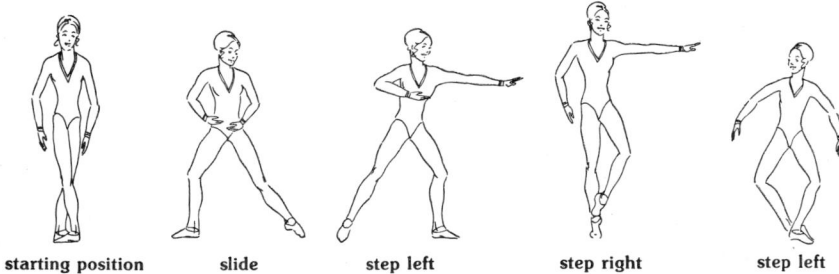

JUMPS AND LEAPS

There are many different types of jumps and leaps that are used in modern rhythmic gymnastics. A *jump* may be done from one foot or two feet and land on two feet. A *leap* is a large jump from one foot to the other. Jumps and leaps are basic elements of a composition. They give a feeling of aerial freedom to a routine.

All jumps and leaps begin and end with a good demi-plié. There are two reasons for this: (1) it enables you to push off from the floor and (2) it allows you to land softly and absorb the shock. Leaps and jumps should show a momentary suspension in the air. Thus, when you reach the highest point of a jump or leap you must get the feeling that you stop in the air for a second. Execute jumps with lightness and good amplitude. Move the arms in harmony with the jump. Do not show tension in the arms and shoulders. Experiment with different arm movements while performing the jump.

1. Changement
A changement is a jump from fifth position to fifth position with the legs changing in the air.

2. Jumps
Try to perform the jumps shown here. They should be executed from both feet to both feet. You may vary the arm positions. You may also precede them with a chassé or glissade.

swan or arch   tuck   cat   straddle

3. Scissor Kick (ciseaux)

The Scissor Kick is sometimes also called a hitch kick. Step forward with the right foot and kick the left leg forward in the air. As the left leg begins downward movement, kick the right leg in the air and land on the left foot. Practice this with the other foot also.

Variations:
a) Do the same movement but kick the straight legs backward instead of forward.
b) Alternate scissor kick forward and backward.

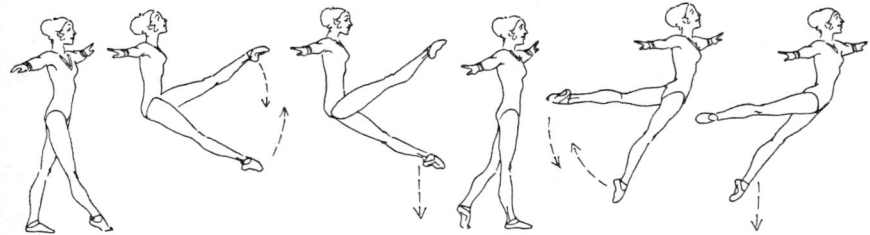

4. Cat Leap (pas de chat)

In gymnastics this is done in the same way as the scissor kick except the legs are bent. Step forward on the right foot, kick the bent left leg forward in the air, and as the left leg descends, kick the bent right leg in the air. Land on the left foot. Circle the arms through fifth position as you leap and open them to second upon landing.

5. Tour Jeté

Step forward on the left foot, kick the right leg forward and quickly scissor the legs as you do a half turn to the left. Land on the right foot in a moderate arabesque position. During the jump the legs must pass close to each other. A tour jeté is usually preceded by a chassé or glissade. To keep the body upright during the tour jeté, circle the arms through fifth position as you turn and then open them to second position upon landing.

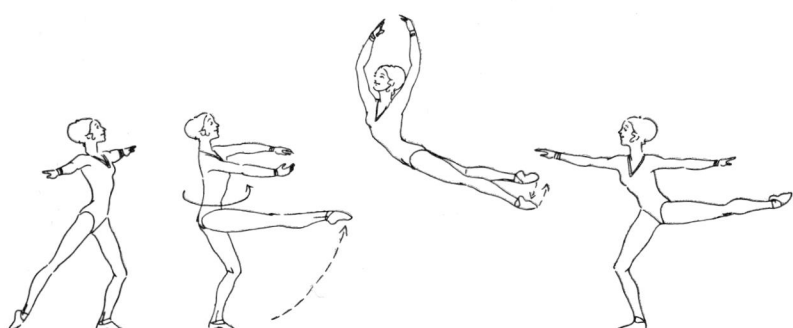

Variation:
Do the same movement, beating the legs together in the height of the jump.

6. Entrechat
Entrechat is a jump with rapid crossing of the legs in the air in which the legs are beaten together. The gymnast jumps into the air from fifth position and rapidly crosses the legs in front of and behind each other and lands in fifth position with the same foot in front. Both legs must beat equally.

7. Cabriole
The cabriole is a jump in which the extended legs are beat together in the air. It differs from the entrechat in that the legs do not change places during the beats; instead, the under leg beats the upper leg from beneath, pushing it even higher into the air.
    Step forward with the left foot, kick the right leg forward into the air, then thrust the left leg into the air and beat the calf of the right leg, sending it higher. Land on the left leg. Also practice with the other foot.

Variations:
a) Do the same movement backward.

b) Do the same movement sideward.

c) Combine front, back and side cabrioles in different ways.

8. Leap (Jeté)
The leap is a jump from one foot to the other. Run forward with long running steps. Then do a series of small leaps instead of running, by increasing the height of the spring. Swing the arms in opposition to the feet.

Variation:
Take a running step with the right foot and leap with the left foot. Continue to move forward in this manner. Try to increase the distance and height of the leaps. Repeat, leaping with the right foot.

run   leap   run   leap

9. Push-leap
Step onto the left foot, bring the right foot behind the left, and demi-plié. Push off with the right foot and leap onto the left foot as the

right leg is extended to the rear. In other words, push with the back foot and land on the forward foot. Repeat, starting with the other foot.

42

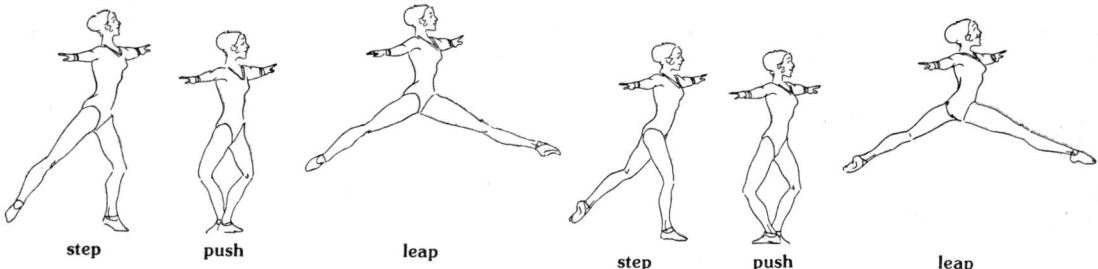

10. Split Leap *(grand jeté)*
A split leap is usually done after two or three running steps in order to get more momentum for this higher and longer leap. Do three steps across the floor to a split leap: run left, right, left, leap; left, right, left, leap; and so on. Repeat with the other foot.

11. Stag Leap
This is similar to the split leap except the forward leg is bent and the back leg is held straight in the air. Go into the leap with a bent leg to show the stag position for a second, then extend the leg into a split leap before landing.

BALANCES

Balances or poses should be held only momentarily to show that the movement is under control. They should not give the feeling of a pause or stop in the routine. They should accent movement patterns and provide a sense of aesthetic beauty in a composition.

Variations of balances are practically unlimited. A few of the frequently used poses are described below. Practice them with various arm positions.

1. Ballet Point
Commonly called a ballet curtsy. Stand in fourth position with the right foot forward. Shift the weight back onto the left foot in a demi-plié as you bend the body slightly and slide the right foot forward in a point. Arm and head positions may vary.

2. Lunges
Lunges may be performed forward or sideward with the supporting leg bent and the other stretched either to the rear or to the side. The body may lean in any direction. Arm and head positions may vary also. An example of a forward and sideward lunge is depicted here.

forward   sideward

3. Arabesque *(scale)*
An arabesque is a balanced position on one foot with the other leg extended to the rear. In ballet there are several arabesque positions but in gymnastics the following two are used most often: (1) the moderate

arabesque, in which the leg is raised to 45° or slightly higher, and (2) the arabesque, usually referred to as a *scale,* in which the leg is raised 135° or higher as the torso is leaning forward. An arabesque can be performed with a bent leg or straight supporting leg and on a flat foot or on the ball of the foot. The position of the arms may also vary.

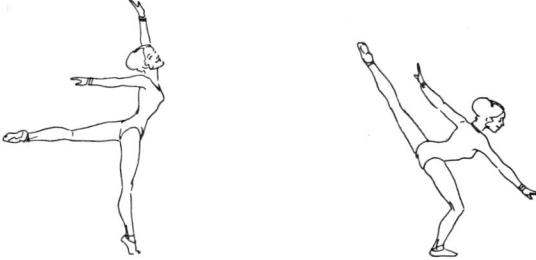

4. Backbend with Leg Lift

This is really a backward scale. Stand on the right foot, lift the left leg upward as high as possible and simultaneously bend the trunk backward. The arms can be held in varying positions. Also practice with the other leg.

5. Croisé Devant

In gymnastics this is simply called *croisé*. Literally, *croisé devant* means "crossed in front." Stand on the left foot and raise the right leg to a semibent position so that the right foot is at about the height of the left knee. Move the arms into third position with the left arm held high. You may twist the trunk to the right and rise to the ball of the foot.

Also practice with the other leg.

6. Attitude

An attitude is a pose on one leg with the knee bent. Turn the knee outward. Usually the arm on the side of the raised leg is curved over the head while the other arm is extended to the side. You may perform this with a bent or straight supporting leg and on a flat foot or on the ball of the foot.

TURNS

Almost all the jumps and leaps given in this chapter can be performed with a half or full turn. All of the above listed balances also can be executed with a turn. These turns will not be mentioned here.

Turns may be done in numerous ways either on both feet or on one foot and either on the floor or in the air. They may start from a step, from a demi-plié and rise to a relevé, or from a step directly onto the ball of the foot (relevé). The direction of the turn may be either outward (turning in the direction of the raised leg) or inward (turning in the direction of the supporting leg). The trunk, arm, and head positions may vary and the free leg may be either straight or bent and placed in any pleasing way. Turns may be of different degrees such as: half turns (180°), full turns (360°) or double turns (720°) or more. A gymnast should not make more than three complete turns.

Turns are a basic element in a routine. They are the most difficult dance movements, consequently, you will need to give a lot of attention to them to learn them correctly. Remember to rise up onto the ball of the foot throughout the turn and keep the body erect with the weight directly over the supporting leg.

Another important element to remember is that the head is the last to move and the first to arrive as the body completes the turn. This is known as *spotting*, which is the technique of keeping one's eyes on a fixed point to the front as long as possible then snapping the head around quickly back to that point. This will give the impression that the head is always facing forward. Spotting prevents the gymnast from getting dizzy. It can be learned easily while practicing a modified chaînés turn.

1. Modified Chaînés Turn

Modified chaînés turns are slow, turning steps across the floor in second position. A half turn is made on each step. For balance, keep the arms in second position throughout the turns.

Stand with the feet together and the arms in second position. When moving to the left, look over the left shoulder at a fixed point at eye level, then step to the left with the left foot, and turn half way around as you snap the head to look over the right shoulder, keeping the same focus point. Step onto the right foot, completing the turn while snapping the head around to look at the same fixed object. Continue in this manner across the room. Concentrate on spotting one point with the eyes throughout the turns. Also practice these turns in the other direction.

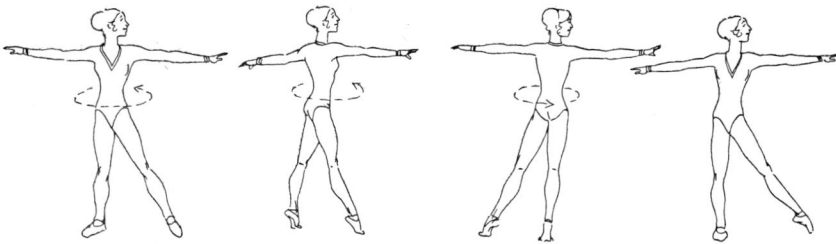

2. Chaînés Turn

This is performed the same way as the modified chaînés turns except the turns are faster and the feet are closer together with heels almost touching. The arms are usually opened to second position on the first step and brought to first position on completion of the turn.

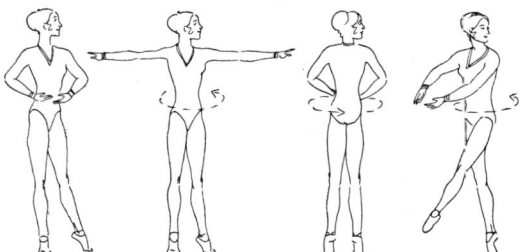

3. Pirouette

The pirouette is a rapid spinning done on one foot. The free foot may be held in various positions (i.e., at the ankle, in attitude, in arabesque, and so on). An example of a simple pirouette is:

Start in fifth position with the left foot in front and the arms held in first position. Do a battement tendu with the left foot to the side as the arms open to second position. Demi-plié in second position while bringing the left arm forward to first position. Then relevé onto the right foot as the left foot is brought to the calf of the right leg. Turn to the left while the right arm joins the left in first position. Open the arms to second position to stop the turn. Remember to spot during the turn.

The Basics: Accompaniment for Exercises, Exercises Without Hand Apparatus

4. Piqué Turn

This is a pirouette in which one steps with a straight leg onto the ball of the foot and completes the turn before returning to a plié position. The free leg may be raised to various positions.

A piqué turn can be best learned by first practicing just the piqué. For example: step onto the ball of the left foot as you bring the right foot to the left ankle. Then plié on the right foot with the left leg extended out to the side. Repeat this several times. At no time does the left leg bend throughout this exercise.

When you are able to perform piqués with good form and balance you may do piqué turns. As you step onto the straight left leg, bring the arms to first position to give additional impetus to the turn. After the turn, plié on the right foot while the arms open to second position. Continue this, moving across the floor. Remember that the eyes must focus on a fixed point in the direction of travel. Also practice this turning to the right.

5. Knee Turn
Kneel on the right knee, left leg bent to the front with toes placed on the floor. Turn to the right while you put the left knee on the floor, placing your weight on it at the completion of the turn. Finish the turn kneeling on the left knee, with the right leg bent to the front and the right toes placed on the floor. Also practice this in the opposite direction.

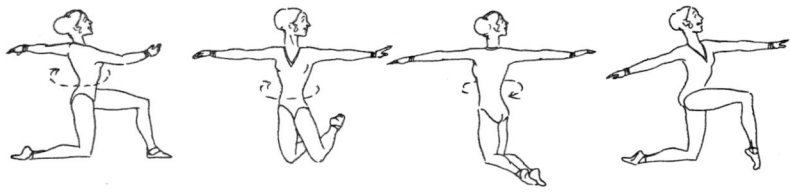

6. Split Turn
The *split turn* is sometimes referred to as a back spin. Do a split on the floor with the left leg in front. Swing the right leg forward in a large circle to an inverted split position and simultaneously roll onto the back. Continue circling the legs wide apart in a large circle until the left leg swings into an inverted split position. Meanwhile, turn completely around to the left on your upper back. Finish the turn by tucking the right leg to the side under the left leg and come to a kneeling position. Perform this turn smoothly and continuously. Do not hold the split positions—just move through them.

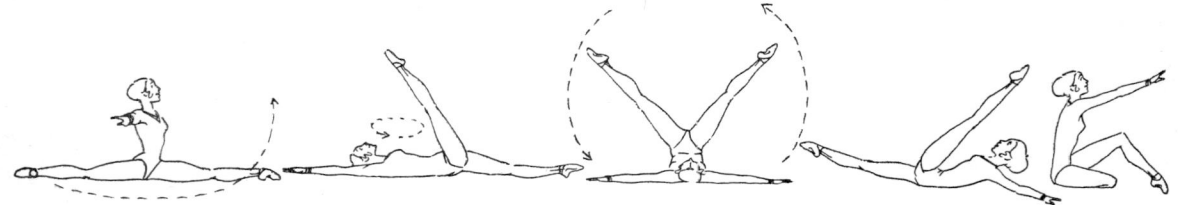

NOTE: To stretch the legs to develop a good split, the hamstring muscles in the back of the thighs and the hip flexors on the front of the thighs must be stretched gradually.

7. Illusion
Stand on the left foot with arms extended to the side and the right leg pointed forward. Step onto the right foot and kick the left leg forward in a high battement, simultaneously swinging the arms overhead. Then

swing the arms and left leg forcefully downward, backward, and upward to an aerial split position while you spin around to the left on the right foot. End the turn with the left foot in a forward battement position.

ROLLS

No acrobatic movements (cartwheels, handstands, aerials, and the like) are allowed in a competitive routine except rolls. Rolls are usually performed in modern rhythmic gymnastics without hands; but practice them first with hand support. When learning rolls, use a mat and remember to keep your back and shoulders well rounded and your head tucked close to your chest. This will help you to make the roll one continuous movement.

Rolls may be executed forward, backward, and sideward. An example for each will be given here.

1. Forward Roll Without Hands

Start from a lunge position with the arms held over the head. Bend forward and tuck the head as the arms move to the side to second position. Roll onto the back of the shoulders and keep rolling to the buttocks and then to the feet. The back of hands and arms contact the mat as you keep them in second position throughout the roll.

Practice this roll from different starting and to various ending positions.

2. Back Shoulder Roll

Start from a long sitting position. Roll backward, lifting the legs upward over the left shoulder as the head turns to the left and the arms move to the side to second position on the mat. As the legs are lowered over the left shoulder, place the left knee on the mat and shoot the straight right leg backward to complete the roll onto the legs.

Practice backward shoulder rolls from different starting and to various finishing positions.

3. Side Shoulder Roll

Stand on the right foot with the left leg extended backward, and the arms in third position with the left arm overhead. Grand plié on the right leg and place the bent left leg behind the right on the mat as you lean to the right side and bring the left arm down to front extension. Keep bending to the side until the left shin and thigh touch the mat; then extend the right leg to the side and simultaneously roll onto the left shoulder. Continue rolling to the left and along the upper back as the left leg also extends into the air and the arms open to second position on the mat. Roll up onto the bent right knee. Repeat to the right side. The different body parts touch the mat smoothly in this order: from left shin, to thigh, to hip and shoulder, to right shoulder, to hip, to thigh, and finally to shin.

TEACHING SUGGESTIONS

1. Do all stretching exercises in a long, continuous movement with no bouncing up and down. This will prevent any strain and over-tension of the muscle.
2. Good posture and form should be stressed in each movement.
3. The whole body should be involved in every exercise. The movement should pass through the whole body as if it were a kind of wave going from one part of the body to another.
4. Include in your lessons exercises which are composed of alternating contraction and relaxation. Gymnasts should learn how to go from extreme extension to complete relaxation so that movement and rest will become continuous.
5. Teach the students how to isolate movement in a particular part of the body while keeping the other parts relaxed. It is just as important to relax the proper muscles as to contract the correct muscles so that one can move smoothly. If muscles do not relax or lengthen when they should, the movement cannot be natural. Relaxation is one key to natural movement. There should be no unnecessary tensions. For example, if the arms are stretched over the head one should not hunch the shoulders or hyperextend the elbows.
6. Help students to see and feel the correct and incorrect positions. In dance studios there are full length mirrors so the students can practice in front of a mirror to obtain the correct leg, arm, and hand positions. In the gymnasium we do not have this aid, so the gymnast must know the feeling of performing correctly. It is helpful to have gymnasts demonstrate before each other and correct each other's movements. This will make them more aware of their own and others' mistakes.
7. Start to teach many of the exercises using a barre. If none is available have the students place a hand against the wall for balance. Most ballet movements should be taught at the barre and then without support. Have the students perform the exercises first on flat feet then standing on toes (on the balls of their feet). Exercises in motion should be taught last.
8. The exercises should progress from simple to more difficult.
9. Sequences or combinations should be started as soon as a few skills have been learned so that continuity of movement is emphasized from the beginning. For example, first teach a few basic movements in each dance category (i.e. steps, turns, poses) and then combine them into a short combination. Let the students perform the combination moving diagonally across the floor.
10. Students should be given the opportunity to move freely and individually, to improvise and to link different kinds of movements together. This will help them to be aware of their own bodies and what they can do in the realm of movement possibilities.
11. Assignments of simple problems for small groups should include experimentation in use of direction—forward, backward, sideward, and around;

in use of levels—high, low; in tempo—fast, slow, accented; in dynamics—forceful, smooth, sustained, and so on. These assignments will help the students compose their own optional routines.
12. Include stretching and strengthening exercises for every muscle in each lesson. Also include dance movements designed to improve form, grace, and posture. Gymnasts must spend as much time learning dance as they do learning to use any hand apparatus.
13. The exercises should be performed to music. It is easier for the student to understand the exercise and do it correctly when she can follow rhythm. Help the students translate the rhythms and moods of the music into movements.

COMPETITIVE RULES

Although exercises without hand apparatus are no longer included in international modern rhythmic gymnastics competition, they are often used in local meets because of the developmental values.

A competitive exercise without apparatus must make effective use of the entire floor area (12 x 12 meters). The exercise must last from one minute to one minute and thirty seconds and it must have a musical accompaniment of just one instrument. The quality of the music should blend with the type of movements and the personality of the gymnast. The rhythm of the exercise must vary. Variation of rhythm is important because it gives life to a performance. There is a 0.10-point penalty for each time that there is a break in rhythm during the exercise.

In addition to the above, there are other points a gymnast must consider when designing a routine. These are: elements of difficulty, continuity, sureness, and elegance of execution.

Common faults in execution are:

Movements	*Faults*
flexion of the trunk	— the arc formed by the body is not an uninterrupted curve.
body waves	— the whole body (that is, all vertebrae and the head) is not participating in the movement.
dance steps	— lack of coordination of the legs with the movements of the trunk and arms.

jumps and leaps	— insufficient amplitude in height and length; incorrect body position; heavy landing
balances	— loss of balance: extra movement of the body or the limbs in order to maintain balance.
turns	— uncertain: placing heel on the floor or hopping.

EXAMPLES OF DIFFICULTIES

A routine of full difficulty must be composed of six medium and two superior movements. For complete classification of these movements consult the F.I.G. Modern Rhythmic Gymnastics rule book. This book is available from the United States Gymnastics Federation. The following examples are given only as guidelines.

Flexion of the Trunk
Medium difficulties: From a stand, bend the upper body backward to a horizontal position, trunk circling around horizontally.

Superior difficulties: From a stand, bend backward and touch floor lightly with the hand; stand on toes and bend the upper body backward to a horizontal position.

Body Waves
Medium difficulties: Body wave forward or backward with arm movements; body wave sideward with arm movements.

Superior difficulties: Sit on heels and straighten up with a body wave, standing on toes (rising up onto the balls of the feet); body wave sideward combined with a turn.

Jumps and Leaps
Medium difficulties: A jump turn (360°) with legs together; cabriole forward, backward, or sideward.

Superior difficulties: A one-and-a-half jump turn (540°) with legs together; cabriole with half turn.

Balances
Medium difficulties (hold one second): Scale forward, backward, or sideward; forward scale, then half turn to horizontal backward scale.

Superior difficulties (hold three seconds): Scale on toes, forward, backward, or sideward; forward scale on toes, then half turn to horizontal backward scale.

Turns

Medium difficulties: A turn (360°) on the toes on one foot; pirouette, bending the trunk backward.

Superior difficulties: Double turn (720°) on the toes on one foot; one-and-a-half turn (540°) with the trunk bending backward.

COMPOSITION

In a routine, the gymnast is expected to demonstrate grace, good balance, flexibility and suppleness, the principles of whole body movement, and flow of motion. A routine should contain a variety of dancing steps, turns, balances, body waves, jumps, and leaps. It is very important to keep balance between these dance elements. Neither category must predominate.

An example of a short composition is given below. Replace some of the suggested moves with easier ones according to your ability.

1. Start with a pose, go into a kneeling position, continue with a stomach roll and a sit turn.
2. Stand up with a half turn and perform two running steps forward and two successive split leaps.
3. Step forward and do three chaînés turns in a curved pattern and swing one leg backward into a scale.
4. Step forward and perform a body wave into a deep backbend.
5. Do two running waltz steps and a cat leap forward in a curved pattern on the floor.
6. Step forward and do an arabesque hop, then swing the rear leg forward into a lunge position as you perform a body wave. Step back to a contraction pose.
7. Chassé forward, step together and do a stag leap from two feet, landing on one foot.
8. Turn around while bending the trunk backward.
9. Chassé forward, step and do an inward double pirouette turn to a ballet point pose.

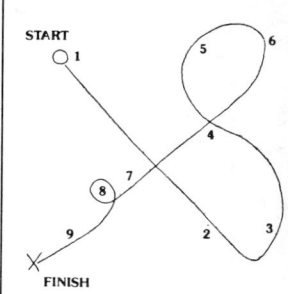

55

Balls

Chapter 3

The ball is one of the oldest and favorite toys of all children. The use of a ball in girl's rhythmic gymnastics was already popular at the various gymnastics schools in Europe in the early 1920s. It is difficult to pinpoint the origin of ball gymnastics. Some people believe that the movement of using the ball in rhythmic gymnastics was started by Hinrich Medau in Germany; others believe it was developed at the Royal Gymnastic Institute of Sweden. It seems to have become popular in many places simultaneously. Regardless of its origin, it has been adopted and further developed by most countries because it develops natural and graceful movements. Recently, ball gymnastics is developing in a new direction under the leadership of the International Gymnastics Federation (F.I.G.—Federation Internationale de Gymnastique). Like all hand apparatus, the ball should never be passive. It should be constantly mobile—rolling, bouncing, swinging, etc.—its movement directing the movement of the body. It should never be held in the hand merely as a decoration while the performer shows her dance talent. The movement of the ball should always be in perfect coordination with the movements of the body and with the music.

EQUIPMENT

The ball should be large enough so that it cannot be grasped by the fingers, but has to rest in the hand and be controlled by balance. It can be either rubber or plastic. For competition the ball must be a minimum of 400 grams (approximately 14 ounces)

and 18-20 centimeters in diameter (approximately 7-8 inches). For
general school use, a rubber playground or a utility ball is the most
economical even though it is not quite heavy enough. For elementary
school children a smaller ball, 14-17 cm in diameter (approximately
5½-6½ inches), is recommended. A six-inch ball is easier to hold in
the hand than an eight-inch one. However, the eight-inch ball develops
better technique and requires more skill because of its greater size and
weight.

Balls can be purchased in different colors, which make ball routines
very appealing in school or club demonstrations. In competition, any
color may be used except gold, silver, and bronze.

CARE OF EQUIPMENT

A ball must be properly cared for if it is to give maximum service. Balls
used in modern rhythmic gymnastics should not be over inflated as this
causes them to lose their resiliency. Over-inflation also makes it difficult
to control movements with the ball. The ball should not feel hard like
a volleyball. The correct number of pounds of air pressure required by
each ball is normally marked on the ball itself; however, in the absence
of a gauge, the correct amount of inflation can be ascertained by
pressing the heel of the hand into the ball. If the ball yields slightly to
pressure, it is sufficiently inflated. During summer vacation, balls that
are not in use should be stored in a cool place.

TECHNIQUES

The gymnast's body should be relaxed, her own movement always
following the movement of the ball. Movements with the ball can be
performed with one or both hands. The ball should always rest in the
hand; it should not be grasped with the fingers. The fingers should be
close together and slightly bent so that the hand can adapt itself to the
form of the ball.

When throwing and catching the ball, the impetus should come from
the center of the body. The movement should come from the feet and
extend through the body to the fingertips. The ball should roll freely out
of the hand, last touching the fingertips. The body and the arms are
fully extended, following the direction of the throw.

When catching the ball, these movements are reversed. First the
body and arms are fully extended toward the ball, and then the fingertips contact the ball and the ball rolls into the palm. The ball can be

caught with two hands or one hand. The entire body should follow the movement of the falling ball and absorb the weight of the ball as it is caught so it is caught softly and silently.

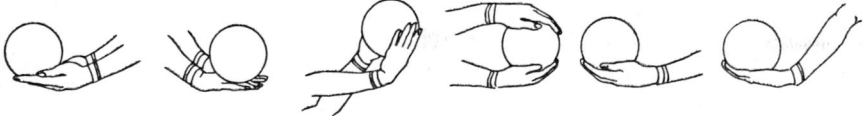

Proper hand position for catching

While bouncing the ball the joints of the body are flexed or extended in accordance with the ball's movement: the knees are flexed when the ball is low and the body is stretched when the ball is high so that the whole body is coordinated with the movement of the bounce. The ball must be pressed, not hit, toward the floor with a firm wrist and with the hand slightly curved over the ball. In order to catch the rebounding ball noiselessly, it must be caught at the top of the bounce.

Correct hand position for bouncing

In balancing and swinging movements the ball remains freely held in the hollow of the hand. This is a new technique which allows for the perfect coordination between the movements of the body and the movements of the ball. The old wrist-grasp technique, in which the wrist was bent at a right angle and the ball rested between the palm of the hand and the forearm, has been eliminated because it caused the ball to move separately rather than in harmony with the movements of the body.

In rolling movements, the hand carries the ball to the floor and the ball rolls smoothly out of the hand last touching the fingertips.

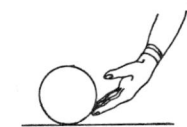

Correct hand position for rolling

The body and the arm follow through with the movement and are extended. During the roll, the ball must not leave the floor and bounce. When picking up the ball these movements are reversed. At the end of the roll the fingertips contact the ball and the ball rolls into the hand. It should be picked up without interrupting the flow of the movement. The ball can also be rolled in various ways on the body or between the hands.

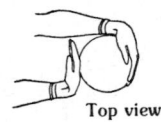

Top view

These movements are very difficult to connect with other movements without disturbing the rhythm of the routine.

MOVEMENTS

When performing exercises based on movements with a ball, the ball should not touch the forearm or other body parts except in movements in which the ball is rolled on the body. When the gymnast holds the ball, it should always rest in her hand; it should not be gripped. It is this means of control of the ball that allows the gymnast to perform with light, free movements. Movements that are similar to conditioning exercises, in which the ball is held in the hand, between the feet, or in some other manner, are not considered modern ball gymnastics.

The whole body should be involved in every exercise. The action is large and ends in a complete extension. The focus should be on the ball so that the movement of the body follows it. Emphasis should be on a relaxed, flowing or swinging type of movement with complete body freedom. All movements should be practiced with both the right and left hand from the beginning in order to develop balanced handling of the apparatus.

The exercises should be performed with music at all times. Waltz rhythm is most conducive to relaxed playful and rhythmical swinging, throwing, rolling, and bouncing movements; however, 6/8, 2/4, or 4/4 meter music works just as well as long as the tempo is correct. The music should not be so slow that it detracts from the life and flowing quality of the movements; nor should it be so fast that the movements cannot be carried out as fully as possible.

Do not be afraid of losing the ball. It is better to lose the ball using the right technique than it is to try and hold on to the ball by grasping it.

THROWING AND CATCHING MOVEMENTS

Throwing movements can be performed in the frontal and sagittal planes. The ball may be tossed by one hand and caught with the same hand, the other hand, or both hands. It can be tossed with both hands and caught with one or both hands. The toss can be low or high. The trajectory or path of the ball in flight can be long or short.

The following is an exercise that develops the proper technique for throwing and catching the ball. Hold the ball in the palm of the hand and let it roll to the end of the fingertips and then back into the hand.

Practice this with the right and left hands separately and with both hands.

When tossing the ball, keep the arms extended. Do not flip the ball into the air, but keep in contact with it as long as possible. Catch the ball high in the air and let the arms fall at the same speed as the ball, catching it noiselessly. The entire body stretches and bends, following the movement of the ball with an up and down motion. In the beginning practice with low tosses, then later with higher and higher ones.

1. Two-Handed Throw
Stand with the knees slightly bent and the ball held in both hands in front of the body. Toss the ball upward, attaining complete body extension. Catch the ball with both hands and absorb the force of the falling ball by bending the hips and knees.

Variations:
a) Clap twice before catching the ball.

b) Do two low throws and one high one. Alternate low and high throws.

c) Toss the ball with two hands, as in the basic movement, but catch the ball with one hand. Toss it up again with both hands and catch it with the other hand.

d) Catch the ball in a deep squat position.

e) Do a changement with the feet while the ball is in the air.

f) Execute a body wave before catching the ball.

2. One-Handed Throw

Stand with the left foot in a forward stride and the weight back on the right foot, while the right hand holds the ball to the rear and the left arm is extended forward. Transfer the weight forward as the right hand tosses the ball upward. Reach up and catch the ball with both hands and transfer it to the right hand again. Repeat several times. Practice this with the left hand also.

Variations:
a) Perform the same movement but catch the ball with the right hand.

b) Throw the ball from the right hand to the left hand and from the left back to the right. Establish a time pattern of throws with alternating hands.

c) Do the same ball toss as in (b) while walking or skipping forward.

d) Perform the same throw as in (b) with scissor kicks or cat leaps.

3. Overhead Throw *(in the sagittal plane)*

Stand holding the ball in the left hand at the left side. Swing the left arm forward and toss the ball slightly upward. Catch the ball from above and swing the arm down and back while bending forward. At the top of the backward swing, throw the ball over the head and catch it in front with both hands.

Variations:
a) Catch the ball with the right hand. Repeat with the right hand.

b) Do the same ball toss while walking or running forward and alternating hands.

4. Overhead Throw *(in the frontal plane)*

Stand with the feet in a wide straddle, the arms extended to the sides and the ball in the right hand. Throw the ball high over the head and catch it with the left hand as the weight is shifted from the right foot to the left. Throw the ball back over the head to the right hand. Help the throw with the side muscles.

Variations:
a) Do the same movement using a gallop step.

b) Do the same ball toss while walking forward.

5. Swing Toss Overhead
Stand in a wide straddle with weight on the right foot, arms extended to the sides and the ball in the right hand. Swing right arm downward toward the left and toss ball from the left overhead. Catch it with the left hand in front of the body and swing left arm back to the side, thus making a complete frontal circle with the arms and the ball. The weight is shifted from the right foot to the left, from the left to the right, and back to the left again during the movement. Reverse the action.

Variation:
Do the same exercise but perform a turn before catching the ball.

6. Swing Toss from Side to Side

Stand in a wide straddle with weight on the right foot, arms extended to the side and the ball in the right hand. Toss the ball from the right to the left low in front of the body as the knees bend and the hips are thrust to the left. Catch the ball with the left hand from above, the palm of the hand facing downward. Immediately swing and toss the ball back to the right side, transferring the weight to the right foot. Continue to toss the ball from hand to hand without stopping. The arms follow the body in a relaxed sideward swinging movement.

Variation:
Do the same ball toss while walking forward or backward.

7. Throw Under the Leg

Stand with the arms extended sideways and the ball held in the right hand. Lift the left leg forward and throw the ball under the leg. Catch it with the left hand. Reverse the action, throwing the ball under the right leg.

8. Throw Under the Arm

Stand with the arms extended sideways and the ball in the left hand. Swing both arms downward and inward. Throw the ball under and over the right arm, while bending the body slightly to the left. Catch the ball in the left hand. Swing the arms back to the sides.

Variation:
Catch the ball with the right hand and swing the arms back to the sides. Repeat with the right hand.

9. Throw Behind Shoulder

Stand with the feet in a wide straddle, the weight on the right foot, the arms extended to the side, and the ball held in the right hand. Bend to the right, swinging the ball downward, and throw it up from behind the right shoulder. Catch the ball with the right hand. Repeat with the left hand.

Variations:

a) Do the same movement but catch the ball with the left hand.

b) Throw the ball from the right hip up behind the left shoulder. Catch it with the left hand. Reverse the direction. Do the exercise from side to side.

10. Throw with the Arm Curled

Stand with the feet in a wide straddle, arms extended to the side and the ball in the right hand. Carry the ball horizontally forward under the flexed elbow, turning the palm inward and upward (the arm is thus curled and the hand is pronated). Throw the ball straight upward. Uncurl the arm (hand is supinated) and catch the ball with the right hand.

Variations:

a) Do the same movement but catch the ball with the left hand.

b) Do the same movement but catch the ball with the arm curled (hand is pronated).

c) Do all of the above mentioned movements while walking forward or backward.

11. Catch with the Arms Crossed
Stand holding the ball with both hands in front of the body. Throw the ball high and catch it with the arms crossed. Bring the hands downward to chest height and roll the ball toward the body, toss the ball upward with the arms crossed and catch it with both hands.

12. Catch on the Back of the Hands
Stand holding the ball in front of the body with both hands. Throw the ball upward with both hands, turn the palms downward, and catch the ball on the backs of the hands. Toss the ball upward from the backs of the hands and catch it with both hands (palms upward).

Variation:
Do the same movement but after the second throw circle the arms backward and catch the ball again on the backs of the hands. While circling the arms bend the right knee forward with the foot touching the left knee.

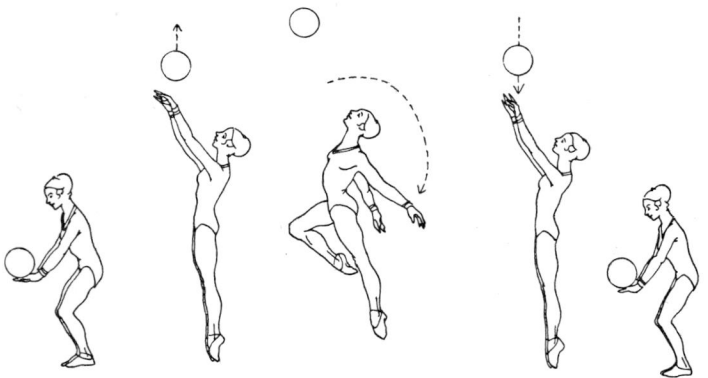

13. Catch Behind the Back
Stand holding the ball in front of the body with both hands. Throw the ball upward and slightly backward and catch it behind the back with both hands. Throw the ball upward and slightly forward from behind the back and catch it in the front with both hands.

Variation:
Do the same movement while walking or running forward.

14. Throw and Run
Stand at one side of the gym with the ball in the right hand. Throw the ball up and forward; then run forward and catch it with both hands before it falls to the floor. Transfer the ball to the left hand and repeat with the left hand.

Variations:
a) Do the same ball toss but catch the ball with one hand.

b) Perform the same movement but turn around before catching the ball.

15. Throw and Leap
Stand with the ball in the left hand. Run, stepping left, right, left and then leap into the air (right leg forward and left leg to the rear) as the ball is tossed upward. Catch it with the left hand while landing on the right foot.

Variation:
Run and leap as above but throw the ball up and forward. Run forward and perform another leap, catching the ball while executing the second leap.

16. Throw and Turn
Stand in a wide straddle with the weight on the left foot, arms extended to the side and the ball in the right hand. Throw the ball high; simultaneously step across with the right foot and turn (360°) toward the left. Catch the ball with the left hand.

side view

Variation:
Throw the ball upward and perform a pirouette or an arabesque turn below it. Catch the ball with one hand.

17. Partner Tossing

Stand facing your partner, each holding your ball in front of your body with both hands. Throw the ball in an arc to your partner. Ball should be tossed from the left side and received on the right side to avoid collision.

Variations:

a) Do the same movement but throw and catch the ball with one hand.

b) Both partners run forward about ten feet apart throwing one ball back and forth between them. Try to increase the distance up to fifteen feet.

c) Same exercise as (b) but use two balls.

BOUNCING MOVEMENTS

Exercises involving bouncing movements can only be performed with the ball and are therefore typical of this hand apparatus. Bouncing movements can be executed using two hands, one hand or alternate hands. When bouncing the ball, the hand is adapted to the shape of the ball and the wrist is held fixed. Bouncing exercises are performed either in place (standing, kneeling, squatting positions, and the like) or while in motion (turning, walking, galloping, and so on). The ball can be bounced in front of the body, in back, on either side or around the body. The ball can be bounced straight down toward the floor or it can be bounced diagonally forward toward the floor.

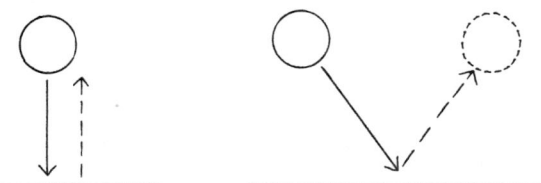

The ball can also be released from the hand on which it is resting and allowed to drop to the floor. This is done without any force and the bouncing of the ball is caused by the weight of the ball.

1. Drop the Ball with an Arm Swing

Stand relaxed but straight, holding the ball in front of the body with both hands. Drop the ball as the arms swing horizontally to the sides and back to the front position, catching the ball with the palms facing upward. The knees and body should "give" with the bounce.

Variation:
Starting in the same position, drop the ball and catch it on the backs of the hands (palms turned downward).

2. Drop the Ball from Overhead

Stand holding the ball in both hands over the head. Arch the back and release the ball, letting it bounce behind the body. Turn and catch the ball with both hands.

Variations:
a) Do the same movement but catch the ball with one hand.

b) Stand in a forward stride with weight in the back on the left foot and the right foot pointed in front. Hold the ball in the right hand over the head with the left arm forward. Body is slightly arched. Release the ball and let it bounce behind the body. Turn 180° to the left and catch the ball with the left hand.

3. Bounce the Ball in a Sitting Position

Sit with legs crossed and the back straight. Bounce the ball with both hands in front of the body. Press the ball with an even force so that it will bounce to the same height each time. Bounce the ball three times and catch.

Variations:
a) Hold the ball in the right hand. Bounce it in a half circle in front of the body from the right side to the left. When the ball is directly in front of the body, the left hand takes over bouncing and continues bouncing to the left without interruption. Use eight bounces to make the half circle. Press the ball evenly and rhythmically. Repeat from left to right.

b) Hold the ball in the right hand. Bounce the ball around the body. Take sixteen bounces to make a complete circle. Start from the right side and continue toward the left as in exercise (a) above. Continue bouncing the ball with the left hand until the ball is directly behind the body. Then quickly turn to the right and continue bouncing with the right hand. Repeat, going in the opposite direction.

c) Perform all of the above exercises both in a kneeling position and sitting on the heels.

4. Bounce the Ball in a Kneeling Position
Kneel on the right knee with the left foot in front. Bounce the ball with both hands as in exercise 3 above.

Variations:
a) Bounce the ball with the right hand from the right side to the left and back in a half circle across the front of the body.

b) Kneel on the left knee and, with the left hand, do the same exercise as in (a) above.

c) Bounce the ball with the right and left hand alternately.

5. Bounce the Ball from a Standing Position *(two hands)*
Stand and bounce the ball in front of the body using both hands. The body should feel elastic, following the movement of the ball with a give in the knees.

Variations:
a) Bounce the ball lower and lower, gradually bending the knees until you are in a deep knee bend. Return gradually to a standing position.

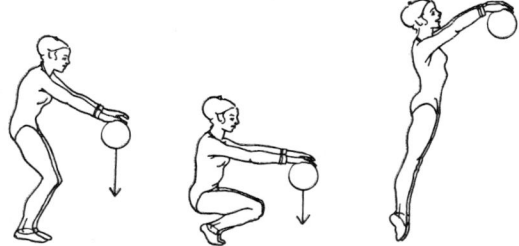

b) Bounce the ball higher and higher, gradually extending the knees until the feet leave the floor with a little jump at each bounce.

6. Bounce the Ball from a Standing Position *(one hand)*
Stand with feet together, holding the ball at shoulder height in front of the body in the palm of the right hand and holding the left arm raised to the side. Bounce the ball three times with the right hand and catch it with the left hand. Repeat the exercise with the left hand. To catch the ball, put the hand (palm down) over the ball as it comes up from the floor and slide the hand under the ball, gently catching it.

Variation:
Bounce the ball with the left and right hands alternately. Stand with the left arm forward and the right arm backward. Bounce the ball with the left hand and then swing the left arm backward while you swing the right arm forward to bounce the ball. When changing from the left hand to the right hand, simply place the right hand on top of the ball and press the ball toward the floor. Continue swinging the arms forward and backward while bouncing the ball with alternate hands.

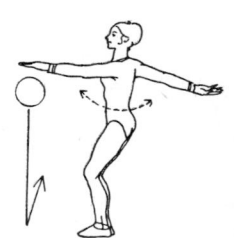

7. Bounce Around the Body
Stand with the ball in the palm of the right hand. Start to bounce the ball in front of the body with the right hand and continue bouncing it

to the right as far back as possible. Turn quickly to the left and, without interruption, continue bouncing with the right hand. Use eight bounces to make a complete circle. Repeat on the opposite side.

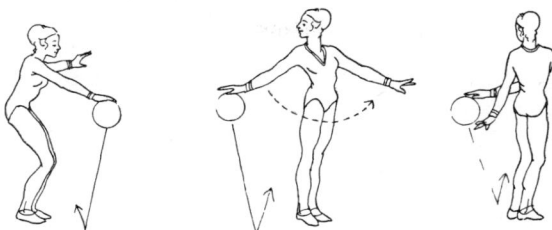

Variations:
a) Use sixteen bounces to make the circle.
b) Do the same exercise but after turning to the left continue bouncing the ball with the left hand.

8. Bounce in Rhythm
Bounce the ball in varying dynamic and time patterns. Stand with the weight on the right foot and the left foot in back of the right. Start with the ball held in front of the body in the palm of the right hand and bounce out different rhythms with the ball. Use one bounce for quarter notes and a double bounce for eighth notes. Bounce the ball with units of equal time first and then try with units of varied time. Practice with the left hand also.

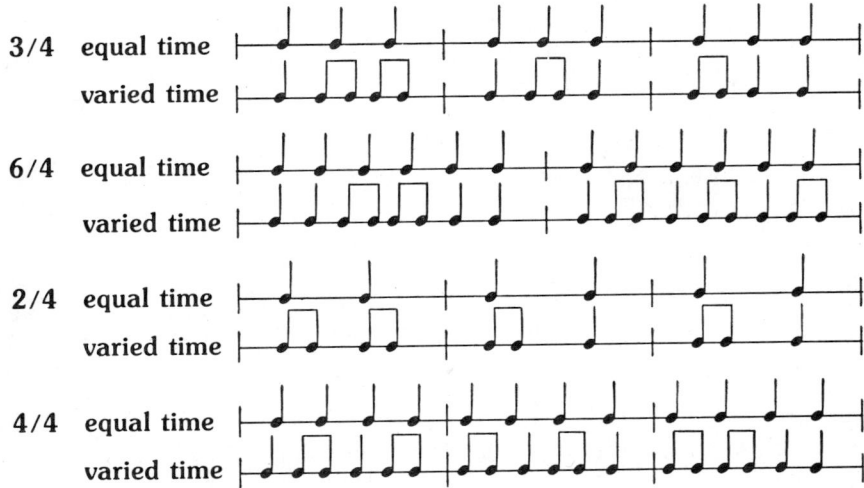

Variation:
Bounce the ball in rhythm with different dance steps.

9. Bounce Across the Body
Stand in a wide straddle with weight on the right foot and the arms extended to the side. Hold the ball in the palm of the right hand. Bounce the ball diagonally over to the left hand, shifting the weight from the right to the left foot. Catch the ball at the top of the bounce with the left hand. Repeat from the left to the right side.

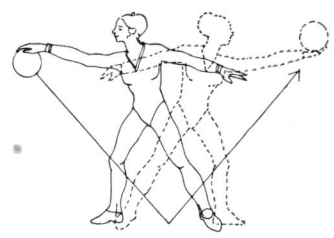

10. Bounce and Turn
Stand holding the ball in front of the body in both hands. Bounce the ball hard with both hands and immediately do a jump turn, catching the ball with both hands on the rebound.

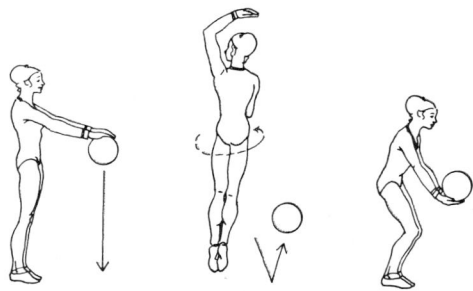

Variations:
a) Start in the same position and bounce the ball hard with the right hand; turn fast to the left and catch the ball with the left hand. Repeat to the opposite side.

b) Perform a pirouette before catching the ball.

c) Bounce the ball hard and execute a double pirouette, catching the ball with both hands.

11. Bounce Under the Leg
Stand with the arms extended to the side and the ball in the right palm. Lift the right leg forward and at the same time bounce the ball diagonally

under the right leg with the right hand. The leg swings outward over the ball. Catch the ball with the left hand. Swing both arms back to the side while lowering the right leg. Repeat the action with the left leg.

Variations:
a) Do the same exercise but catch the ball with the same hand.

b) Start in the same position and bounce the ball diagonally under the left leg. The left leg swings high inward over the ball. Catch it with the left hand.

c) Repeat (a) and (b) with a step-hop.

d) Start in the same position. Bounce the ball on the floor in front, swing the right leg inward over the ball and bounce the ball two more times with the right hand. Reverse the motion using the left hand.

e) Start in the same position, bounce the ball in front of the body and swing the right leg inward over it. Make a complete turn to the left. Catch the ball with the left hand. Reverse the movement.

12. Bounce While Walking

Walk forward with springy steps. Bend the knees when the ball is low and stretch up on the toes when the ball is high. Follow the movement of the ball with your whole body. Bounce the ball diagonally forward with the right hand as you take each step.

Variations:
a) Repeat with the left hand.

b) Walk backward while bouncing the ball.

13. Bounce While Running
Run forward while bouncing the ball with the right hand. Take two running steps with each bounce. Repeat with the left hand.

14. Bounce While Skipping
Skip forward on alternate feet. Bounce the ball with the right hand once with each skip. Repeat, bouncing the ball with the left hand.

Variation:
Skip clockwise in a small circle and bounce the ball with the right hand. Turn 180° to the left and reverse the movement, skipping counterclockwise.

15. Bounce with Grapevine Steps
Stand in a wide straddle with the weight on the right foot, the left toe supported to the side, the arms extended to the sides, and the ball in the palm of the right hand. Step to the left with the left foot, cross the right foot in front (or in back) of the left and step left with the left foot. (Step, cross front, step, and reach.) Bounce the ball with the right hand three times and catch it with the left hand, reaching to the side. Repeat, stepping toward the right side.

Variations:
a) Do the same exercise but bounce the ball with the right and left hands alternately.

b) Continue moving to the side with the grapevine pattern. Step with the left, cross with the right in front, step with the left, cross with the right in back, and so on.

16. Bounce with Chassé
Chassé with the left foot forward and bounce the ball twice with the right hand. On the second bounce catch the ball in the left hand. Repeat the chassé to the right, bouncing the ball with the left hand.

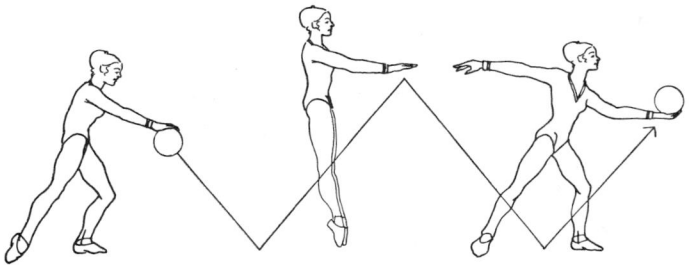

Variation:
Do the same exercise but add a hop between the chassé steps. (Hop on the right foot; chassé forward with the left foot; hop on the left; chassé forward with the right.)

17. Bounce with Leap
Stand with the ball in the right hand. Step with the left foot and leap on the right foot. The ball is bounced with the right hand once on each leap. The left arm is extended to the side.

Variation:
Run and leap. Step left, step right, step left, and split-leap with the right leg forward. The ball is bounced twice on the right side, on the first and third steps. Practice on the left side also.

18. Bounce with Side Gallop
Stand in a wide straddle with weight on the right foot. Gallop four times sideways to the left with the arms forward, bouncing the ball with both hands during each gallop. Repeat to the right.

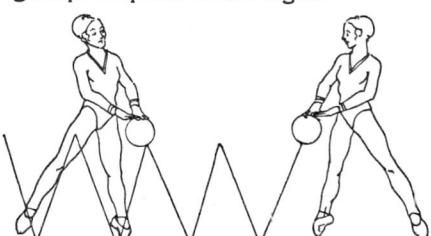

Variations:
a) Same starting position. Do side gallops to the left, bouncing the ball with the right hand. Repeat to the right, bouncing the ball with the left hand.

b) Start in the same position. Do two gallops to the left with the left foot leading, do a 180° turn to the left, and then continue to the left with the right foot leading. Turn 180° to the right and repeat the exercise from the beginning. Bounce the ball with both hands during each gallop.

c) Bounce the ball with one hand (hand opposite from leading foot) while doing variation (b).

19. Bounce with Scissor Kick
Stand with the arms extended to the sides, holding the ball in the right hand. Step to the left, kick the right leg forward into the air, followed immediately by the left, and land on the right foot. Bounce the ball once on each jump. Repeat several times. Practice the same jump on the opposite side.

Variations:
a) Do the same movement with kicks to the rear (scissor kick backward).

b) Alternate a scissor kick forward and a scissor kick backward, bouncing the ball once with each kick.

c) Do the same exercises as described above but bounce the ball twice with each scissor kick.

d) Scissor jump over the bouncing ball. Bounce the ball with the right hand diagonally under both legs as they scissor kick over the ball. Catch the ball with the left hand. Reverse the movement.

20. Partner Bounces
Stand facing a partner with the ball in the right hand. Bounce the ball to the partner on the right side and catch the partner's ball with the left hand. Bounce the ball to the partner with the left hand, on the left side, to avoid collision. Do this several times. Each person should bounce the ball simultaneously. If bouncing with two balls is difficult practice with one ball first.

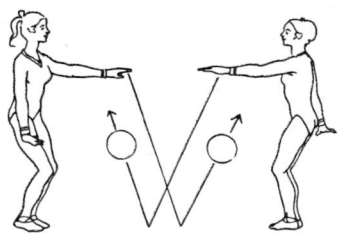

Variations:
a) Both partners run forward, about eight feet apart, bouncing one ball back and forth between them. Try to increase the distance up to fifteen feet.
b) Do the same exercise as in (a) but use two balls.

ROLLING MOVEMENTS

The ball may be rolled on the floor or on the body in various ways. Rolling the ball without bouncing it requires skill. One must stretch the body toward the rolling ball and perform the movements smoothly.

1. Roll in Sitting Position
Sit with the legs extended on the floor in front of you, the arms extended to the sides, and the ball held in the right hand. Holding the legs straight, raise them up off the floor and roll the ball under them to the left hand. Lower the legs, then raise them again and repeat the movement to the left.

2. Roll in Prone Position
Lie in a prone position with the arms extended to the side and the ball on the floor under the right hand. Raise the head, shoulders, and chest off the floor, roll the ball under the chest to the left hand, and relax. Repeat with the left hand.

3. Roll in Kneeling Position

Kneel with the knees about eighteen inches apart, the arms extended to the side, and the ball in the right hand. Roll the ball with the right hand in front of the body and to the left, letting the ball roll up into the left hand while shifting weight to the left. Reverse the movement.

Variation:

From a standing position, kneel down onto the left knee, extending the right leg forward on the floor. Extend the arms to the side and hold the ball in the right hand. Swing the right arm upward and backward in a circle and roll the ball forward in the sagittal plane. Stand up, run after the ball, and lift it up with both hands. Repeat the same movement with the left hand.

4. Roll in Standing Position

Stand in a wide straddle with the arms extended to the side and the ball in the right hand. Roll the ball along the floor to the left and catch it with the left hand while shifting weight to the left and bending the trunk. Reverse the movement.

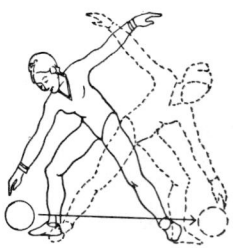

Variations:

a) Do the same movement with a gallop step to the side.

b) Roll the ball from the right to the left. Chaîné turn to the left and bend forward, letting the ball roll into the left hand. Repeat with the left hand.

5. Run with Roll

Stand with the arms extended to the side and the ball held in the right hand. Bend forward and roll the ball across the floor in the sagittal plane. Run forward beyond the ball and let it roll into the right hand, with the right arm curled. Uncurl the arm and repeat the movement. Practice with the left hand.

Variations:
a) Run after the ball, make a complete circle around it, and run forward before catching it.
b) Do the same movement but run beyond the ball and turn halfway around to catch it.
c) Repeat (b) and after catching the ball throw it up in the air, turn halfway around, catch the ball, and roll it forward again.

6. Run and Leap with Roll
Stand with the arms extended to the sides and the ball in the right hand. Roll the ball forward, run and leap beyond it, bend forward, curling your arm as you do so, and let the ball roll into your hand from behind you.

Variation:
Do the same movement but after catching the ball toss it forward over the head.

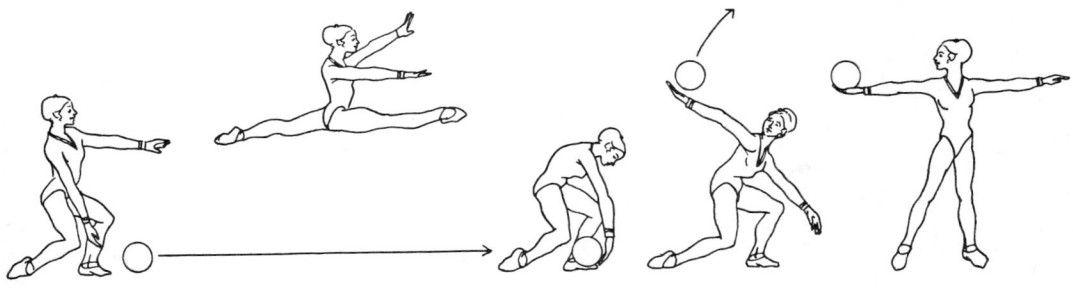

7. Leap over Rolling Ball

Stand with the arms extended to the side and the ball in the right hand. Run alongside the rolling ball and leap sideways over it with the right leg; continue to run left, right; and leap sideways over the ball with the left leg. Run and leap several times over the rolling ball then bend forward and catch it, arm curled.

Variations:

a) Do scissor leaps over the ball.

b) Do cat leaps over the rolling ball.

8. Tour Jeté over Rolling Ball

Stand in a front stride position with the arms extended to the side and the ball in the left hand. Roll the ball forward, glissade on the left alongside the ball, and tour jeté to the left over it. Reach down and let the ball roll into the left palm upon completion of the movement.

Variation:
Do the same movement but finish the tour jeté in a kneeling position, then catch the ball as before.

9. Roll Between the Hands

Stand in a forward stride with weight in front on the right foot and the left foot pointed in the rear. The ball is held in front with both hands. Roll the ball between the palm of the right hand and the back of the left hand, quickly changing the position of the hands as it rolls. Roll the ball inward several times and finish by reaching over the head with the ball while shifting the weight back to the left foot. Then roll the ball several times outward between the hands to return to the starting position.

Balls

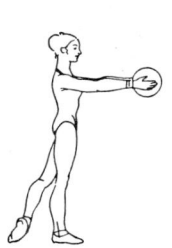   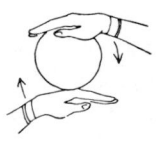

Variation:
Start the same rolling exercise, moving from a deep squat position to a complete extension of the body. Roll the ball several times and finish with a toss in the air.

10. Roll on the Legs
Sit with the legs extended in front of you on the floor. Hold the ball out in front of you with both hands. Tilt the trunk backward and lift the legs up toward the ball and let the ball roll down the legs toward the chest. Then lift the upper body and lower the legs so that the ball rolls back. Repeat.

11. Roll on the Arms
Stand with the arms stretched in front of the body. Hold both arms together and slightly above the horizontal. Balance the ball in supinated hands (palms of the hands facing upward) and, giving a very slight upward impetus to the ball, pronate the hands (palms facing downward) and let the ball roll down the arms toward the body while taking two small steps forward. Step backward and lower the arms below the horizontal so the ball rolls back into the palms of the hands. Toss the ball upward and catch it. Repeat the movement.

Variations:
a) Do the same movement but catch the ball on the backs of the hands.
b) Start the movement the same as above but when the ball is at the chest swing the arms horizontally to the sides and the ball will drop between the arms in front of the body. After the ball bounces to the floor, catch it on the rebound.

12. Roll on One Arm *(palm up)*
Stand in a front stride position with weight in front on the right foot and the left foot in the rear. The arms are extended forward and the ball is held in the right hand. Let the ball roll down on the right arm while stepping back on the left foot. Push the ball with the left hand so the ball will roll back into the right palm while taking two steps forward, finishing in a ballet position.

13. Roll on One Arm *(palm down)*
Stand with the arms extended to the sides and the ball in the palm of the right hand. With a very slight toss of the ball upward, turn the palm downward and let the ball roll along the right arm to the shoulder. Let the ball drop behind the body, then twist to the left, and catch the ball on the rebound with the left hand. Repeat with the left hand.

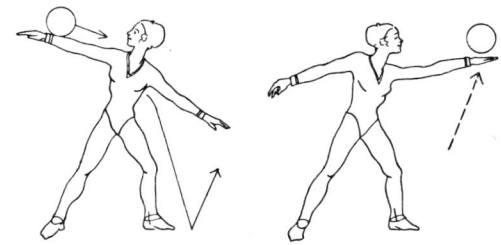

14. Roll Along the Arms *(in front)*

Stand with the arms extended to the sides and the ball in the right hand. Raise the right arm slightly above the horizontal, let the ball roll along the right arm, across the chest and down along the left arm into the left palm. Keep the head and chest high and the body slightly bent to the left. Repeat with the left hand. NOTE: this exercise is very difficult and needs a lot of practice.

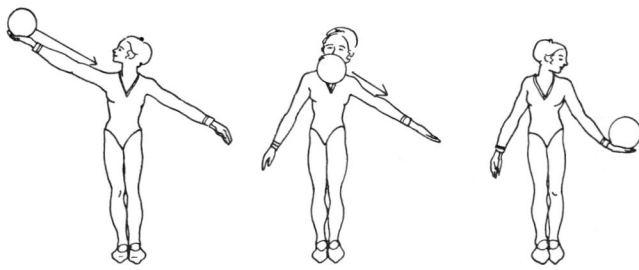

Variation:
Combine the roll with waltz steps forward.

15. Roll Along the Arms *(in back)*

Stand with the arms extended to the sides. Curl the right arm and hold the ball in the right hand. Roll the ball along the right arm, across the back of the neck and down along the left arm. Catch it with the left hand. Keep the body bent forward and toward the left, and the head slightly tucked. This exercise is also very difficult and requires much practice.

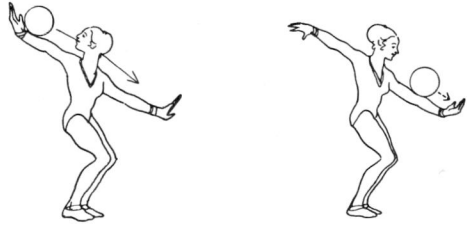

Variation:
Do the same movement but catch the ball with the arm curled (palm of the hand turned backward and upward).

16. Roll on the Neck and Arm

Stand with the arms extended to the side and the ball in the right hand. Bend the right elbow, place the ball on the right shoulder and push it with the right hand across the back of the neck. Let the ball roll down on the left arm into the palm of the hand. Repeat with the left hand.

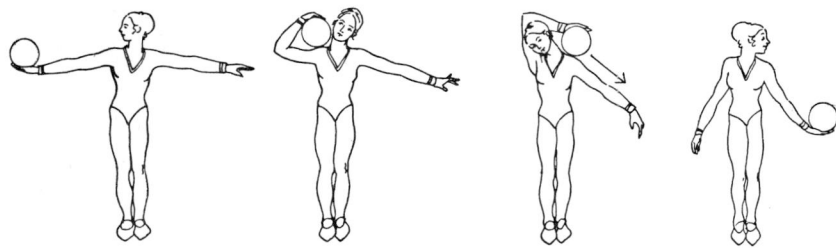

Variation:
Let the ball roll down along the right arm to the right shoulder. Roll the ball completely around the neck (front, left side, back) with the left hand and let it roll back along the right arm to the right palm. Practice this also with the left hand.

17. Roll on Back

Practice this exercise first in a kneeling position, sitting on the heels. Hold the ball in front with both hands. Bend forward and place the ball behind the head with the arms bent and the elbows out. Let the ball roll down on the back and simultaneously swing the arms sideward and backward to catch the ball behind the back with both hands. Then roll it back on the back over the head and catch it with both hands in front. Repeat.

Variations:
a) Do the same movement with one hand.

b) Do the same exercise in a standing position.

18. Roll on Arm and Back

Stand with the arms extended to the sides and the ball in the left hand. Give a very slight impetus to the ball, turn the left palm downward, let the ball roll along the left arm, down the left shoulder and back toward the waist. Catch it behind the body with both hands.

Variations:

a) Do the same movement but catch it with the right hand.

b) Repeat (a) in a lunge position.

19. Ball Rolling to Partner

Stand, facing a partner, each holding your ball in your right hand. Roll the ball to the partner on the right side and receive the partner's ball with the left hand. Roll the ball with the left hand to the partner on the left side. Repeat several times. Each person rolls the ball simultaneously.

Variations:

a) Both partners walk forward, about eight feet apart, rolling one ball back and forth between them. Increase the distance up to fifteen feet.

b) Perform the same movement as in (a) but use two balls.

c) Do a turn before catching the rolling ball in all of the above exercises.

SWINGING MOVEMENTS

Swinging movements can be performed with one or two arms in the sagittal, frontal, or horizontal planes. Movements with two arms, in which the ball is held lightly between the hands, are easy. Movements with one arm, in which the ball is balanced in one hand, are quite difficult. Swing the arms freely from the shoulder. Do not worry about dropping the ball while learning the exercises. Do not grip the ball or press it against the wrist. If the arm is swung properly, the ball will feel heavy at the bottom of the swing and light at the top. Let the body give during the swinging action. Follow the ball with your eyes.

1. Swing Backward and Forward
Stand with the arms extended horizontally forward and the ball in the right hand. Swing the right arm backward and forward on the right side two times. At the end of the second forward swing change hands and repeat the movement with the left hand. Do not toss the ball to change hands.

Variations:
a) Do the same movement with a forward stride, shifting the weight forward and backward with the ball.

b) Do the same movement with a glissade forward.

2. Pendular Swing
Stand on the right foot with the right leg bent, the left leg extended slightly forward, the trunk slightly bent forward, and the ball in the right hand behind the body. Move the weight to the front foot on the forward swing; move the weight to the back foot, while bending forward, on the backward swing. The arm is like a pendulum, it swings forward until it reaches its highest point, then swings backward to reach the highest opposite point.

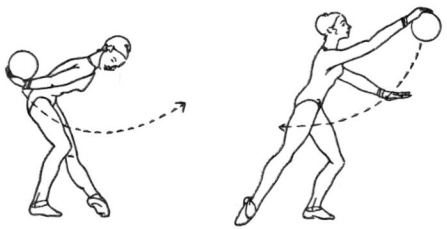

Variations:
a) Repeat the movement while walking forward in a waltz rhythm (1-2-3) during the forward swing and walking backward (4-5-6) on the backward swing. Practice also with the left arm.

b) Let the ball fly slightly upward in front of the body. Catch the ball from above with the same hand and swing it backward.

c) Do the same variation as in (b) with a step forward and change hands in the front. Swing the ball backward on the opposite side. Repeat movement.

3. Circling in Sagittal Plane *(forward)*
Stand with the right arm extended backward, the ball in the right hand and the left arm extended forward. The body is slightly rotated to the right. Swing the right arm in a complete circle downward, forward, upward and backward. Repeat the movement several times. Practice with the left arm too.

Variation:
Do the same movement with a chassé or two walking steps forward with each circle.

4. Circling in Sagittal Plane *(backward)*
Stand with the arms extended forward and the ball in the right hand. Swing the right arm downward, backward, upward over the head, and downward again. Switch the ball to the left hand and repeat on the opposite side.

Variations:
a) Take two walking steps forward or backward with each circle.

b) Glissade forward or backward with each circle.

c) Do one and a half circles with the right arm, toss the ball forward over the head and catch it with the left hand. Repeat to the left side.

5. Body Wave
Stand with the arms extended forward and the ball held in the right hand. Do a body wave while swinging the right arm downward to the side, backward, and over the head. Drop the ball into the left hand and repeat with the left arm.

Variations:
a) Do the same movement with a step forward or backward.

b) Do the same movement but instead of dropping the ball into the left hand bounce it on the floor. Catch it with the left hand and repeat.

c) Hold the ball in front of the body with both hands. Bring the ball downward, inward in front of the body and reach over the head as the body wave movement is done. Repeat several times.

d) Do the same movement as in (c) but perform the body wave in a kneeling position.

6. Swing Across the Body
Stand in a wide straddle with weight on the right foot, the arms extended to the sides, and the ball held in the right hand. Swing the right arm downward across the body to the left, switch the ball into the left hand, and swing the left hand across to the right side. Transfer the weight from side to side while swinging the ball.

Variation:
Swing the right arm to the left, back to the right, and to the left again before transferring the ball into the left hand. Repeat with the left hand.

7. Circling in the Frontal Plane
Stand in a wide straddle position with the arms extended to the sides and the ball in the right hand. Make one and one half circles in the frontal plane by swinging the right arm downward, upward over the

head and downward again to the left side. Transfer the weight and sway the body from side to side while swinging the ball. Transfer the ball to the left hand and do a one-and-a-half circle in the opposite direction.

Variations:
a) Do the same movement with a gallop from side to side.

b) Repeat (a) but transfer the ball to the opposite hand with a toss.

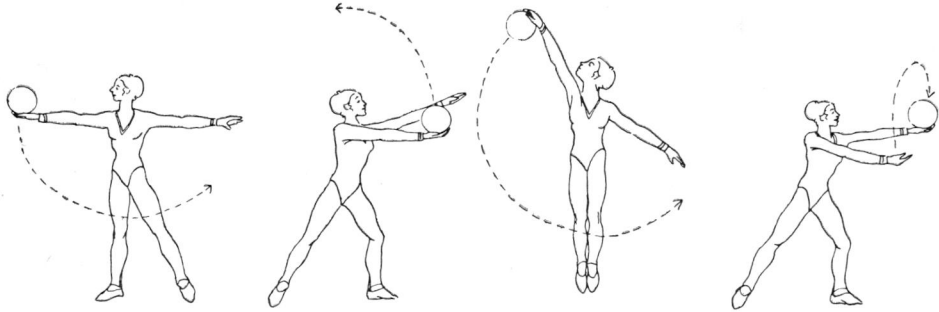

8. Circling Across the Body
Stand with the arms extended to the side, the right arm curled, and the ball in the right hand. Swing the right arm downward across the body to the left, upward over the head, and downward again across the body to the left. Transfer the ball to the left hand. Repeat the movement on the opposite side.

Variations:
a) Do the same exercise, but after the one-and-a-half circle throw the ball over the head and catch it with the right hand at the right side of the body.

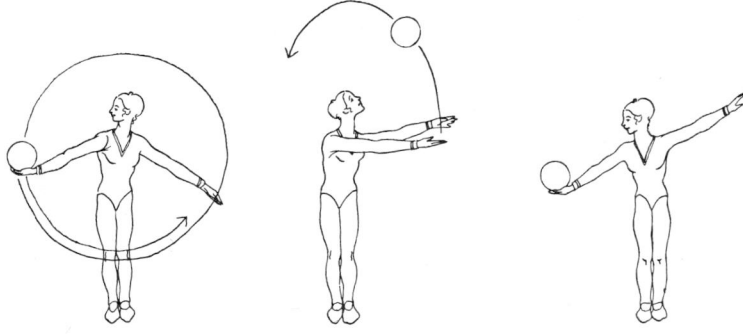

b) Repeat (a), catching the ball with the arm curled.

9. Circling Around the Body

Stand with the arms extended to the sides and the ball in the right hand. Swing the ball in the horizontal plane across in back of the body to the left. Transfer the ball to the left hand. The left hand carries it to the front. Switch it into the right hand. Practice this several times, then repeat in the opposite direction.

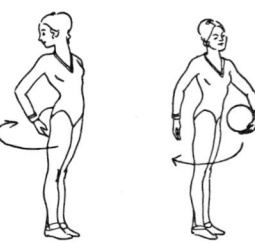

Variations:

a) Do the same movement while performing a chaîné turn.

b) Do the same movement while doing a pirouette or arabesque turn.

10. Figure Eight with Both Arms

Stand in a wide straddle with the arms extended to the right side and the ball in both hands. Make a figure eight from the right to the left in front of the body with the ball. The whole body follows the ball, transferring the weight and pushing the hips from side to side with the swinging ball.

11. Figure Eight with One Arm

This movement is exactly the same as number ten but is performed with either the right or left arm. The arm and hand rotate inward and outward in continuous successive motion.

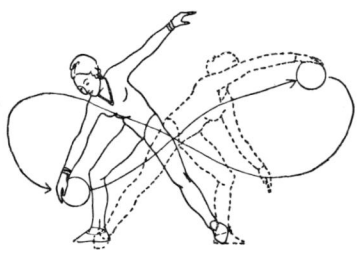

12. Glissade–Tour Jeté

Stand in a front stride position with weight on the right foot and the ball in the right hand. Extend the right arm backward and the left arm forward. Do two and a half backward circles with the right arm in the sagittal plane (exercise 4) while doing a glissade forward on the left and a tour jeté. End in an arabesque with the left leg extended to the rear, the right arm obliquely forward and the left arm backward.

BALANCING MOVEMENTS

In these types of movements the ball is balanced freely in the hollow of the hand.

1. Balance the Ball While Curling and Uncurling the Arm

Stand in a wide straddle position with the arms extended to the sides and the ball held in the right hand. Carry the ball horizontally forward under the flexed elbow, turning the palm of the hand inward and upward (curl the arm). Return to the starting position, reversing the movement (uncurl the arm). Practice also with the left hand.

Variations:

a) Start from the same position. Start the turning from the shoulder. Turn the palm downward, backward, and upward. Reverse the movement to uncurl the arm.

b) Curl and uncurl the arm while walking forward.

c) Toss the ball lightly with the arm curled and catch it in the same hand with the arm uncurled.

d) Repeat (c), catching the ball with the arm still curled.

e) Throw the ball over the head with the arm curled, and catch the ball with the other hand (arm curled).

f) Repeat (c), (d), and (e) with a walk, chassé, or waltz step forward.

2. Spiral

Stand in a front stride position with the left foot in front, the arms extended to the side and the ball in the right hand. Move the right arm parallel to the floor across in front of the body. Flex the elbow, and turn the palm of the hand inward and upward while carrying the ball in a circle under the elbow until the arm is extended toward the left. The trunk is bent forward. Continue carrying the ball to the left over the head, circling above the head as the body bends backward. Return to the original position. The entire body participates in circling the ball. The horizontal circles should be large and parallel to the floor. Repeat with the left arm.

  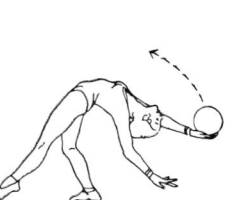 

Variation:
Do the same movement with walking or waltz steps forward.

3. Reverse Spiral

This exercise reverses the movement described in exercise 2. Carry the ball from the right side backward, toward the left and above the head as the body bends backward. Continue the movement, carrying the ball forward. Bend the right elbow, move the ball in a circle toward the body and under the body as the body bends forward. Carry the ball back to the starting position. Repeat the movement with the left arm.

4. Spiral Turn

Stand with the arms extended to the sides and the ball in the left hand. Cross the left leg in front of the right and do a full turn to the right while doing a spiral. Finish in a front stride position, with the weight on the right foot in front.

Variations:
a) Do the same movement but start low, with the knees bent, then stretch and finish high on the toes.

b) Repeat (a) but execute two spiral movements while doing the turn.

c) Do the same movement but turn on one foot. The other leg may be extended or bent in various pirouette turns.

5. Balancing Ball While Turning

Stand with weight on the left foot, the right toes supported to the side. The ball is held in the right hand. Step to the right on the right foot and turn with a moderate arabesque turn to the right with the left leg extended to the rear. During the turn, the right arm circles overhead, the palm of the hand is turned upward, and the left arm is extended to the side. The arms must move with the movement of the trunk, otherwise the ball will drop.

Variation:
Do the same movement but at the end step forward with the left foot and catch the ball in front with crossed hands—right hand over left. Do another turn to the right. Turn on the ball of the left foot with the right leg extended backward. The ball is held in the curled left hand and circles overhead.

MOVEMENTS WITH TWO BALLS

Most of the movements that have been described for one ball can also be performed with two balls. Exercises with two balls are difficult and should be attempted only by advanced students. First efforts will probably not be too successful but by the third practice period improvement should be noticed. Routines with two balls are very spectacular in gymnastic demonstrations. It is important that the two balls have the same resiliency.

1. Throw Two Balls Simultaneously

Stand with the arms extended to the side. Throw the balls upward and forward simultaneously with both hands, and catch them with the same hands.

Variations:
a) Do the same toss, cross the arms, and catch the balls with the opposite hands.

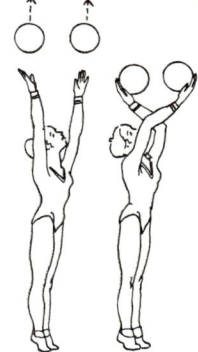

b) Swing arms down and forward, crossing them in the front, and throw the balls upward. Uncross the arms and catch each ball with the other hand.

2. Throw Two Balls Alternately

Stand with the arms extended to the side. Throw the ball up with the right hand. Catch it and simultaneously throw the other ball up with the left hand. Establish a time pattern of throws with alternating hands.

Variation:
Do the same exercise while walking forward.

3. Bounce Two Balls Simultaneously

Kneel, holding a ball in each hand about a shoulder width apart. Bounce the balls in a half circle in front of the body, from the right side to the left. Repeat from the left to the right. Press the balls with even force so they will bounce to the same height. Keep the balls close to the hands by having the hands follow the balls as they bounce.

Variations:

a) Do the same movement from a standing position.

b) From a standing position bounce the balls with both hands in front of the body. Focus straight ahead.

c) Repeat (b) while walking, running, or skipping forward.

4. Bounce Two Balls Alternately

Stand with the arms extended to the side, a ball resting in each hand. Bounce a ball in front of the body first with the right hand, then with the left. Continue bouncing the two balls alternately, establishing a rhythmic pattern.

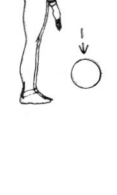

Variation:
Do the same movement while walking or running forward or backward.

5. Overhead Throw

Stand with the arms extended to the side. Throw a ball over the head with the right hand. Then pass the other ball in front of the body from the left hand to the right. Catch the first ball with the left hand. Repeat this several times. Practice also to the other direction.

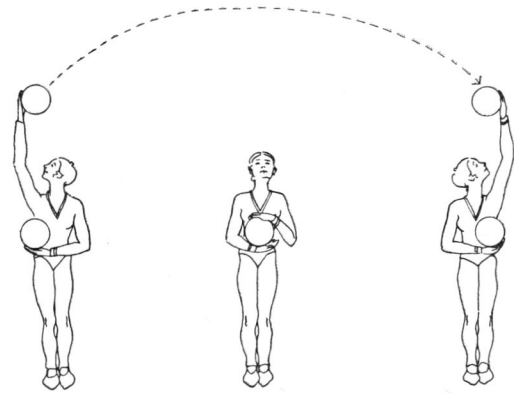

Variation:
Do the same exercise while walking forward or backward.

97

6. Juggle Two Balls

Juggling requires concentration and perfect timing.

Stand with the arms extended to the sides, a ball resting in each hand. First throw ball number 1 upward with the right hand. When this ball is overhead move ball number 2 over to the right and throw it up with both hands. Catch ball number 1 on the left with both hands. Movement must be continuous, always throwing one ball and before catching it, releasing the other ball.

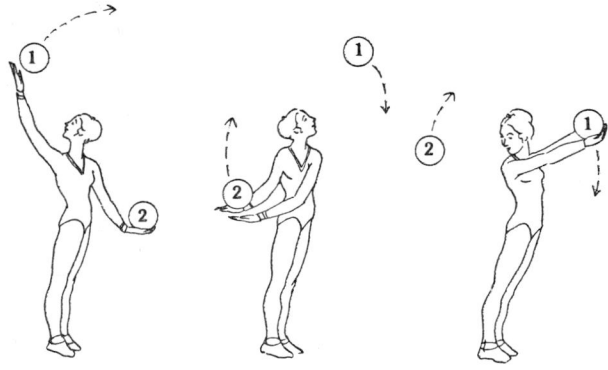

Variation:
Do the same movement while walking or running forward or backward.

~~~~~~

TEACHING SUGGESTIONS

~~~~~~

1. Good basic ball handling techniques must be taught before introducing more complex exercises.
2. Progress from the simple to the more complex movements.
   Allow the students to work alone with the ball before they work with a partner. Students should work with one ball before attempting routines that require the use of two or three balls.
3. New movement combinations should be gone through first without the ball. Once the combination itself has been perfected, the coordination of the movements with the ball is less difficult.
4. Sequences or combinations should be started as soon as students have learned enough skills so that continuity of movement is emphasized from the beginning.
5. Give students the opportunity to create their own sequences. This will help them to discover the limitless possibilities of movements with the ball. It will also help them develop their own creativity and individuality.
6. The exercises should be performed with music at all times. Waltz rhythm is the best to get the relaxed playful rhythmical swinging, throwing, rolling, and bouncing movements; however, 6/8, 2/4 or 4/4

meter music works just as well, as long as the tempo is correct. The music should not be so slow that it loses the life and flowing quality of the movements or so fast that the movements cannot be carried out to their fullest possible range.
7. Students should not be afraid of losing the ball. It is better to lose the ball and use the right technique than to try and hold on to the ball by grasping it.
8. Movements that are similar to conditioning exercises, in which the ball is held in the hand, between the feet, or in some other manner, are not considered modern ball gymnastics.
9. All movements should be practiced with both the right and left hand from the beginning in order to develop balanced handling of the apparatus. If the movements with the ball are described for only one side, the reader should reverse the movements for the other side.

COMPETITIVE RULES

The *area* for ball gymnastics in competition is 39⅓ square feet (12 x 12 meters). The performer, who should use the entire area, should plan a choreographic design that allows for the best use of each corner and all the floor space. There is a penalty for stepping out of the area.

Any type of *music* may be used but it must be appropriate for both the movement and the temperament of the gymnast. The selection of music should allow for a variety of rhythms with slow and fast passages. Only one instrument may be used for accompaniment. If the musical accompaniment is not in harmony with the gymnast's movements there is a penalty.

The *duration* of individual routines, according to the F.I.G. rules, is one minute to one minute and thirty seconds. If the exercise is too long, 0.30 point is deducted, if it is too short, 0.05 point is deducted for each second.

There are certain points the gymnast must consider in the *execution* of the routine. These are: proper rhythm, continuity of the exercise, and sureness and elegance of execution. The rhythm of the exercise is important because proper rhythm allows for better execution and it makes a more pleasing composition. Lack of harmony between the movement and the ball is penalized.

Other penalties found in execution are: loss of the ball, grasping the ball with the fingers, bouncing the ball with a slapping noise, causing the ball to hop during a roll, throwing the ball with a flat hand, catching it noisily, and supporting the ball on the forearm. Unnecessary movement of the arms or legs to maintain balance is penalized each time it occurs. All jumps or leaps must have an amplitude and all turns must be performed with confidence or there is a penalty.

EXAMPLES OF DIFFICULTIES

The individual optional routine should contain six elements of medium difficulty and two elements of superior difficulty. At least three difficulties must be performed with the left hand. For complete classification of movements consult the F.I.G. rule book. The following examples of types of difficulties are given only as guidelines.

Throwing and Catching

Medium difficulties: Throw the ball upward with a turn and catch it with one hand; throw the ball upward and catch it with two hands behind the back.

Superior difficulties: Throw the ball upward with a pirouette (turn on one foot) and catch it with one hand; throw the ball upward while running forward and catch it with both hands behind the back while still moving.

Bouncing

Medium difficulties: Bounce the ball while performing a 360° turn; bounce the ball while doing scissor kicks.

Superior difficulties: Bounce the ball without interruption while doing a double pirouette (720° turn); do scissor kicks over the ball.

Rolling

Medium difficulties: Do jumps over the rolling ball; roll the ball on one arm and catch it with the other hand.

Superior difficulties: Perform turning jumps over the rolling ball; roll the ball along both arms.

Swinging

Medium difficulty: Swing toss the ball overhead.

Superior difficulty: Swing toss the ball over the head with a turn.

Balancing

Medium difficulties: Curl and uncurl arm while walking; spiral with waltz steps.

Superior difficulties: Throw the ball with curled arm over the head and catch it with the other hand (arm curled); spiral with pirouette or with jumps.

COMPOSITION

Balls

Before attempting to compose a complete routine of one minute and thirty seconds or longer, it is best simply to combine a few of the skills you have learned. In your combinations try to include a variety of movements at different levels and to plan an interesting floor pattern. The following is an example of a composition using only skills that have been presented in this chapter.

1. Bounce the ball under the left leg.
2. Run forward in a figure eight while performing swing tosses from side to side.
3. Swing toss overhead from right to left hand.
4. Spiral with the left hand, in a lunge position.
5. Roll the ball on the floor.
6. Turn to the left, run, leap, and catch the ball.
7. Throw the ball overhead in the sagittal plane and catch it.
8. Lunge, then turn on the floor while swinging the right arm backward and forward.
9. Throw the ball up in a forward motion.
10. Run forward and catch the ball behind the back.

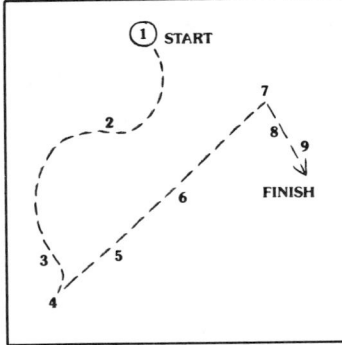

Floor pattern for composition

102

GROUP EXERCISES

Balls

In competition the group exercise is performed by six gymnasts. The length of the exercise may range from two minutes and thirty seconds to three minutes. The space within which the group must remain is 39⅓ square feet (12 x 12 meters). The exercise should have pleasing floor patterns and should be composed of at least six formations. During the routine there must be at least four exchanges of balls between members of the group.

Ball exercises can also be used very effectively with large groups for school demonstrations. The examples presented here are for a group of six girls and may easily be adapted to larger groups.

FLOOR PATTERN EXAMPLES

1. Six girls form a reverse T-formation in the center of the area. With four chaînés turns, circling the ball around the body, they end in the second formation.

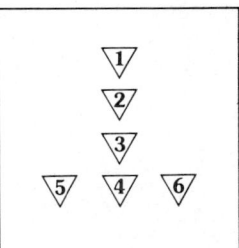

2. Girls in two parallel lines, facing each other. Throw the ball up and let it drop. Run forward into the third formation and catch the partner's ball on the rebound.

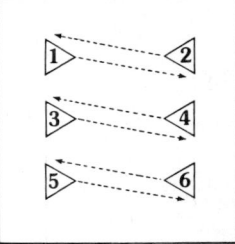

3. Girls in two parallel lines, facing in opposite directions. Waltz run forward in a circle while performing overhead throws. End in the fourth formation.

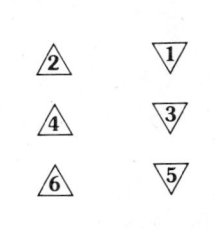

4. Stand in a circle, facing counterclockwise. Leap as you toss the ball and catch it; step scissor kick as you bounce the ball and catch it, forming the fifth formation.

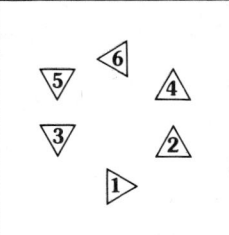

5. Form two symmetrical triangles, facing in opposite directions. Spiral while walking forward into the sixth formation.

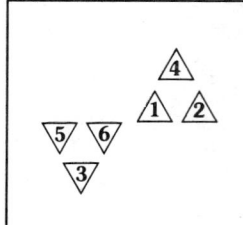

6. Four girls form a diamond and two girls stand in front on either side.

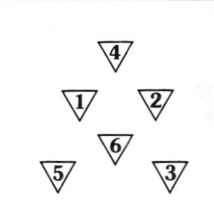

EXCHANGE EXAMPLES

1. Circle formation, facing counterclockwise.
   Take four skips forward, bouncing the ball with each skip. The last bounce must be higher so each girl is able to catch the ball on the rebound from the girl in front. Repeat.

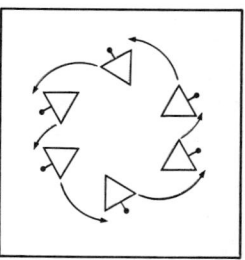

2. Circle formation, facing inward, ball in right hand. Throw the ball overhead to the left to the next girl who catches it with her right hand. Repeat.

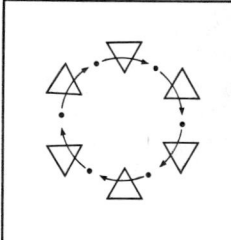

3. Circle formation, facing counterclockwise. Throw the ball upward and backward over your head, then run forward. Catch the ball from the person in front. Repeat.

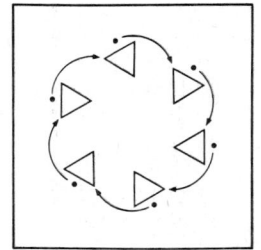

4. Two parallel lines, one behind the other. In the first line each girl holds the ball in her right hand. Number 1 throws the ball overhead to the left to number 3. Simultaneously number 3 passes the ball with a swing toss to number 2's right hand and number 2 passes her ball to number 1. Number 3 catches the ball from number 1 with her left hand and quickly passes the ball in front of her body to the right hand. Repeat. In the second line students hold the ball in their left hands and perform the same exercise in the opposite direction.

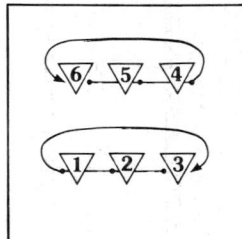

SUGGESTED GROUP ASSIGNMENT

The problem-solving method of teaching has been recently utilized in physical education. Setting up a problem to be solved by students through experimentation has greatly encouraged creativity. The teacher should present a problem to the class in written form so that they have the written material in front of them. She should then allow the students ample time to attack the problem.

The following is an example of a problem the author used in modern gymnastic classes with high school and college students.

Problem: Work out the following formations using creating transitions. Be imaginative and use your sense of adventure to arrive at the assigned patterns.

1. Patterns

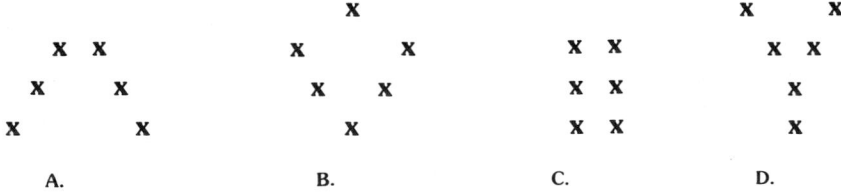

2. Be sure to include the following movements:
   throwing and catching   swinging   rolling
   bouncing   balancing

105

3. Make use of different levels.

4. During the execution there must be at least two exchanges of balls between members of the group.

5. The formations must be worked out in the sequences shown. Be sure to use the balls and accompanying steps in harmony with and of the same quality as the music.

*Music—*Franz Lehár "Gold and Silver Waltz"—arrangement by Harriet Jones

Musical breakdown:
32 measures
3/4 meter
8 bars—medium soft and light
8 bars—crisp, bouncy
16 bars—smooth, grandiose

"The Gold and Silver Waltz" is suitable for ball gymnastics since it implies a happy, gracious mood and therefore allows for large flowing movements.

Music for Ball Group Assignment

107

Ropes

Chapter 4

Jumping rope is a very old activity. English sports books printed around 1800 mention it as a favorite game of girls and boys. The winner of the game was the person who jumped over the rope the most times without interruption. Children today still enjoy jumping rope and almost every child is familiar with the activity.

Besides being a favorite game, jumping rope is beneficial. It develops cardiovascular fitness, a sense of rhythm, and total body control. Because of this, boxers, football players, and other athletes use rope jumping as one means of developing cardiovascular endurance and strengthening their feet and legs.

The rope jumping done in modern rhythmic gymnastics, however, is quite a different activity from that done by a child at play or an athlete in training. Jumping rope as a form of dancing with a rope emerged at the 1967 Third Modern Rhythmic Gymnastics World Championships in Copenhagen, Denmark, when the compulsory routine was a rope routine. This routine combined rope jumping with numerous variations of dance steps, turns, jumps, and leaps. The exercise was accompanied by lively and playful music.

Since use of the rope develops endurance, elasticity, strength, rhythm, coordination, speed, and agility, the Eastern European countries, who have long been leaders in modern rhythmic gymnastics, recognize the rope as one of the most important hand apparatuses in the junior modern gymnastics program. It is also one of the most commonly used hand apparatuses in the high schools of these countries because it is considered to be the best developer of physical fitness while the equipment is inexpensive.

EQUIPMENT

The official F.I.G. rope is a hemp rope without handles which may be reinforced in the middle. The enlarged long center section of a reinforced rope gives proper distribution of weight which allows the gymnast to perform many of the new skills. The length of the rope depends upon the height of the gymnast. It is measured by having the gymnast stand on the center of the rope with one foot and hold the ends in her hands. The rope should be long enough for the hands to be held at shoulders height with the arms extended.

For school, a sash cord No. 9 or 10 can be used. This rope is heavy enough to be swung effectively and change speed quickly. It may be purchased for a few dollars by the coil or by the foot. The rope should be cut in 3 or 4 different lengths (perhaps 8, 9, and 10 foot lengths). Tape the ends of each length with a different color tape. This will both allow quick identification of the length of the rope, and prevent the rope from raveling.

Knotting the ends of the rope makes the rope easier to handle (even competitors do this). Also, if you need to shorten a rope without cutting it, knotting the ends will do the trick.

TECHNIQUES

The rope can be used in its full length or it can be folded in half (doubled), or into fourths (quadrupled). The rope should be held with the wrists relaxed and the hands holding the end knots either loosely between the thumb and the index finger so that the rope rotates in the hands, or between the index and middle fingers (in much the same way as one would hold a cigarette).

If the rope is being held in both hands, it may be held with the arms far apart, with the arms crossed, or with the hands close to each other. Both ends of the rope may also be held in one hand.

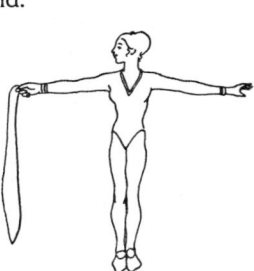

If exercises are performed with proper technique, there will be no slack in the rope during the exercise.

Be sure to maintain good posture. The body should be erect rather than bent during jumps. The feet must be close to the floor and stretched when in the air and the knees must be slightly bent in landing.

During the swing the rope should not touch the floor but rather pass slightly above it. Also, the rope should not touch the trunk or any other part of the body except during movements in which the rope is wrapped around the body.

In rope jumping, the first swing of the rope starts from the shoulders and consecutive swings come from the wrists. If any swings after the first come from the shoulders the movement of the rope will be jerky and not coordinated with the leg work. During the jump, the toes should be pointed while the feet are in the air. The jump need not be high, just sufficient for the rope to pass smoothly under the feet. The landing should be light and with the knees bent.

Rope swinging movements are initiated from the shoulders, the elbows, or the wrists with the entire body following the direction of the rope.

MOVEMENTS

Begin with simple rope jumping exercises and progress to more difficult ones as you feel your ability develop.

As soon as you have learned a few skills, try putting together sequences or combinations. This will help you develop a good feeling for continuity of movement.

Rope exercises should always be performed with music. Schottische rhythms, polkas, and other lively folk dance melodies are the most suitable for rope jumping. Popular music also may be used if the rhythm is good.

Use gymnastic shoes for rope jumping. Never jump on concrete, cement, or marble floors or practice too long because this may be injurious to the metatarsal arch and may cause shin-splints.

Rope movements are divided into: jumping, swinging, wrapping, balancing, and tossing movements.

JUMPING MOVEMENTS

The jumps are executed with the rope single, double, or quadruple. The turns of the rope are made forward, backward, or laterally.

The rotation of the rope can be slow (two jumps on each swing), regular (one jump for each turn of rope), and fast (one jump for each two turns of the rope). During slow rotation the arms are extended; in regular turns the arms are bent; and during fast spinning only the wrists rotate.

The gymnast should learn basic jumps and running steps with forward and backward rope swings before attempting any other movements. The rope may pass under the feet every third, second, or single jump or running step.

Jumps may be divided into the following categories:

a) Starting with both legs and finishing on both.

b) Starting on both legs and finishing on one.

c) Starting with one leg and finishing on both.

d) Starting with one leg and finishing on the same leg.

e) From one leg to the other.

The goal in rope jumping is lightness and perfect coordination of movements of the arms, legs, and trunk.

1. Basic Forward Jump
Stand holding the rope in back of the body with the arms raised to the sides. Swing the rope up, overhead, and forward; jump with both feet to clear the rope and then jump again (a small jump) as the rope passes over the head. This is called a double jump. Repeat.

Variations:
a) Do the same exercise with a single jump for each turn of rope.

b) Jump over the rope with a single jump with the feet together; jump with the feet apart (straddle position); jump with feet together; and so on.

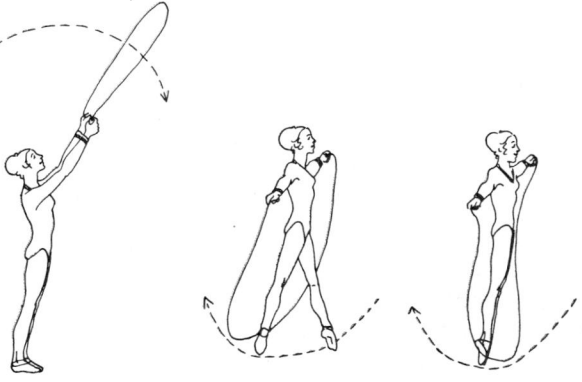

c) Jump with each swing: feet apart; feet crossed, right leg in front of left; feet apart; feet crossed, left leg in front of right; feet apart; and feet together.

d) Jump with feet together; feet apart in front stride position, right foot in front; feet together; feet in front stride position, left foot in front; feet together; and so on.

2. Basic Jump Backward

Stand holding the rope in front of the body with the arms extended to the sides. Swing the rope up, overhead and backward. Jump over the rope and then jump again as the rope is above the head. Do a double jump with each swing.

Variations:
Do the same variations as in exercise 1 but swing the rope backward.

3. Step-Hop Forward

Stand holding the rope in back of the body with the arms extended to the side. Swing the rope slowly up, overhead, and forward. Step forward over the rope with the right foot, and hop on the right as the rope passes above the head. During the hop the left leg is extended forward with the toes pointed. Repeat the step-hop with the left foot.

Perform this exercise first in place then moving across the gymnasium.

Variations:
a) Do the same exercise extending the free leg backward.

b) Repeat (a) extending the free leg sideward.

c) Alternate extending the leg forward, sideward, and backward.

d) Step forward on the right as the rope is overhead; hop over the rope on the right foot. Then step forward on the left and hop over the rope on the left foot. Continue the step-hop, alternating sides.

e) Do all of the above exercises with a regular rope swing, taking one step-hop for two turns of the rope.

4. Step-Hop Backward
Stand holding the rope in front of the body with the arms extended to the sides. Turn the rope backward, step backward over the rope with the right foot, and hop on the right as the rope passes overhead. During the hop the free leg is bent to the rear. Repeat the step-hop with the left foot. Practice first in place, then moving across the gymnasium.

Variations:
Do the same variations as in exercise 3 but while swinging the rope backward.

5. Cradle
Stand in a forward stride position, with the left foot forward and the weight back on the right foot as the left foot is pointed. Hold the rope in back of the body. Turn the rope slowly forward. Rock from the back foot to the front foot while stepping over the rope with the left foot, with the right leg extended backward and the body leaning slightly forward. Rock back while the rope is above the head. Rock from back foot to front foot on each jump over the rope. Also practice with the right leg in front and the left leg back.

rock forward

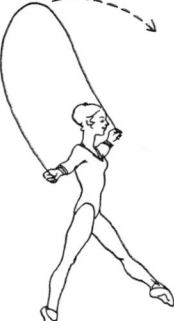
rock backward

Variation:
Reverse the above movement and turn the rope backward.

6. Pendulum Swing

Stand with the feet together and the rope held in front of the body. Swing the rope slowly backward and jump forward over it. Do another small jump while extending the arms backward to force the rope to stop its upward swing. Then swing the rope forward and jump backward over the rope. Jump again while extending the arms forward to stop the rope's upward swing and reverse its direction. The rope swings back and forth under the feet in a pendulum fashion.

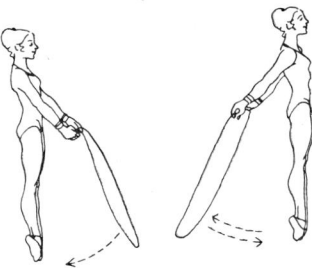

Variations:
a) Do the same movement with a single jump.

b) Combine the pendulum swing with a basic jump forward and a basic jump backward.

7. Running

This exercise may be done in place or while moving across the gymnasium. Stand holding the rope behind the body with arms extended to the sides. Take two running steps forward for each slow forward swing of the rope. The rope passes under the same foot each time. Also practice starting with the other foot.

Variations:
a) Run forward but swing the rope backward.

b) Run forward, turning the rope forward quickly. Take one running step for each swing.

c) Run backward with a slow backward swing. Take two running steps for each swing.

d) Run backward, turning the rope backward quickly. Take one step for each swing.

e) Run backward while turning the rope forward.

8. Gallop

Stand holding the rope in back of the body with arms extended to the sides. Perform four gallop steps to the left side over the rope as the rope is turned forward. There should be one turn of the rope for each gallop step. During the jump the legs are extended with toes pointed. When landing, the weight is kept on the right foot. Reverse the movement, moving to the right.

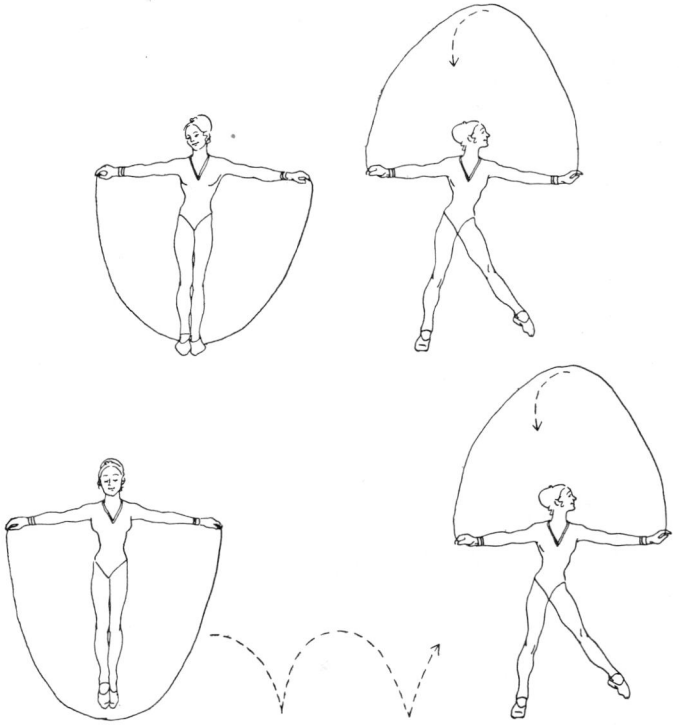

Variations:
a) Do the same exercise while turning the rope backward.

b) Gallop forward, bringing the same foot forward each time. Practice leading with both legs.

c) Stand with the right leg in front. Gallop forward and step-hop to change the leading leg. Repeat with the left leg. Take two turns of the rope for each gallop and step-hop. The rope goes under the feet on the gallop and again on the step-hop.

9. Front Cross
Stand holding the rope in back of the body with the arms extended to the sides. Swing the rope up and overhead. As the rope starts downward, cross the arms in front and jump over the rope with the arms crossed. Keep the arms crossed until the rope is again overhead, then uncross the arms and do a basic forward jump in the normal manner. Continue the above pattern. Practice crossing the right arm in front, then crossing the left arm in front.

Remember that when the arms are crossed, the rope area is decreased, therefore, lower the hands as the arms are crossed and cross the arms far enough so that the elbows are together in order to form a good loop.

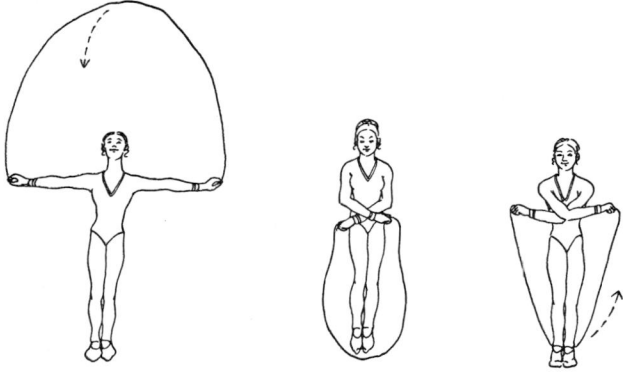

Variations:

a) Run forward while turning the rope forward with the arms alternating between crossed and uncrossed.

b) Step-hop forward with the arms crossing and uncrossing while turning the rope forward.

c) Do a forward jump with a double turn of the crossed rope. This exercise is considered difficult because only a few students are able to swing the rope with enough force to make a double turn while the arms are crossed.

10. Back Cross
Stand holding the rope in front of the body with the arms extended to the side. Start with a basic jump backward as in exercise 2, then cross

the arms in front of the body and continue jumping with the arms crossed, and then open the arms and again do a basic jump backward. Continue the above pattern, crossing first the right arm in front and then the left arm in front. Crossing and uncrossing of the arms must be performed smoothly on the upward swing just before the rope passes over the head.

Variations:
Do the same variations as in exercise 9 but swing the rope backward.

11. Double Turn
Stand holding the rope to the rear with the arms extended to the sides. Perform a basic forward jump with the rope passing under the feet twice before landing. In order to do this, the jump must be higher than normal and the rope speeded up. The fast spinning rope will make a whistling sound.

This exercise can be learned most easily if it is combined with two or three basic jumps performed with single turns of the rope and then going on with the double turns in which the rope swings twice as fast.

Variations:
a) Do two squat jumps (see exercise 13) while turning the rope forward. Then, without stopping, straighten up and jump with a double turn of the rope.

b) Do any leap or jump with a double turn of the rope.

c) Perform the above-mentioned movements while turning the rope backward.

12. Triple Turn
The triple turn is very challenging and can be accomplished by only a few gymnasts because exceptional speed and timing are required to be

able to perform this movement. When attempting this exercise, shorten the rope, hold the arms low, and stay in the air as long as possible by bending the knees during the jump.

Stand holding the rope to the rear with arms extended to the sides. Swing the rope up, overhead and forward. Jump high in the air as the rope goes under the feet. Bring both knees upward to the chest (into a tuck position) as the rope passes under the feet for the second time. Hold the tuck position until the rope swings under the legs for the third time. The rope must be spun forward quickly and forcefully with the wrists in order to make three turns on one jump.

13. Squat Jump
Squat, holding the rope behind the body with the arms extended to the sides. Keep the hips low and the back straight. Swing the rope up, overhead, and forward and jump over it in a squat position. Repeat this exercise two or three times but do not overdo it or the ligaments in the knees will become irritated.

Variations:
a) Alternate squat jumps with basic forward jumps. For example, do two squat jumps, straighten up and do two basic forward jumps and so on.

b) Do all the above exercises while swinging the rope backward.

14. Schottische Step
Stand with the rope in back of the body, arms extended to the sides. Schottische step forward: step, step, step, hop. On the hop the free leg is swung forward or backward. The rope is turned forward and goes under the feet on the first and third steps. Repeat, starting with the other foot.

Variations:
a) Perform the schottische step to the rear while turning the rope backward.

b) Perform the schottische step with three running steps and a hop, as it is sometimes performed in American folk dances.

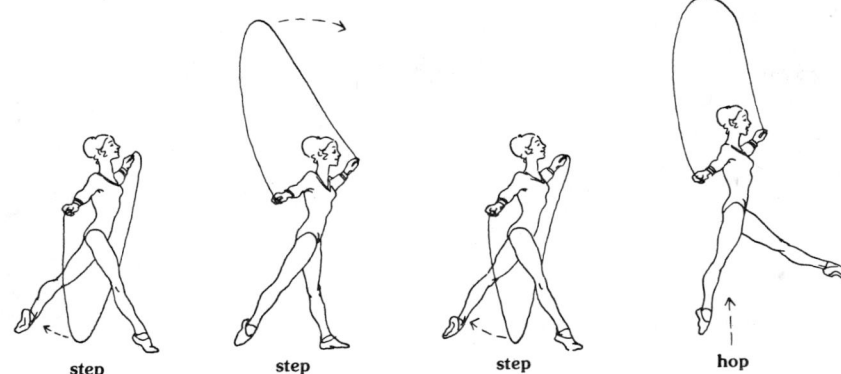

15. Polka Step
Stand holding the rope to the rear, arms extended to the sides. Swing the rope slowly forward while performing the fast polka step. The polka step is a "hop-step-close-step" with the hop, which is quick, coming on the up-beat. Hop over the rope, then do the step-close-step forward as the rope passes over the head. Repeat the polka step with the other foot.

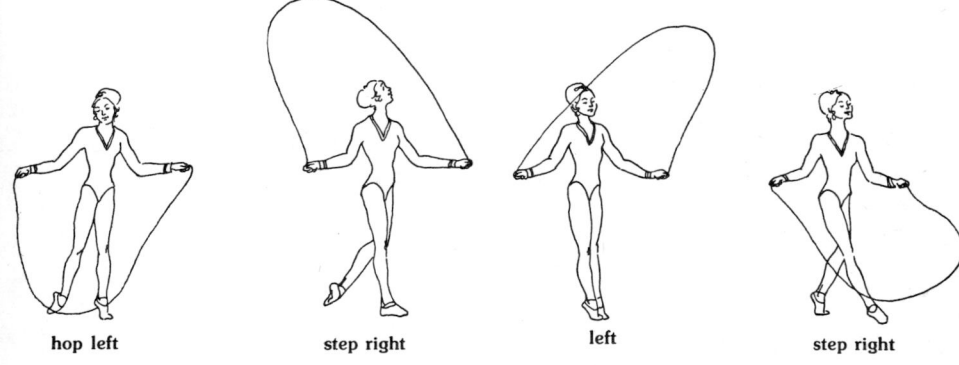

16. Jumps
Stand with the rope in back of the body, arms extended to the side. Do two basic forward jumps and on the third jump perform a tuck jump and land on both feet. The rope passes under the feet on each jump.

Variations:

a) Perform a cheerleader jump instead of the tuck jump.

b) Do the basic exercise but on the third jump extend the legs and split them forward and backward in the air.

c) Performing the basic exercise, on the third jump split the legs with both knees bent, forward and backward in the air. Land on the front foot.

17. Scissor Kick

Stand with the rope to the rear and the arms extended to the sides. Perform a scissor jump forward while turning the rope forward: step on the left foot, kick the right leg forward and up, kick the left leg forward and up to follow the right leg, and land on the right foot. The rope passes under the feet on both the step and the scissor kick.

Variations:

a) Perform a scissor jump forward followed by a scissor jump backward while turning the rope forward.

b) Perform a scissor jump backward while turning the rope backward.

18. Cabriole

Stand with the rope in back of the body, arms extended to the sides. Swing the rope up, overhead, and forward. As the rope approaches the floor, thrust the left leg sideward into the air. Then push off with the right foot and thrust the right leg into the air beating the calf of the left leg with the right leg as the rope passes beneath the feet. Land on the right foot. Repeat. Also practice this to the right side.

Variations:
a) Do the above movements alternating sides. After landing on the right foot, immediately shift the weight to the left foot to be ready to swing the right leg sideward.

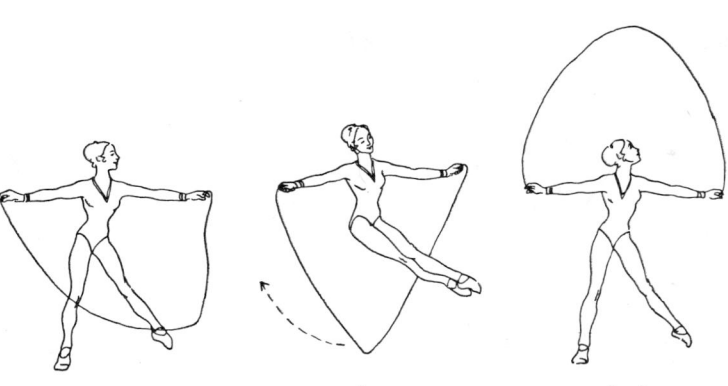

thrust leg   beat   land

change   jump

b) Do the same movement forward.

c) Do the same movement backward.

d) Do all the above movements with bent legs.

19. Leaps
Stand with the rope held to the rear, arms extended to the sides. Take one running step forward on the left foot; leap on the right. Continue this pattern, passing the rope under the leaping leg. Also practice leaping on the left foot.

Variations:
a) Do several leap steps successively. The rope turns twice as fast as above to pass under the feet with each step.

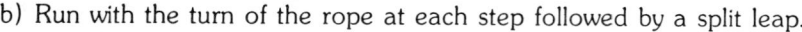

b) Run with the turn of the rope at each step followed by a split leap.

c) Repeat (b) with a stag leap.

d) Do cat leaps turning the rope forward or backward. The cat leap is performed in the same way as the scissor kick (exercise 17), except that the legs are bent.

20. Side Leg Swinging *(cowboy kick)*

Stand on the right foot with the rope in front, the left leg extended to the side, the left arm held high above the head, and the right arm low in front of hips. Keep the left hand high and swing the rope to the left, across the back to the right, and across the front by circling the left wrist in a counterclockwise direction.

As the rope is brought to the left side, kick the left leg through the rope; step-hop on the left foot as the right leg is lifted to the side while the rope is behind the body. Swing the rope forward under the right leg and step-hop on right foot while the rope is twisting in front of the body. Continue the step-hops with the free leg swinging alternately to left and right side while the rope is circling.

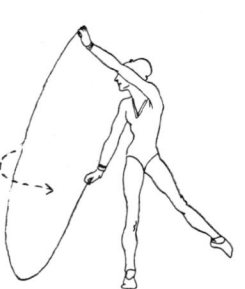 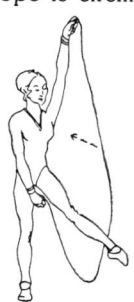  

hop right   **under left**   **hop left**   **under right**

Variations:
a) Circle the arms as above but hold the right arm high above the head and the left arm low in front of the hips.

b) Turn the rope in a clockwise direction with the hand above the head.

c) Do the same movement but hold the lower arm in back of the body instead of front.

d) Do the above exercises with a 180° turn at each leg kick to the side.

21. Oblique Turn
Stand with the rope at the right side, the left arm held high above the head and the right arm stretched sideways in an oblique position. Swing the rope to the left and jump over it. Continue to turn the rope and jump over it again. The rope is turned in a similar way as it is in exercise 20.

Variations:
a) Squat jump over the rope as it passes through the oblique plane.

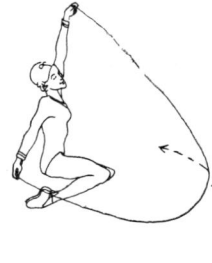

b) Try different jumps through the loop.

c) Perform the jump over the rope with 180° or 360° turns.

22. Lateral Turn
Many of the movements listed above can be performed while turning the rope laterally from side to side rather than forward or backward. Perfect the basic jump using a lateral turn before attempting any other skills.

Stand with the left arm in front, right arm to the rear. Hold one end of the rope in each hand, with the rope hanging down on the left side of the body. Swing the rope up, overhead, and downward on the right side of the body, and jump over it. Continue jumping while focusing forward. Practice with the right arm in front as well as the left.

Variation:
Do the same exercise, but let the rope hang down on the right side of the body and turn the rope in the opposite direction from right to left.

23. Forward-to-Backward Turn
Stand with the rope to the rear, arms extended to the side. While jumping forward (see exercise 1), as the rope starts downward, instead of letting it go under the feet, swing both arms to one side of the body and make a half-turn in that direction. The rope is allowed to continue its arch while the body does a 180° turn; then the arms are separated above the head and the rope is now turning backwards. Continue with backward jumps. Practice turning to both sides.

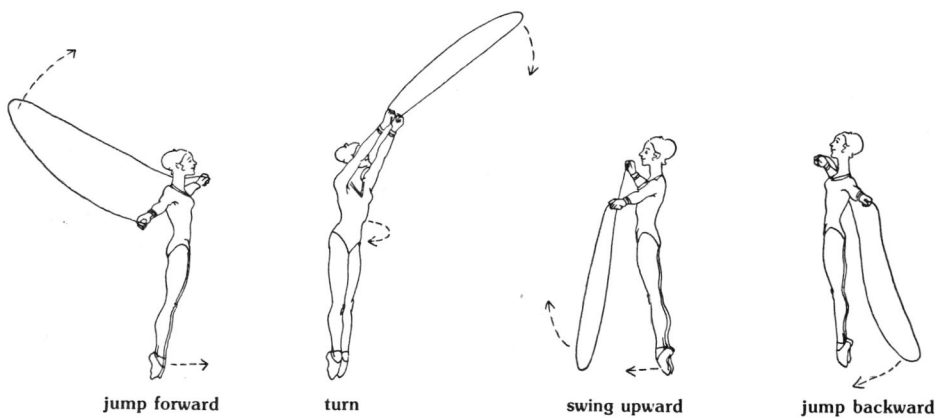

jump forward   turn   swing upward   jump backward

Variation:
Do the same movement while performing step-hops or other dance steps.

24. Backward-to-Forward Turn
Stand with the rope in front, the arms extended to the sides. While performing a basic jump backward, make a half-turn as the arms come overhead and then continue jumping forward. Do not allow the rope to swing out to the side. Turn while the arms are still up and the rope is overhead.

Variations:
a) Do the same movement while running or performing step-hops or other dance steps.

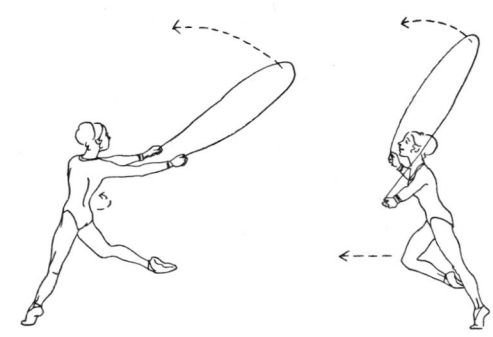

run backward   turn   run forward

b) Alternate forward-to-backward-to-forward turns with different dance steps.

25. Folded Rope Turn
Fold the rope in half and stand holding the folded rope in the right hand above the head. Swing the rope to the left in a horizontal circle above the head and then swing it in the same direction slightly above the floor while passing over the rope with a jump. Also practice swinging the rope with the left hand.

Variation:
Do a few running steps and then perform different leaps while swinging the folded rope under the legs.

26. Double-Folded Rope Jump

This exercise is very challenging and can be performed successfully by only a few gymnasts because it requires exceptional speed, timing, and shoulder flexibility. Before attempting to jump over a double-folded rope (the rope is folded in half and then in half again), practice this skill over a folded rope (folded in half once) held in both hands.

Stand holding the double-folded rope in front of you in both hands. Swing the arms downward and jump over the rope in a squat position. Repeat a few times.

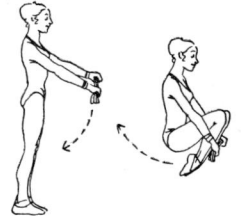

Variation:
The same exercise can be done while the rope is circling backward.

27. Partner Jumping *(using one rope)*

Stand next to your partner facing the same direction as she does. Put your **inside** arm around your partner's waist and hold the end of the rope with the outside hand. Both partners swing the rope together. The girl on the right turns the rope with her right hand while the girl on the left turns it with her left hand. Do jumps forward or backward on both feet, on one foot, or on alternate feet; or walk or run forward or backward. The rope may be turned either forward or backward.

Variation:
Partners face in opposite directions while performing the above movements.

28. Partner Jumping *(using two ropes)*

Stand next to your partner facing the same direction as she does. Each girl turns her partner's rope with her inside hand. Both partners swing the ropes together, turning them both either forward or backward. You may jump forward or backward on both feet, on one foot, on alternate feet, or you may walk or run forward or backward.

 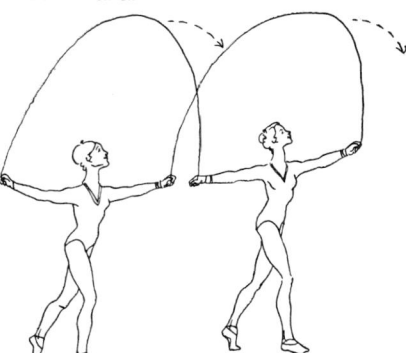

SWINGING MOVEMENTS

127

Ropes

Swinging skills are performed with a single, doubled, or quadrupled rope. The rope can be held in one or both hands. Movement of the rope is initiated from either the shoulders, the elbows, or the wrists. The possible variations and combinations of arm, lower arm, and wrist circles are limitless.

The rope may be swung in vertical, lateral, and horizontal planes. The swing of the rope forward, backward, or sideward should be followed by movement of the total body.

Vertical swings are executed in front and in back of the body or head in the frontal plane.

Lateral swings can be executed on the left or right side of the body. The best example is the figure eight in which the rope circles from side to side in the sagittal plane.

Horizontal swings are executed by moving the rope around the body, above the head, and below the legs in the horizontal plane.

1. Swing in the Frontal Plane

Stand in a wide straddle position with the arms extended to the sides holding the folded rope in the right hand. Swing the right arm downward, upward over the head, and downward again toward the left side, making one and a half circles in front of the body. Transfer the rope to the left hand and make one and a half circles in the opposite direction. The whole body should follow the movement of the rope.

Variations:

a) Do the same movement with a gallop from side to side.

b) Repeat (a) while turning the rope with hands close together.

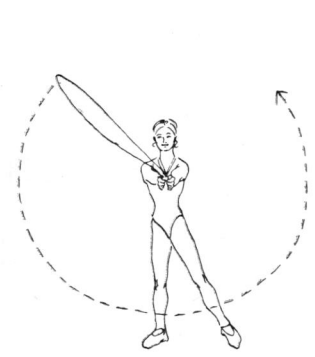
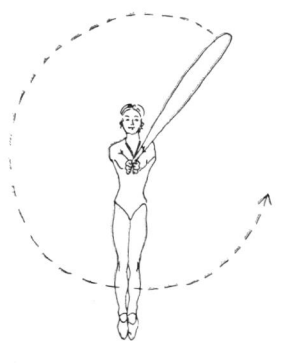

2. Sitting and Circling *(quadrupled)*

Sit on the right buttock, with both legs bent and the feet to the left side. Hold the quadrupled rope in the right hand at the right side. Swing the rope inward with the right hand making two circles in front of the body with it. On the third circle, rise to both knees, transfer the rope to the left hand, and then shift your weight to the left buttock. Shift your weight from side to side while circling the rope in front of the body.

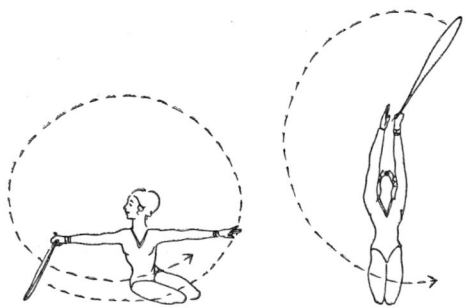

3. Figure Eight Front-to-Back

Stand holding the rope in front of you with both hands. Circle the rope inward in front of the body toward the left, over the head, and then bend the elbows and circle the rope inward in back of the body toward the right, then over the head and then straighten the arms. Repeat several times and then alternate directions. Keep the arms parallel during the movement.

4. Figure Eight Sideward

Stand holding the rope in front of the body with the arms extended to the sides. Swing the right arm upward to the left over the horizontal left arm and circle the right arm downward and backward outside of the left shoulder. Then circle downward and backward with the left hand. Continue with a swing downward and backward outside of the right shoulder with the right arm. Repeat the movement. To be able to do this movement smoothly the trunk must rotate with the movement of the arms. The arms must pass through the sagittal plane, must be kept straight. Practice this also in the opposite direction.

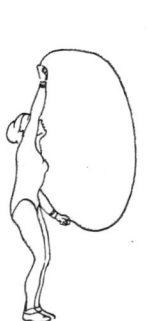

Variation:
Do the same movement while moving forward or backward, with either walking or dancing steps.

5. Kneeling and Circling

Kneel on both knees holding a quadrupled rope in front, in the right hand. Swing the rope downward, backward, and upward in the sagittal plane, while simultaneously doing a body wave. Repeat several times and then alternate sides.

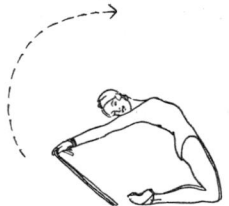

6. Swing in Sagittal Plane

Stand holding the rope in front of you with both hands close together. Swing the rope forward in a circle on the right side of the body. Repeat several times and then alternate sides.

Variations:

a) Do the same movement while circling the rope backward.

b) Circle the rope either forward or backward from side to side in a figure eight.

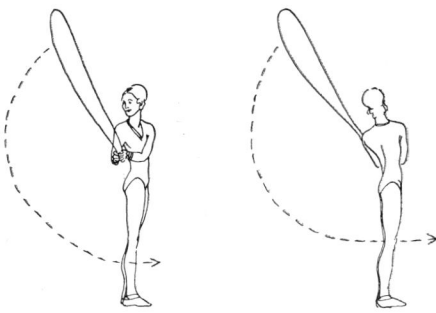

c) Do a body wave while circling the rope.

d) All the above movements may be performed by holding the rope in one hand, either right or left.

e) All the above swinging movements may be done while moving forward or backward, with either walking or dancing steps.

7. Swing and Forward Jump

Stand holding the rope in front of you with both hands close together. Swing the rope downward, backward, and around, circling it on the right side of the body. When the rope is overhead, separate the arms and swing the rope forward and downward. Jump over it, bring the hands together and swing the rope on the left side of the body. Continue the movement, separating the arms and jumping over the rope, then swinging the rope to the right side of the body, and so on.

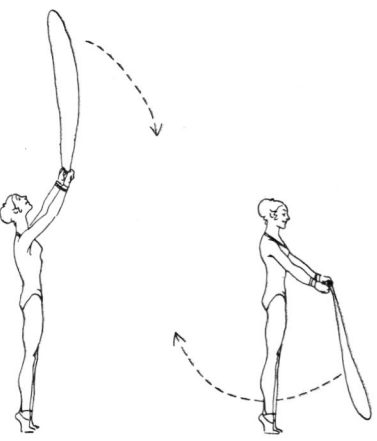

Variations:
a) Swing the rope to the right side, then to the left side, then jump over it forward.
b) Do two swings at the right side, jump over it twice then do two swings at the left side.
c) Do the above alternating swings and jumps while moving forward with either walking or dancing steps.

8. Swing and Backward Jump
Do the same exercises as described in exercise 7 but swing the rope in the opposite direction and jump over it backward.

9. Swing and Sideward Jump
Stand holding the rope in front of the body with both hands close together. Swing the rope to the right in front of the body, then upward and overhead, and then separate the hands (left hand forward, right hand to the back) while you swing the rope downward on the right side of the body and jump over it. Bring the hands close together overhead and swing the rope down in front of the body. Alternate the vertical swing with the lateral jump several times.

Variations:
a) Do the same exercise, but turn the rope in the opposite direction.
b) Alternate two swings in front with two sideward jumps.

10. Swing in Rhythm
Swing the rope in varying dynamic and time patterns while performing alternate lateral swings and forward jumps.

4/4 meter: Swing the rope from the shoulders with the arms straight. Swing it twice on the left side then do one basic jump forward. Then swing the rope twice on the right side and do one basic jump forward. Repeat several times.

♩ ♩ ♩ ♩
Swing, swing jump

3/4 meter: Do the same exercise as described under the 4/4 meter but initiate the swings from the elbows. The 3/4 meter does not allow time to straighten the arms during the swings.

♩ ♩ ♩
Swing, swing jump

2/4 meter: Do the same exercise but the 2/4 meter requires that the swings be done in double time, so perform them from the wrists.

♩ ♩
Swing, swing jump

11. Swing and Quadruple the Rope

Stand with the left foot in a forward stride, with the weight back on the right foot, and holding the doubled rope in the right hand in front of the body. Make two forward circles with the folded rope on the right side of the body. Transfer the weight forward and do a quarter-turn to the right as you catch the center of the folded rope with the left hand. Step on the right foot and simultaneously catch the end of the rope with the right hand. You will be ready to do a double-folded rope jump. (See rope jumping exercise 26.)

12. Swing Overhead

Stand holding both ends of the rope in the right hand. Perform horizontal circles inward overhead. Repeat with the left hand.

Variations:

a) Perform horizontal circles outward overhead.

b) Do the same movement while moving forward or backward, with either walking or dancing steps.

c) Do the same movement performing pirouettes and other kinds of turns.

d) Do an inward horizontal circle over the head with the left arm while doing a forward step. Without stopping do a low inward horizontal circle in front of the body while performing a scale on the left leg.

e) Perform the above movements holding the rope with both hands close together.

13. Swing Under the Leg

Stand holding both ends of the rope in the right hand, out to the side. Swing the rope low inward, jump over it and continue the circle. Repeat with the left hand.

Variation:
Do a few running steps and then leap or jump as the rope passes under the legs.

 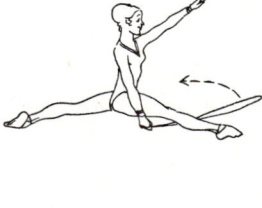

14. Swings over the Head and Under the Leg

Stand holding both ends of the rope in the right hand, over the head. Circle the rope inward above the head then swing the right arm down and circle the rope in the same direction slightly above the floor level, passing over it with a jump. Practice also with the left hand.

Variations:

a) Do a few running steps while circling the rope a few times above the head then leap or jump as the rope is circled under the legs.

b) Do the same movement as (a) but perform a 360° turn with the jump.

15. Turns with Horizontal Swing

Stand holding both ends of the rope in the right hand out to the side. Perform chaînés turns to the left while swinging the folded rope horizontally around you at waist level, by changing hands. Change the rope to the left hand in front of the body and pass it to the right hand in the rear.

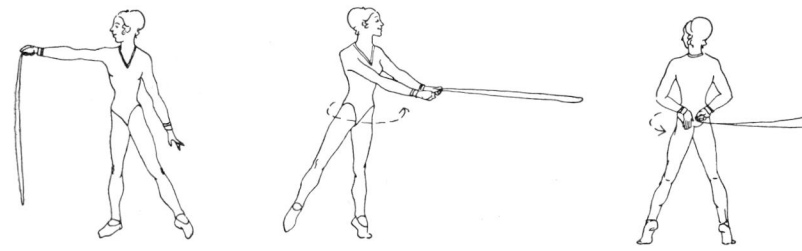

Variations:

a) Do a 360° turn on the right leg simultaneously circling the rope horizontally around you by changing hands.

b) Do a seat turn in hook sitting position while swinging the rope horizontally around you.

c) Swing the rope in a horizontal circle above the head. Then, without stopping, circle the rope around the body by changing hands. Continue to swing the rope above the head and around the body while doing several consecutive turns.

16. Kneeling Turn
Kneel on the right knee, holding both ends of the rope out to the side in the left hand. Bring the left knee across in front of the right knee and place your weight on it as you turn to the right. Step on the right foot, then on the left while turning the folded rope horizontally around the body at waist level by changing hands. Repeat to the opposite side.

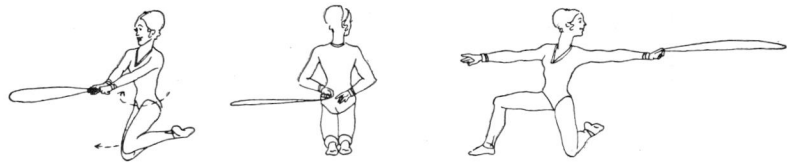

17. Circling Around the Body
Stand with the feet in a wide straddle and the weight on the right foot; extend the arms to the right and hold the rope in both hands. Shift the weight to the left foot as the rope swings to the left in front of the body. Continue swinging the rope toward the rear by arching the trunk backward. Then transfer your weight back to the right foot finishing in the original position. The rope completes a full horizontal circle around the body. Also practice this movement toward the opposite side.

Variation:
Do the same movement by holding the rope in one hand—either right or left.

18. Circling Around with a Twist

Stand holding the rope with both hands, left arm extended overhead and right arm to the side. Swing the left arm across the body, simultaneously bend the right arm and turn the right hand inward and under the forearm, then swing the twisted right arm over the head toward the left side. Continue the circle around the body with the trunk arching backward and finish in the original position. Do this exercise continuously a couple of times then repeat it to the opposite direction.

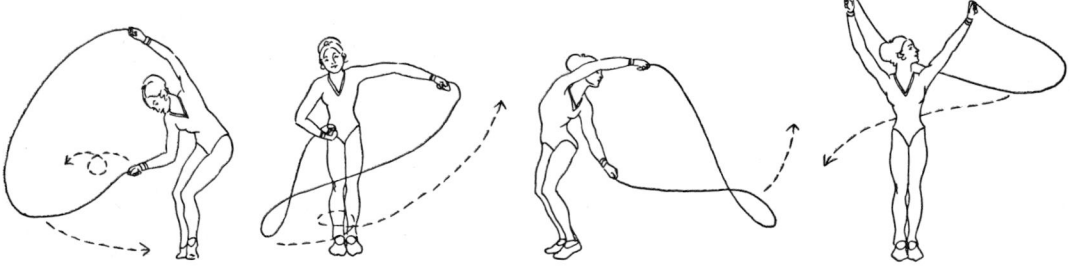

Variation:
Do the same exercise while performing turns or pirouettes.

19. Horizontal Swing with Straight Rope

Stand in a wide straddle with weight on the right foot holding the folded rope in the right hand at the side. Swing the rope inward horizontally overhead and let go of one end allowing it to swing far out. Continue swinging the rope above the head while turning to the left and catch the center of the straight rope with the left hand. Then catch the end of the rope with the right hand.

20. Partner Swinging

Stand facing your partner, holding one end of your rope and one end of your partner's rope in your hands. Swing both ropes from side to side shifting the weight with each swing from one leg to the other. On the third swing raise and make a complete turn with three steps, on the fourth step swing the ropes down on the opposite side. Reverse the movement.

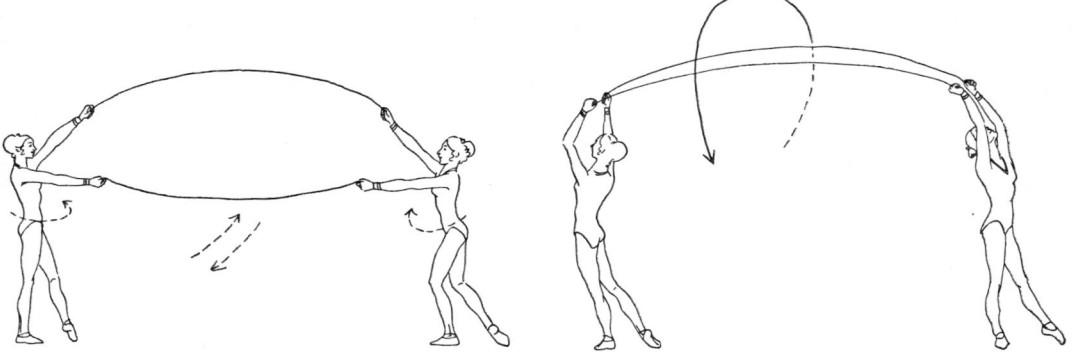

WRAPPING MOVEMENTS

The rope can be wrapped around any body part, but most commonly it is wrapped around the waist. Wrapping movements are used as connecting and resting elements in a routine.

1. Wrap Around Waist

Stand holding the rope in front of you in both hands, with the left arm in front of the waist and the right arm above the head. Swing the rope back, to the right and across the front by circling the right forearm in a counterclockwise direction above the head until the rope is wrapped around the waist. To unwrap, the rope is turned clockwise with the right hand.

Variations:

a) Do the same exercise but after unwrapping the rope continue to swing it clockwise, rewrapping it around the waist. To unwrap it again, turn the rope counterclockwise.

b) Circle the rope as above but move it in the opposite direction by holding the left arm high above the head and the right arm in front of the hips.

c) Do the same movements while doing a turn.

d) Wrap and unwrap the rope; then swing it around the body (see rope swinging exercise 17) and wrap and unwrap the rope in the opposite direction.

2. Wrap Around with Folded Rope
Stand, holding the folded rope by the right hand at the right side. Do a chaîné turn to the left, simultaneously swing the rope horizontally in front of the body to the left and wrap it around the waist. To unwrap, do a chaîné turn to the right while swinging the rope in the same direction.

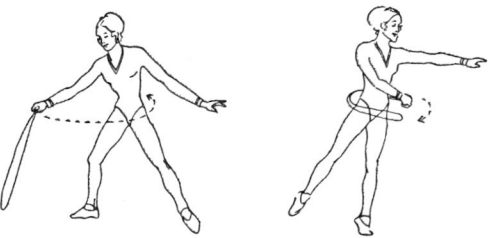

Variation:
Do the same exercise but after wrapping the rope around the body exchange hands and unwrap it with the left hand.

3. Wrap Around with Straight Rope
Stand in a wide straddle with weight on the left foot and the arms stretched out to the sides. Hold the folded rope in the left hand. Swing the rope to the right side, back to the left side and let go of one end,

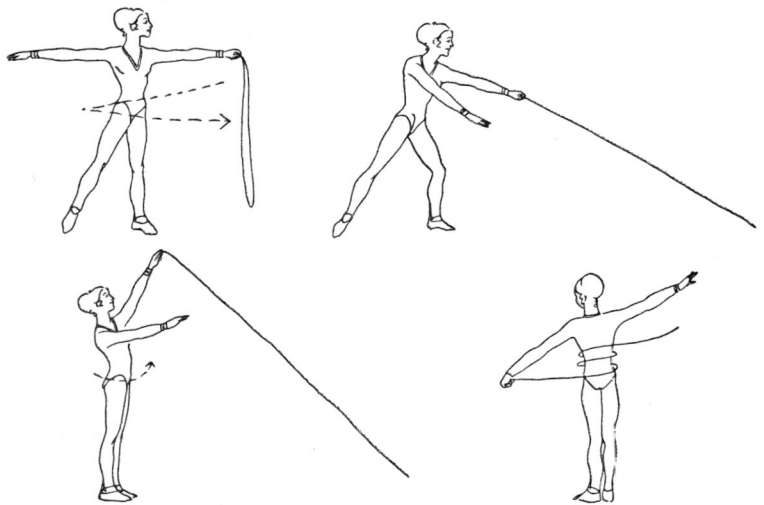

allowing it to swing far out in front of you as you perform a quarter turn to the left. Swing the straight left arm backward and upward and turn into the rope toward the left, wrapping it around the waist. To unwrap, turn to the opposite direction. This can make a nice finishing movement for a routine.

4. Wrap Around the Arm
Stand holding the rope in front of the body in both hands, with the arms extended to the right side. Swing the rope forward, upward, and around by circling the right wrist in a clockwise direction until the rope is wrapped around the right arm. Turn the wrist counterclockwise until the rope is unwrapped from the arm. Repeat the movement, wrapping the rope on the left arm.

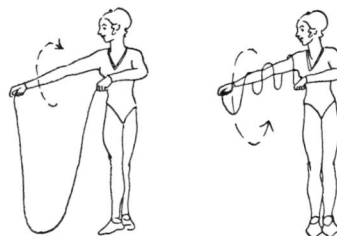

Variation:
Do the same exercise but reverse the direction in which the rope is circled.

BALANCING MOVEMENTS

The number of possible balancing movements is unlimited. These movements can be performed by varying the positions of the arms, legs, trunk and head.

Balancing movements serve two purposes. They add variety to a rope routine and they help the gymnast regain her breath. Balancing movements, however, should be held only long enough to show control. They should be connected with other movements and should not disturb the rhythm of the routine. They must show a good body line with the rope creating an artistic whole.

1. Rope Hooked Around the Leg
Stand or kneel, holding the rope in front of you with both hands, with the arms extended to the sides. Place one foot on the rope and raise that leg forward, or sideward. Keep the rope taut. By changing arm

positions, different effects may be created. The following sketches depict a few of the many possibilities.

140
Modern Rhythmic Gymnastics

2. Arabesque
Stand holding the rope in front of you with the arms extended to the sides. Place the left foot over the rope. Bring the rope ends together in front of the body and exchange the ends. Then return the arms to the side, crossing the rope above the foot. Step over the rope with the right foot and pull the left leg backward into a scale keeping the rope taut. Lower the leg, step back over the rope with the right foot, and uncross the rope by changing hands.

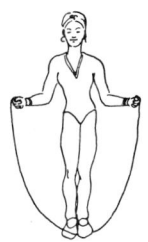  

side view

3. Scale with Folded Rope
Stand, holding the folded rope in the right hand in front of the left leg. Place the left foot over on rope then raise it backward, resting the foot on the rope, while performing a scale.

4. Balancing with Double-Folded Rope
Hold the double-folded rope with both hands. Try to perform the depicted exercises with varying arm, leg, trunk, and head positions. Find

different ways of going into and coming out of these balancing movements. These movements can be used as connecting elements in a routine.

TOSSING AND CATCHING MOVEMENTS

Tossing and catching movements are the most difficult of the rope exercises. The rope can be tossed with one or both hands. It can be caught with one hand at each end or with one or both hands on one end. In many throwing movements the rope will rotate in the air. Tossing and catching skills are usually combined with swinging and jumping movements.

1. Swing and Catch
Stand, holding one end of the rope with the right hand. Run forward as you swing the long straight rope forward and upward, then run backward and catch the other end of the rope with the right hand. Repeat this several times and then practice the movement with the left hand.

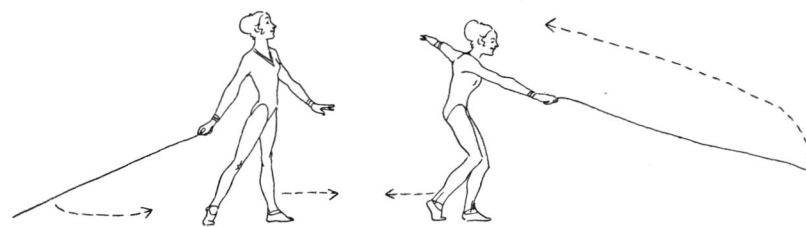

Variation:
Do the same movement but catch the rope with the left hand.

2. One-Handed Release
Stand, holding the rope at each end in front of the body with arms extended to the right. Swing the rope to the left, back to the right (left

arm under right arm) and release it with the left hand. The free rope end will fly over your head. Catch it at the left side with the left hand. Repeat on the opposite side.

3. Backward Swing and Toss
Stand, holding the rope at each end in front of the body with the arms extended to the sides. Turn the rope backward while running or skipping forward. With straight arms toss (release) the rope in front above the shoulders. The left side of the rope will change places with the right side as it makes a complete turn in the air. Catch the ends of the rope with both hands and continue running or skipping forward while turning the rope forward.

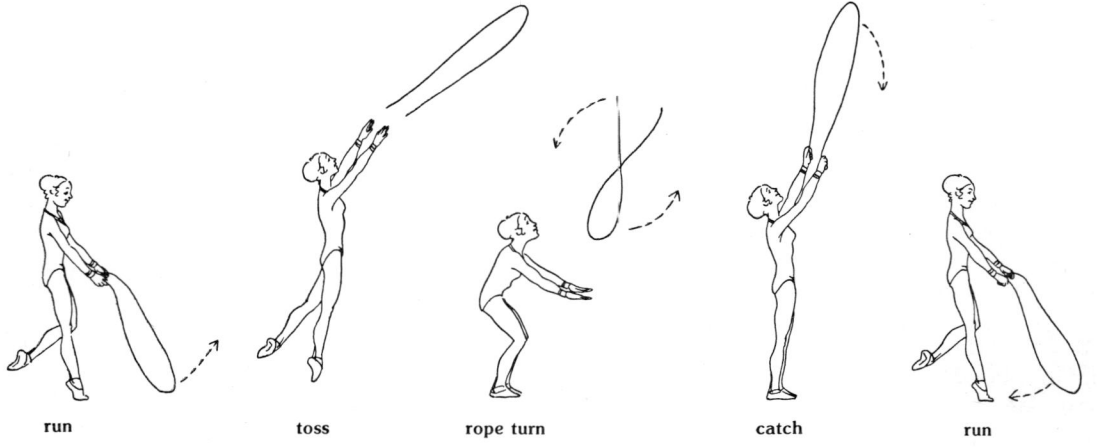

run   toss   rope turn   catch   run

Variations:
a) Do the same exercise but swing the rope forward before the release.

b) Do the same exercise but perform a turn as the rope makes a complete turn in the air.

4. Sideward Swing and Toss
Stand, holding the rope at each end with both hands at the right side. Swing the rope from the right to the left and throw it obliquely upward on the left side. The rope will make a complete turn in the air over the head. Catch the ends of the rope with both hands on the right side. Repeat. Practice this also to the opposite side.

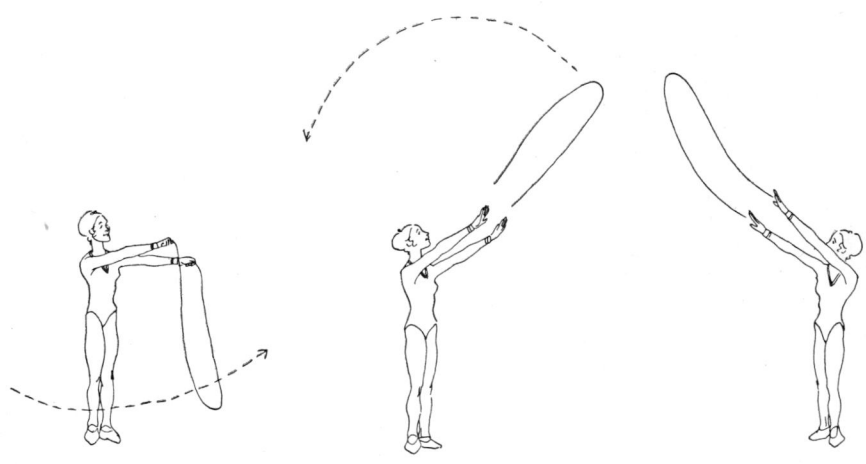

Variations:
a) Do the same movement but catch both ends of the rope with the right hand.

b) Do the same movement by holding the rope in one hand.

5. Folded Rope Toss
Stand with the feet together holding both ends of the rope in the right hand. Swing the rope forward, overhead, backward, and forward again in the sagittal plane and then release it obliquely upward in front of the body. The rope will make one complete turn in the air. Catch both ends

of the rope in the right hand. Reverse sides. In the beginning, practice with low tosses, then later with higher and higher ones.

Variations:
a) Do the same movement with a forward stride, shifting the weight forward and backward with the rope.
b) Do the same movement but throw the rope up in an arc and forward, then run forward and catch it with one or both hands.
c) Toss the rope up high and let it turn two times in the air before catching it.
d) Toss the rope upward in front of the body with the right hand and catch it with the left hand. Alternate sides.
e) Throw the rope up with the right hand, do a half-turn and catch it with the left hand.

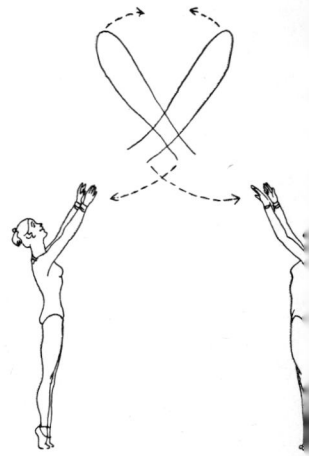

6. Partner Tossing
Stand, facing your partner, each of you holding a folded rope in front of your body with the right hand. Swing the rope backward then forward and toss it to your partner. The rope should do a half-turn in the air. Catch your partner's rope with your left hand.

TEACHING SUGGESTIONS

1. The rope can be held with the thumb and index finger, with the other fingers resting on the rope, or it may be held between the index and middle fingers in much the same way as one would hold a cigarette. In either case it should be held loosely, with relaxed wrists so that it rotates in the hands.
2. During the swing the rope should not touch the floor but rather pass slightly above it.
3. The rope should not touch the trunk or any other part of the body except during movements in which the rope is wrapped around the body.
4. The rope should remain taut during the different movements. Slack in the rope during the course of a movement indicates poor technique.
5. Good posture should be emphasized. The body should be erect rather than bent during jumps. Stress that the feet must be close to floor and stretched when in the air and the knees must be slightly bent in landing.
6. Exercises should progress from simple to more difficult.
7. Start your girls on sequences or combinations as soon as they have learned a few skills so that continuity of movement is emphasized from the beginning.
8. Students should be given opportunity to create new sequences. This will help them discover the limitless possibilities of movements with the rope.
9. Stretching exercises in which the rope is used as an aid to increase flexibility are not considered modern jump rope gymnastics.
10. Exercises should always be performed with music. Schottische rhythms, polkas, and other lively folk dance melodies are the most suitable for rope jumping. Popular music may also be used if the rhythm is good.
11. Students should be given homework assignments—routines five minutes long that can be tested in class for improvement. The homework should be changed every week.
12. Students should use gymnastic shoes for rope jumping. They should never jump on concrete, cement, or marble floors or practice jumping too long because this may injure the metatarsal arch and cause shin-splints.
13. When learning the basic skills the class should be in staggered lines with ample space between students so ropes will not touch.
14. Because of the strenuous nature of rope jumping, the class should be divided into groups, with one group practicing while the other observes, or the skills should be alternated—i.e., students do some jumping, then some swinging, and then perhaps some balancing exercises with the rope.
15. Class organization for teaching rope jumping. The following are suggested formations that lend themselves well to teaching locomotion movements:

    a) Class in a single circle, counting off by two's. Number 1's jump toward the center and back while number 2's rest or perform swinging or balancing exercises. Then number

2's jump toward the center and back while number 1's rest, and so on.

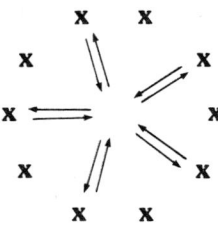

b) Line the class up in fours or sixes across the side of the gymnasium. One line moves forward as far as possible, then they divide and walk back along the side of the gymnasium and step to the rear of their respective files. The second line begins when there is room enough behind the first one—usually after the fourth musical measure. Then the next line follows, and so on. This allows each line to have a rest period.

c) Divide the class into two lines, each starting at opposite rear corners of the gymnasium. Students move diagonally forward to the opposite corner, lines crossing at the center, and walk along the side of the room and step to the rear of the other line. Repeat movement from the other corner. The next girl in each line begins when there is sufficient room behind the girl in front of her, and so on. This pattern may also be done with partners moving side by side.

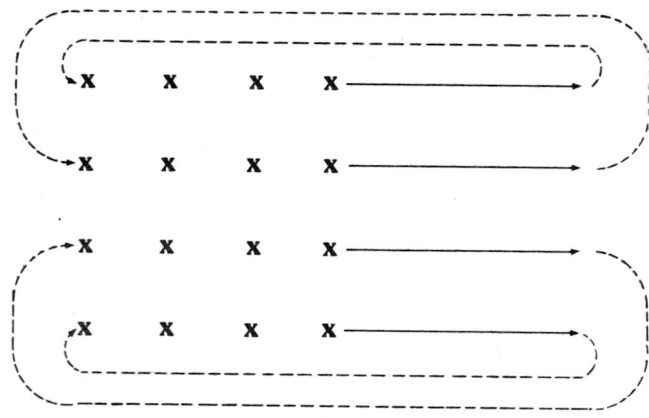

COMPETITIVE RULES

The dimensions of the *area* shall be 12 m x 12 m (39⅓ square feet) clearly marked with white lines. The *duration* of a rope routine is from one minute to one minute and thirty seconds. The clock starts as soon as the gymnast begins a movement of the exercise and will stop when she maintains her final position. The *music* should be appropriate for rope exercises. The selection of the music should be phrased to retard fatigue and finish with the concluding movements of the gymnast. If the musical accompaniment is not in harmony with the movements this will be penalized. Only one instrument may be used for accompaniment.

A perfect exercise is one that is presented with elegance, ease, and confidence and in good rhythm with no faults in *execution*. Common faults in execution are: clasping the rope in the hand instead of holding it lightly, tangling the rope, failure to jump over the rope, touching the body with the rope (unless performing wrapping movements), touching the floor with the rope, slack in the rope during a movement, losing the end of the rope, throwing the rope in the wrong direction, and dropping the rope. Other penalties found in execution are: feet not arched and legs bent on jumps, jumps which are not light and elegant, turns executed without sureness, and poor coordination between steps and movements of the rope.

EXAMPLES OF DIFFICULTIES

Jumping
Medium difficulties: Gallops to the side with a turn of the rope for each gallop step; jumping with double turns of the rope.

Superior difficulties: Jump over the quadrupled rope held in both hands; basic forward jump with a double turn of the crossed rope.

Swinging
Medium difficulties: Figure eight sideward; 360° turns with horizontal swing around waist level.

Superior difficulties: All the movements of the rope in figure eight carried out with consecutive 360° turns or with large jumps.

Tossing and Catching
Medium difficulties: All exercises involving throwing the rope.

Superior difficulties: Backward swing and toss, catch the rope with both hands and continue skipping forward while turning the rope forward; folded rope toss, catch it with both hands and jump over it.

NOTE: Throwing a knotted rope is not considered an element of difficulty.

COMPOSITION

The basic elements of a rope routine must be included in the exercise to ensure an appropriate and correct composition. Consequently, the rope routine should include jumping, swinging, wrapping, balancing, tossing, and catching movements. In competition the exercise should contain six medium and two superior difficulties. It is unwise to perform a greater number of difficulties than required unless the amplitude and form are of high standard. Too many difficulties cause the gymnast to tire, make more technical and executional errors, and thus receive a lower score. It is better to do some simpler skills with elegance than to select difficult skills and labor through them.

Before attempting to compose a complete routine of one minute or longer, it is best to put together a few learned skills into several combinations. In your combinations, include a variety of movements with rhythmic and dynamic changes, as well as with changes in speed. It is important to learn how to get into and out of a skill smoothly. The "before" and "after" movements are almost as important as the difficult skill itself. One of the things one should remember is that skills must be tied together in an interesting manner by using dance and other movements.

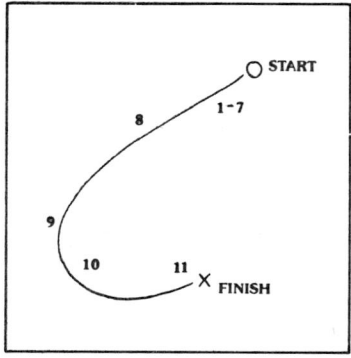

Floor pattern for composition

The composition should be done in a quick, lively tempo, and without interruption. An example of a composition from the skills already presented, is as follows:

1. Swing and quadruple the rope.
2. Squat jump over quadrupled rope turned backwards.
3. Stag leap jump with double folded rope held above the head. Start the jump from both feet and finish it on both.
4. Swing the rope backward with both hands close together from side to side in a figure eight while doing two running steps in place.
5. Two running steps in place while quickly turning the rope backward.
6. Basic jump with double turn of the rope backward.
7. One hand release with the left hand and catch.
8. Swing the rope forward with both hands close together from side to side in a figure eight, while running forward. Separate arms and continue to swing the rope forward while performing a split leap over the rope.
9. Bring feet together and circle the rope twice around the body with a twist while doing a 450° turn to the left.
10. Bring the hands together and transfer the folded rope to the right hand. Swing the rope overhead while performing a knee turn, a stomach roll to sitting position and a "push-up" with the left hand to standing position.
11. Transfer the folded rope above the head to the left. Swing the rope from the right side to the left side in front of the body and let go of one end of the rope. Wrap the full length of the rope around the waist and finish the combination with a pose.

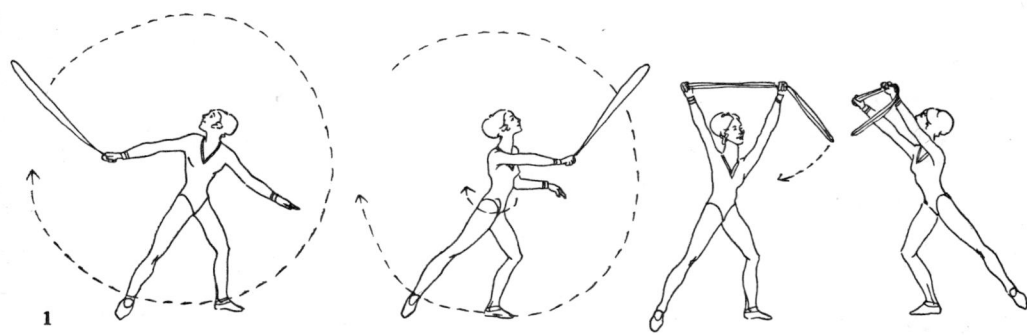

1

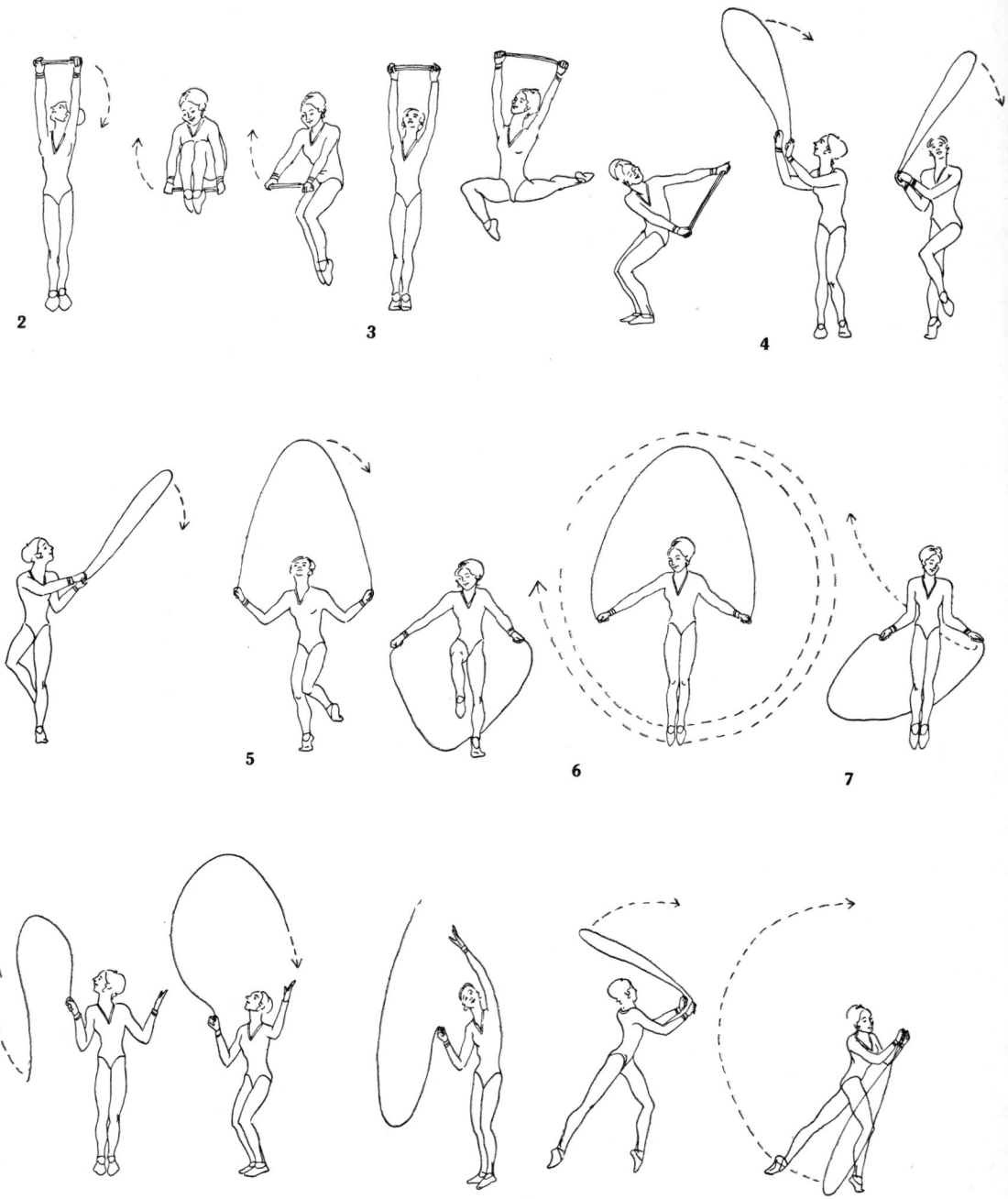

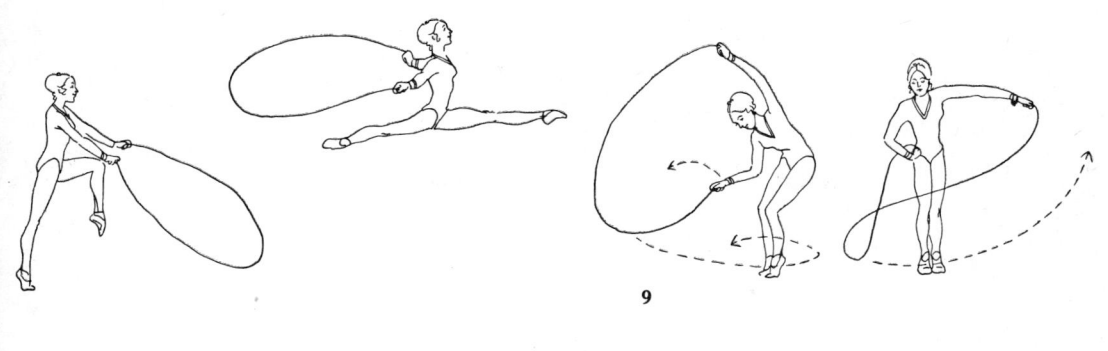

9

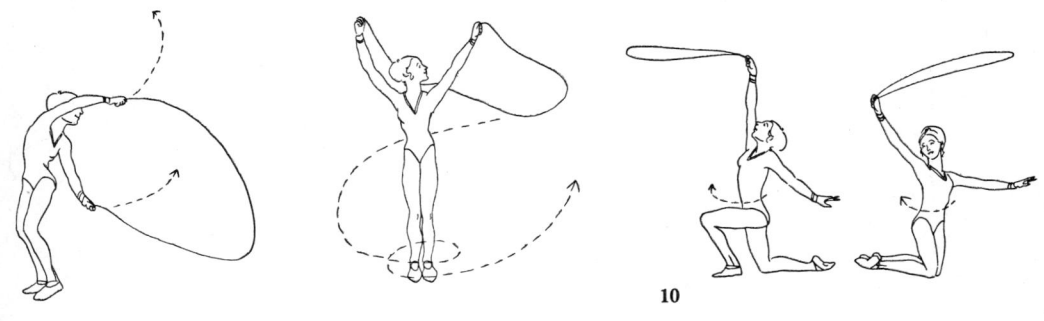

10

GROUP EXERCISES

The rope is also a commonly used hand apparatus in group exercises. In the sixth Modern Rhythmic Gymnastics World Championships in Rotterdam, Holland, it was first included for team competition. In the seventh World Championships in Spain it was employed again. For the six member team three balls and three ropes were used.

The area used for group exercises is 12 meters by 12 meters (39⅓ square feet) and the gymnasts must perform within this area. It is not considered to be a fault if the rope passes over the line as long as the gymnast does not actually go outside the area herself. The time limits are two minutes and thirty seconds to three minutes. The exercise must include at least six different formations, but long-distance changeovers are not required. The following are suggestions for group formations and exchanges.

FLOOR PATTERN EXAMPLES

1. Six girls form a reverse V-formation. Do a figure eight in the sagittal plane with the ropes and continue with four step-hops to form the second pattern. Gymnasts 3 and 4 step-hop forward, 1 and 6 step-hop backward, and 2 and 5 stay in place.

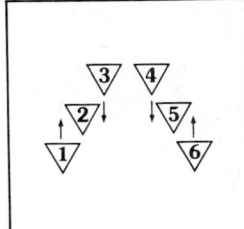

2. V-formation. Perform gallop steps to the side. Gymnasts 1, 2, and 3 do gallop steps to the right and then do a half-turn. Gymnasts 4, 5, and 6 perform gallop steps to the left.

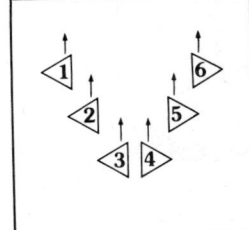

3. Straight-line formation. Follow the leader (number 6) and run forward into an S-formation while turning the rope forward with arms crossed and uncrossed. Then bring the rope above the head and transfer it to the left hand.

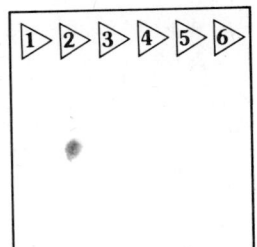

4. S-formation. In the corner of the floor area each girl does a quarter turn and continues to run diagonally forward while performing overhead and underleg swings with folded ropes.

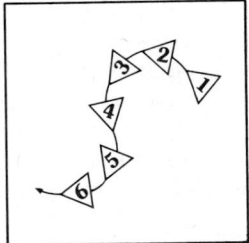

5. Diagonal line formation. Do chaînés turns, turning the folded rope horizontally around the waist to arrive in the next formation.

6. Two symmetrical triangles, facing each other. Perform a scale with the folded rope.

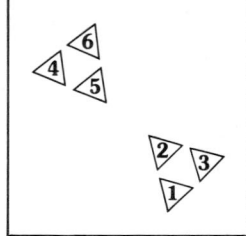

EXCHANGE EXAMPLES

1. Diagonal line formation. Partners facing each other holding folded rope at each end with arms extended. Take one step forward and place your folded rope above your partner's head and down around your partner's waist, then wait for your partner to place her rope around your waist. Take a small step to the left with the left foot and place the right foot behind the left, giving a light pushing action and be ready to step on the left foot again. Let go of your rope and grab hold of your partner's, so as to exchange ropes. Continue with a swinging movement.

2. Two-line formation. Lines face and move toward each other with running steps. Simultaneously gymnasts swing the folded rope forward in a circle on the right side of the body with the right hand. When partners meet each other they do a deep knee squat and then stand up and smoothly exchange ropes. They run back to their original places while swinging the folded rope backward in a circle on the left side of the body with the left hand. The exchange must be smooth so as not to break the rhythm of the swing.

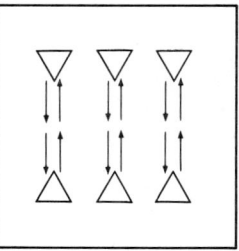

3. Circle formation, facing counterclockwise. Swing the straight rope twice above the head then wrap it around the girl's waist in front of you and let it go. Do chaînés turns to unwrap the rope.

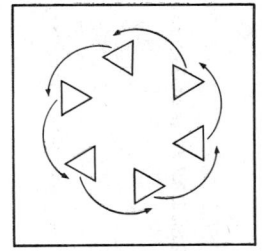

4. Two parallel lines, facing each other. Stand, holding both ends of the rope in the right hands. Do a body wave while swinging the rope backward in a sideward figure 8 pattern. Then toss the rope to your partner. The rope will do a half turn in the air. Catch your partner's rope.

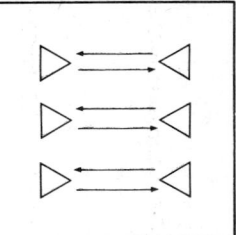

SUGGESTED GROUP ASSIGNMENT

Group assignments will foster creativity, imagination, and intellectual involvement.

Problem: There are five formations given. Be sure you work out the formations in order (e.g., from number 1 to 2 to 3, etc.). Plan smooth and logical transitions with steps that harmonize with the music. Be imaginative and experiment with different ways of arriving at the assigned places. Explore different levels, directions, and qualities of movement and make full use of the available space.

Formations:

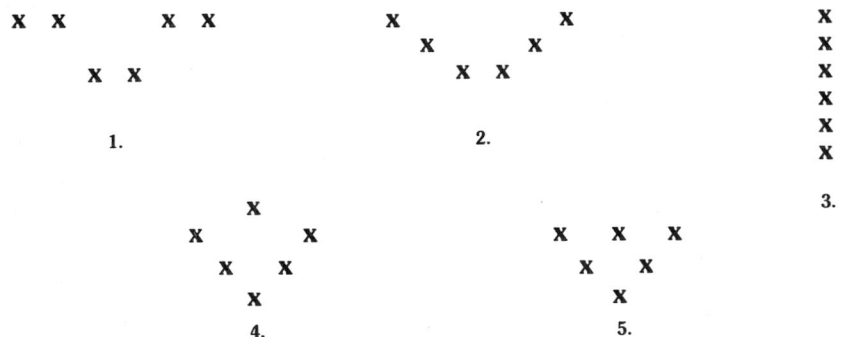

155

Music: Medley—arrangement by Harriet Jones

Musical breakdown:
20 measures
  4 measures 4/4—schottische, dynamic, grand
  8 measures 2/4—soft, smooth legato
  4 measures 2/4—gypsy dance
  4 measures 4/4—grand and dynamic

Music for Rope Group Assignment

Hoops

Chapter 5

Hoops were first used by the famous German rhythmic gymnastics leader, Hinrich Medau. For the 1936 Olympic games he choreographed a gymnastic routine in which he used hoops to represent the five interlocking rings of the Olympic symbol. This immediately made hoop gymnastics popular and since that time gymnastics schools all over the world have used hoops in their programs.

At first, the hoop was used merely as decoration; it had little physical developmental value. Within a short time, however, numerous new and difficult techniques were developed and the hoop became a very valuable hand apparatus. With the hoop practically every technical element applying to all of the other hand apparatuses may be utilized. Consequently, exercises with the hoop can demand high technical development and skill. Because the Committee for Modern Rhythmic Gymnastics of the International Federation of Gymnastics (F.I.G.) recognized the usefulness of the hoop in the developmental stages of this new sport, the hoop has been included in every Modern Rhythmic Gymnastics World Championship since the first one in 1963.

The hoop can be used very effectively in small or large demonstrations, because it is a very spectacular hand apparatus.

EQUIPMENT

The hoop may be made of wood or plastic, but must weigh a minimum of 300 grams (approximately 11 ounces) irrespective of the material. It may be painted any color except gold, silver, or bronze or it may be left as the natural wood. The hoop itself must be round. The material making up the rim of the hoop may be round or square.

Hoops used by adults should have an interior diameter of 80–90 cm (approximately 31½–35½ inches), while hoops used by children and juniors should be approximately 60–75 cm (23⅝–29½ inches) in diameter. The size of the hoop should depend on the size of the gymnast. Gymnastics clubs and schools sometimes use larger hoops (38 inches) for demonstration purposes.

CONSTRUCTION OF HOOPS

A hoop can be made by taking a piece of smooth plastic hose or tubing, forming a circle with it, and joining the two ends by forcing them onto a small wooden dowel until the ends of the tubing meet. Both ends are then tightly stapled together. Some school groups have reported using this type of cheap hoop satisfactorily although they are not as effective or as easy to handle as the commercial hoop constructed from laminated beech wood.

TECHNIQUES

Movements with the hoop can be performed with one or both hands. The hoop is held lightly with the thumb and fingers encircling it. Do not be afraid of losing the hoop. It is better to lose the hoop, using the right technique than to try and hold on to the hoop by grasping it too tightly.

Strive for good posture and natural total body movements with the hoops at all times. Practice alternately with right and left hand from the very first day, so that you immediately get used to working with both hands. The free arm should also participate in the movement.

There are five kinds of grips used with the hoop:

1. Regular grip (overgrip)—with one or both hands, palm(s) facing downward.

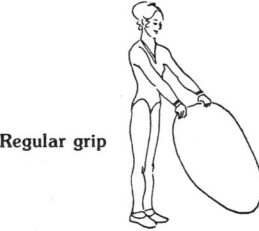
Regular grip

2. Reverse grip (undergrip)—with one or both hands, palm(s) facing upward.

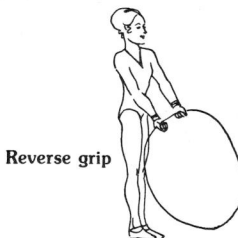
Reverse grip

3. Inside grip—with one or both hands, palm(s) facing outward and little finger(s) upward.

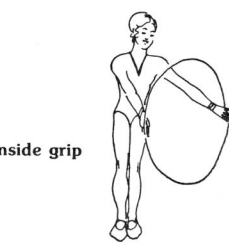
Inside grip

4. Outside grip—with one or both hands, palm(s) facing inward and thumb(s) upward.

Outside grip

5. Mixed, or combined, grip—one hand holds the hoop with a different grip from that of the other. For example, one hand holds the hoop with an overgrip while the other with an undergrip.

Mixed grip

161

Hoops

When holding the hoop with both hands, the hands may be held close together, a shoulder width apart, or as far apart as possible.

The position of the hoop in regard to the body may be specified according to levels of elevation (hip level, chest level, overhead and so on) and to movement planes (frontal, sagittal, and horizontal).

Frontal plane

Sagittal plane

Horizontal plane

Swinging movements should be performed by bending and stretching the arm during the swing, so that the hoop will not touch the floor. At the beginning of the movement the arm is straight, in the middle the arm is bent, and at the end the arm is straight again. When swinging the hoop horizontally, the arm is usually kept straight.

In *turning* movements the hoop may be spun around its horizontal axis, which passes through the center of the hoop on a line parallel to the ground, or its vertical axis which passes through the center of the hoop on a line perpendicular to the ground.

When the hoop is spinning around its horizontal axis it may spin forward or backward, depending upon whether the top of the hoop moves away from the front of the gymnast (forward) or toward the front of the gymnast (backward). When the hoop is spinning around its vertical axis it may turn either to the right or to the left. Turning movements may be performed with one or both hands but they must be combined with movements of the trunk or with dancing steps.

In *circling* movements, the hoop usually rotates between the thumb and index finger and on the palm and back of the hand. In some movements the hoop will rotate only around the thumb, or it may rotate first around the thumb and then around the straight fingers. Moving the hoop from the thumb to the fingers must be carried out smoothly and without change in the rhythm of rotation. Changing the hoop from one

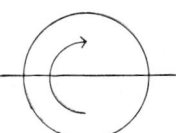
Horizontal axis

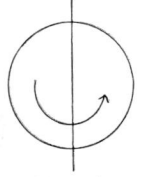
Vertical axis

hand to the other during circling should be done with a continuous movement. This can be achieved by placing the free hand near the circling hand. If changing in front of the body, put the little fingers close together, the hoop turns between the thumb and index finger, palms facing upward. If changing in back of the body, the thumbs are together for the change, since the hoop will circle around the thumbs, palms facing to the rear.

The hoop can be *tossed* and caught by one or both hands. The throw should start either from the shoulders or wrists. Tossing movements can be performed in the various planes and directions. The hoop should be caught between the thumb and index finger and the entire body should follow the movement of the falling hoop.

The hoop may be *rolled* on the floor or on the body in various ways. During the roll the hoop must not vibrate, bounce, or change its plane or direction. The rolling hoop should be picked up without interrupting the rhythm of the movement.

Jumping through the hoop is done with a technique similar to that used when jumping over a rope. All the movements should be smooth, and the body movements coordinated with the hoop movements.

MOVEMENTS

Most of the basic skills should first be attempted in a stationary position. When you have gained control of the hoop, repeat the skills with locomotion movements. As you master the various moves, combine them into short sequences with the music in order to get the feeling of arranging movements with a continuous, flowing quality on various planes and levels.

Music should be used at all times. Waltz rhythm is very suitable for hoop exercises.

The hoop movements are divided into: swinging, turning, circling, throwing, catching, rolling, and passing the body through the hoop.

SWINGING MOVEMENTS

The hoop may be swung with one or both hands in the frontal, sagittal, or horizontal planes. Swinging movements can be done either forward or backward, inward or outward, to the left or to the right. The movements should be very large; this can be achieved by reaching after the hoop and following its movement with the whole body. There should always be good alignment between the body and the hoop. The process of changing the hoop from one hand to the other must be smooth without interrupting the swing.

1. Swing Across the Body

Stand in a wide straddle with weight on the right foot, the arms extended to the sides, and the hoop held in the right hand with an inside grip (palm facing backward). Swing the hoop downward across the body to the left, then swing it back to the right side. Transfer weight from side to side while swinging the hoop. Repeat the movement several times. Practice with the left hand too.

Variations:

a) Do the same movement while walking or running forward or backward.

b) Do the same movement holding the hoop with both hands using an outside grip.

c) Swing the hoop in a large circle in the frontal plane while performing a 360° turn.

2. Swing and Lean

Stand holding the hoop in front of the body with both hands, using an outside grip. Swing the hoop to the left and then upward over the head into a right side lean. Then swing the hoop over the head to the left and back to the original position. Repeat the movement to the opposite side.

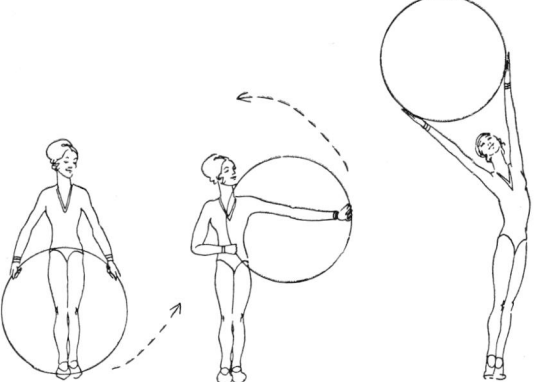

Variation:
Do the same movement while walking forward or backward.

3. Change Hands in Front of the Body *(frontal plane)*
Stand in a wide straddle with weight on the right foot, the arms extended to the sides, and the hoop held in the right hand with palm facing backward. Swing the hoop downward and upward in front of the body then change hoop to the left hand (palm upward) and swing it to the left side. The hoop will do a turn in front of the body. Repeat to the opposite side. Transfer weight from side to side as you follow the movement of the hoop.

Variations:
a) Do the same movement but cross the left arm in front of the right before changing the hoop to the left hand.

b) Do the same movement while doing walking or dancing steps.

4. Change Hands Behind Body *(frontal plane)*

Stand in a wide straddle with weight on the left foot, arms extended to the side and the hoop in the left hand with palm facing forward. Swing the hoop downward, and then upward in back of the body; then change the hoop to the right hand (palm facing backward) and swing it to the right side. Repeat to the opposite side. Shift the weight from side to side with the hoop swing.

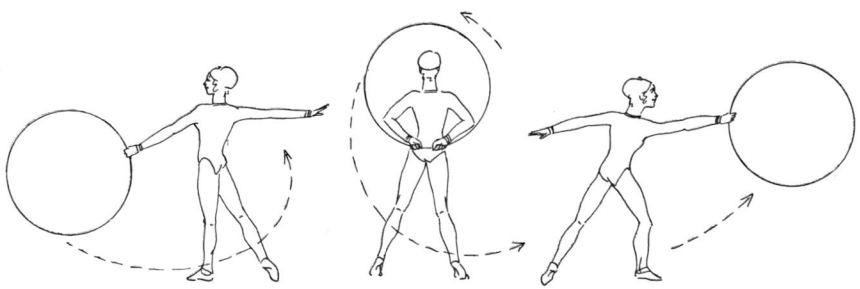

Variation:
Do the same movement with various walking or dancing steps.

5. Change Hands Overhead *(frontal plane)*

Stand in a wide straddle with weight on the right foot, arms extended to the side, and the hoop in the right hand, the palm of the hand facing forward. Swing the hoop downward across the body to the left, back to the right and upward over the head. Change hands over the head and swing the hoop to the left side. Reverse the movement, starting with the left hand. Shift the weight from side to side with the swinging hoop.

Variations:
a) Do the same movement using a side gallop step. (When the hoop is in the right hand do a gallop to the left.)

b) Do the same movement while walking forward or backward.

6. Change Hands Under the Leg *(frontal plane)*
Stand with the arms extended to the sides, holding the hoop in the right hand, with palm of the hand facing backward. Raise the right leg forward and at the same time swing the hoop under the leg. Then change hands and swing the hoop to the left side. Reverse the movement, starting on the left side.

Variations:
a) Pass the hoop under the lifted leg while doing a 360° turn.

b) During a leap, swing and pass the hoop under the legs.

7. Swing Backward and Forward
Stand with the arms extended forward, holding the hoop in the right hand with the palm facing inward. Swing the hoop backward and forward on the right side twice. At the end of the second forward swing change hands and repeat the movement with the left hand. Follow the movement smoothly with the whole body.

Variations:
a) Do the same exercise but change hands after the first forward swing.

b) Do the same movement with a forward stride, shifting weight forward and backward with the hoop.

c) Repeat the movement with walking or dancing steps.

8. Change Hands Behind the Body *(sagittal plane)*
Stand in a front stride position with left arm extended over the head and right arm extended forward. Hoop in the left hand, palm facing inward. Swing the arms downward to the rear while performing a ballet point. Change hands in the rear, then swing the hoop forward with the right hand. Repeat this movement with the right hand.

Variations:
a) Do the same movement with a chassé backward on the backward swing and a chassé forward on the forward swing.

b) Pass the hoop behind the body while performing a scissor jump or a cat leap.

9. Swing to Backbend

Stand in a front stride position with right foot in front, arms at the sides and the hoop held in the right hand with palm facing inward. Swing the hoop upward, overhead, and to the rear into a deep backbend position, while shifting the weight to the left foot. Then swing the hoop back to the original position. Practice with the left hand also.

Variations:
a) Do the same movement but lift the front leg while doing the backbend.

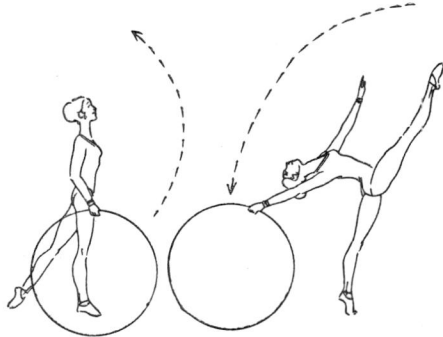

b) Do the same movement while walking forward with walking or dancing steps.

10. Swing Around the Body

Stand with the arms extended to the sides and the hoop held horizontally in the right hand, the palm of the hand facing downward. Swing the hoop horizontally to the left in front of the body and transfer it to the left hand. The left hand carries the hoop to the back of the body, where it is passed to the right hand. Practice this several times, then repeat in the opposite direction.

Variations:
a) Do the same movement while performing a chaîné turn.

b) Pass the hoop horizontally around the body, changing hands in front of and behind the body while doing a pirouette or arabesque turn.

c) Perform different types of jumps while swinging the hoop horizontally around the body.

11. Swing Overhead

Stand with the arms extended to the side, with the hoop held horizontally in the right hand, and the palm of the hand facing downward. Swing the hoop to the left in a large circle over the head, then pass it to the left hand in front of the body. Repeat with the left hand, circling the hoop to the right. Note, the hand must smoothly change from an over grip (palm facing downward) to an under grip (palm facing upward) at the far left side. This is accomplished by turning the hoop over. The whole body must follow the swinging hoop in order to keep it in the horizontal plane and to keep the movement continuous.

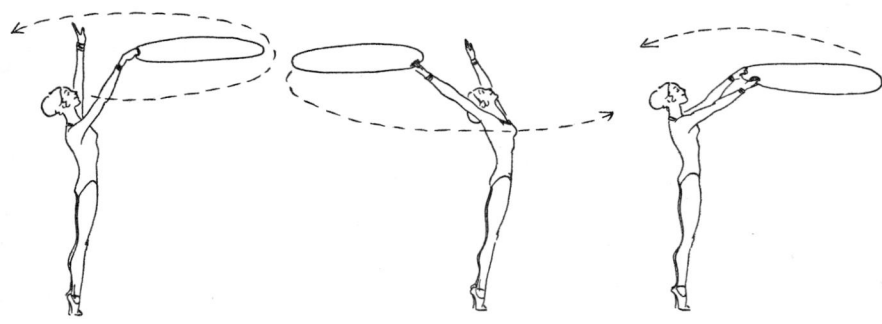

Variations:
a) Do the same movement while moving forward or backward, with either walking or dancing steps.

b) Do the same movement while performing different kinds of turns or pirouettes.

12. Figure Eight in the Sagittal Plane

Stand with the arms extended forward and the hoop held perpendicular to the floor in the right hand with the palm of the hand facing outward. Keeping the hoop perpendicular to the floor, move the right arm across to the left side, crossing it over the horizontal left arm. Swing the hoop downward, backward and around, making the first loop of the figure eight on the left side. When the right arm is overhead switch the hand to reverse grip (palm upward) and swing the hoop downward, backward and upward to sketch the second loop of the figure eight on the right side of the body. To be able to do this exercise smoothly the arm and hand must rotate inward and outward in a continuous successive motion. Practice with the left hand also.

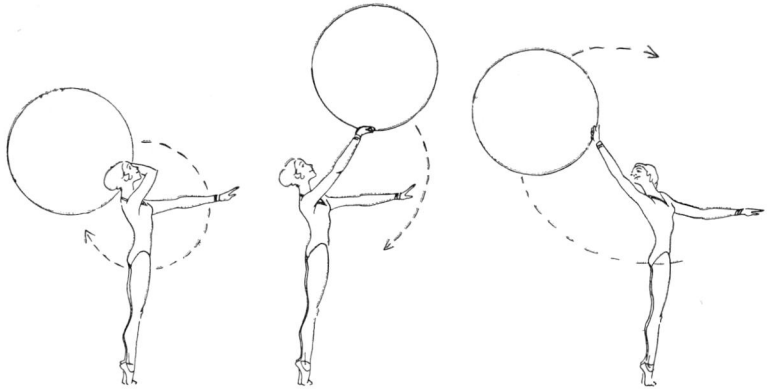

Variations:

a) Do body waves while executing the figure eight.

b) Do the same movement while moving forward or backward with either walking or dancing steps.

c) Do the same movement but swing the hoop in the opposite direction.

13. Figure Eight in Frontal Plane

Stand with the arms extended to the sides, holding the hoop in the right hand with the palm of the hand facing backward. Swing the hoop inward in front of you, toward the left, overhead, then bend the elbow (palm facing upward) and swing the hoop inward in back of the body. Repeat several times, then practice it with the left hand also.

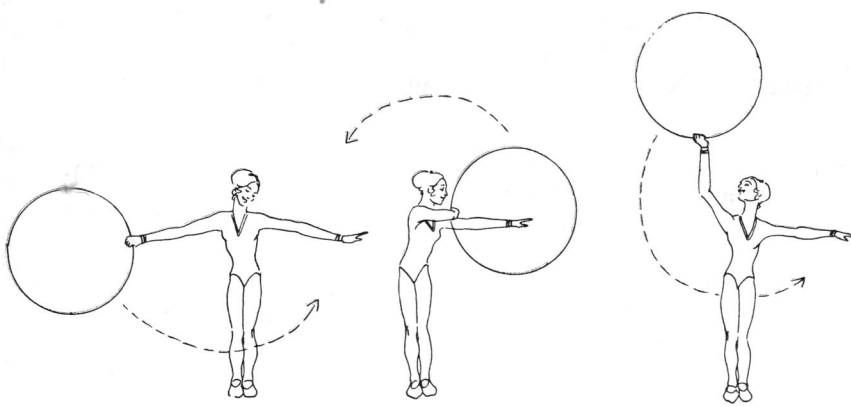

Variations:
Do the same movement while moving sideward, forward or backward with either walking or dancing steps.

14. Figure Eight in Horizontal Plane
This movement is performed exactly the same way as the spiral with the ball. Stand with the arms extended to the side, the hoop held horizontally in the right hand, palm facing upward. Swing the hoop parallel to the floor across in front of the body. Flex the elbow, turn the palm inward and upward while swinging the hoop in a circle under the elbow until the arm is extended toward the left. Continue swinging the hoop in a large circle to the left, over the head and back to the original position. Repeat several times and then practice with the left hand also.

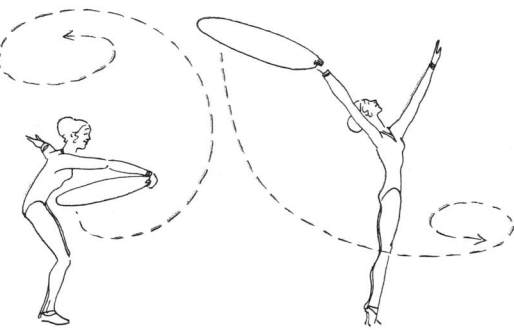

Variation:
Do the same movement with walking or waltz steps forward.

15. Poses

Try to perform the poses depicted below. Find different swinging movements for going into and coming out of these balances. These positions are used only to emphasize the beginning or the end of a movement pattern. They should be held only long enough to show good balance and control.

TURNING MOVEMENTS

The hoop may be turned around its horizontal or vertical axis by spinning it with the thumb and fingers or by turning it by using arm movements.

1. Turning in Frontal Plane

Stand in a wide straddle holding the hoop in front of the body. Hold the hoop with an outside grip in both hands on the opposite sides. Transfer weight to the left foot and swing the hoop to the left, upward over the head into a side bend to the right as the arms move into fourth position. The left arm forms a half circle above the head and the right arm forms a half circle in front of the body as you look through the hoop. Repeat the movement to the opposite side.

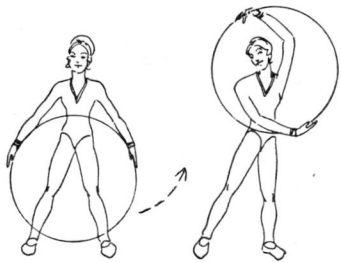

Variations:
a) Do the same movement, holding the hoop with an inside grip.

b) Perform balancé from side to side doing a sidebend on each balancé.

c) Combine this movement with a grapevine step.

2. Turning in Sagittal Plane
Stand in a front stride position with the weight on the right foot in the rear. Hold the hoop at the right side of the body with a mixed grip—the right hand using an inside grip, the left hand an outside one. Shift the weight forward to the left foot while turning the hoop backward over the head, keeping the hands in place on the hoop. Then transfer the weight backward as you turn the hoop forward back to the original position. Practice this on the left side also.

Variations:
a) Do the same movement but hold the hoop with an outside grip.

b) Do the same movement, but when turning the hoop forward kneel down and change the right-hand grip from an inside to an outside one and lean slightly forward.

3. Turning in Horizontal Plane

Stand with arms extended over the head, the hoop held horizontally with an outside grip. Turn the hoop to the right by swinging the left arm to the right as the right arm moves to the left. End with arm crossed in front of the head. Then reverse the movement to return to the starting position. Repeat to the opposite side.

Variations:

a) Combine the exercise with dancing steps.

b) Do the same exercise with a backbend.

4. Horizontal Spin

Stand holding the hoop horizontally in front of the body in both hands, using an outside grip. Spin the hoop with three fingers—thumb, index, and middle fingers—outward away from you.

Variations:

a) Do the same movement but turn the hoop in the opposite direction, inward toward you.

b) Combine the horizontal spin with different kinds of walking and dancing steps.

c) Do the same turning of the hoop while doing a pose.

5. Vertical Spin

Stand holding the hoop vertically in the right hand, with the palm of the hand facing downward. Turn the hoop either to the left or to the right with three fingers while performing various types of turns, walking, or dance steps. Practice with the left hand also.

Variations:
a) Change the spinning hoop from one hand to the other in front of the body without interrupting the rotation of the hoop.
b) Lift one leg forward and at the same time change the spinning hoop from one hand to the other under the leg without interrupting the motion of the turning hoop.
c) Do the same movement as in (b) while performing a 360° turn.

6. Spin on Floor

Stand holding the hoop vertically in the right hand, the palm of the hand facing downward. Place hoop on floor in front of you and spin it around in either a clockwise or counterclockwise direction. Remove the hand and let the hoop spin free. Catch it before it falls. Practice this with the left hand also.

Variations:
a) Run or dance around the spinning hoop.
b) Do a 360° turn while hoop is spinning.
c) Do a pirouette while lifting the raised leg above the spinning hoop.

7. Jump over Spinning Hoop

Spin the hoop as described in exercise 6, then scissor jump over it. This movement requires good coordination and good timing in order to jump over the hoop without touching it.

CIRCLING MOVEMENTS

Circling movements are initiated from the elbow or wrist. The hoop may be circled in the frontal, sagittal, and horizontal planes around the hand, between the thumb and the index finger, or on only the thumb. The gymnast's body should follow the circling hoop. The hoop should be circled smoothly without any vibrations. Most of the time circling is performed with the arm held straight, but relaxed.

1. Circle in Front of the Body

Stand with the arms extended to the sides, holding the hoop in the right hand with palm of the hand facing forward. Circle the hoop inward by straightening the fingers and thumb and releasing their grasp on the hoop.

The hoop circles between thumb and index finger and on the palm and the back of the hand. First make only one circle and at the end of the circle grasp the hoop again with palm facing forward. Then do two or three circles in a continuous manner. Practice with the left hand also.

Variations:
a) Do the same movement but circle the hoop in the opposite direction—outward.

b) Stand in a wide straddle and circle the hoop three times across the body to the left, then circle it three times back to the starting position. Transfer weight from side to side while circling the hoop.

c) Repeat (b) with gallops from side to side.

d) Do the same movement while moving forward or backward with either walking or dancing steps.

2. Change Hands in Front of the Body

Stand with arms extended to the side, holding the hoop in the right hand with the palm of the hand facing forward. Circle the hoop inward in front of the body then change the hoop from the right to the left hand without interrupting its rotation. This can be achieved only by placing the left hand inside the hoop near to the circling right hand with palm facing upward. Then perform the movement to the right.

Variations:
a) Circle the hoop two times with the right hand then two times with the left hand and swing it to the left side.

b) Repeat (a) but continue swinging the hoop upward over the head. Change hoop over the head to the right hand and swing it to the right side. Repeat the exercise.

c) Do the same movements with various walking and dancing steps.

d) Perform the above movements while circling the hoop in the opposite direction.

3. Circle in Front of the Arm

Stand with the arms extended to the sides and the hoop in the right hand, the palm of the hand facing backward. Circle the hoop in front of the arm inward around the base of the thumb while releasing the

grasp of the hoop by straightening the fingers. At the end of the circle grasp the hoop with palm facing forward. Practice with the left hand also.

4. Circle in Back of the Arm
Stand with the arms extended to the sides and the hoop held in the right hand, the palm of the hand facing forward. Circle the hoop in back of the arm inward around the thumb, and end the circle with palm facing backward. Practice with the left hand also.

5. Combination of Circles in Front and in Back of the Arm
Make an inward circle in front of the arm around the thumb as in exercise 3, then without stopping make a circle in back of the arm around the thumb as in exercise 4. This movement should be done in a smooth continuous way without stopping the hoop between the circles.

6. Change Hands in Back of the Body
Stand with arms extended to the sides and the hoop in the left hand with palm facing forward. Circle the hoop inward around the thumb and when it is behind the body, change hands without interrupting the rotation of the hoop. This can be done only by placing the right thumb near to the left one with palm facing backward and the hoop circling freely around the thumbs. Repeat the movement to the left side.

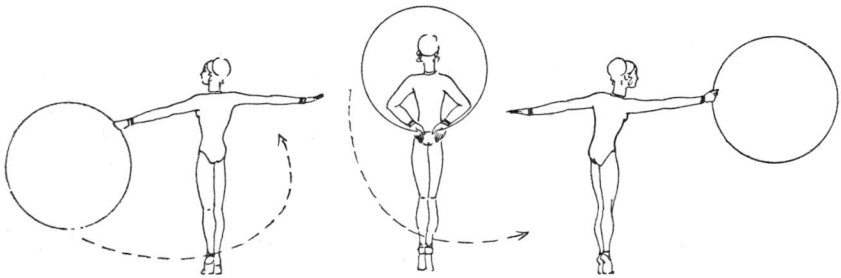

Variation:
Do the same movement while moving sideward, forward, or backward with either walking or dancing steps.

7. Combination of Front and Back Hand Changes
Stand with arms extended to the side and the hoop in the right hand with palm facing forward. Circle the hoop inward behind the body and change hands. Immediately circle the hoop with the left hand outward in front of the body and change hands. Repeat this several times and then practice it to the opposite direction.

Variations:
a) Perform chaînés turns to the left while circling the hoop around you in the frontal plane, by changing hands.
b) Do any kind of 360° turn while changing the hoop from one hand to the other behind the back and in front of the body.

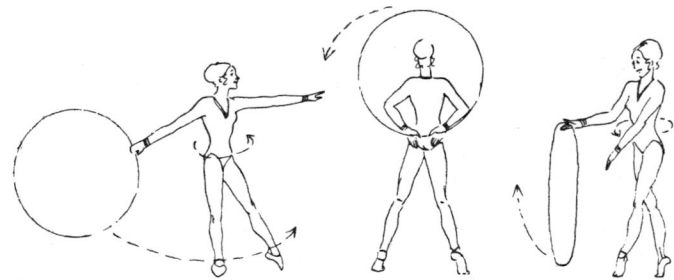

8. Combination of Front and Back Circle
Stand with arm extended to the side and the hoop held in the right hand palm facing forward. Circle the hoop inward in front of the body, then circle inward in back of the body and pass hoop to the left hand. Repeat the movement with the left hand.

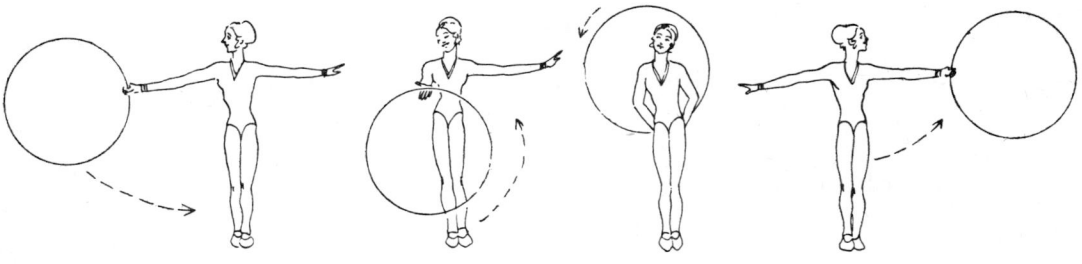

Variations:
a) Do the same movement but reverse it by circling first in back of the body, then in front of the body and change hands.
b) Perform the above movements while moving forward or backward with either walking or dancing steps.

9. Circle Back of the Head and Front of the Body
Stand with right arm extended over the head, left arm in side extension. Hold the hoop in the right hand with palm facing forward. Circle the hoop inward around the thumb behind the head, then smoothly change the fingers from the outside to the inside of the hoop and circle it outward in front of the body. Practice with the left hand also.

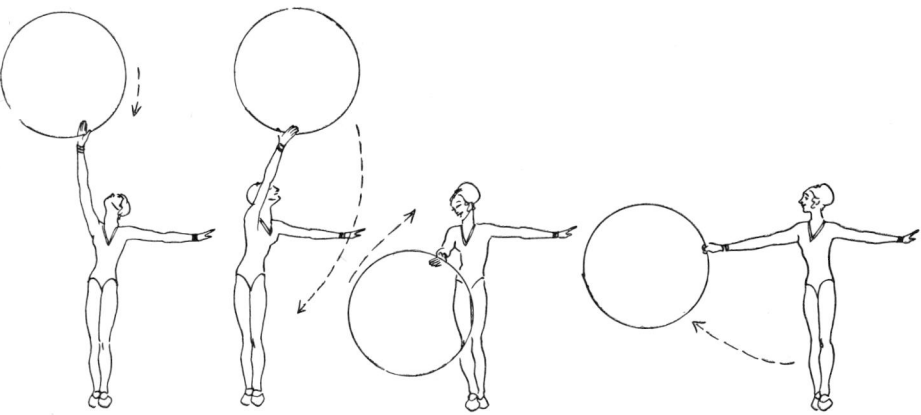

Variation:
Do the same movement while moving forward or backward with walking or dancing steps.

10. Circle in Sagittal Plane
Stand with the arms extended to the sides and the hoop in the right hand, the palm of the hand facing upward. Circle the hoop several times forward with straight arm, palm facing downward. Then circle it several times backward. Practice with the left hand also.

Variations:
a) Circle the hoop at the side in the sagittal plane—twice with arm bent then once with arm straight. Repeat this pattern several times.
b) Circle the hoop twice with arm bent as in (a) then straighten the arm over head and circle the hoop once. Repeat this pattern several times.

c) Repeat (b) with two running steps and a leap. During the leap the hoop is circled with the arm straight.

d) Circle the hoop in the sagittal plane while executing different types of jumps or leaps.

11. Circle to Backbend
Stand in a front stride position with weight on the right foot in the front, arms extended to the side and the hoop held laterally in the right hand, palm facing upward. Circle the hoop several times upward, over the head to the rear in the sagittal plane while shifting the weight to the left leg and executing a deep backbend.

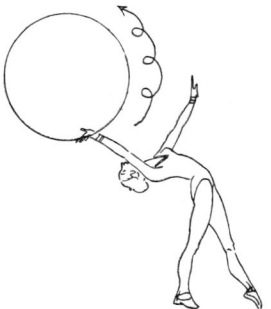

12. Horizontal Circle in Front of the Body
Stand with arms extended to the side and the hoop held horizontally in the right hand with palm facing downward. Swing the hoop inward and circle it several times, with a straight arm between the thumb and fingers, in front of the body. Practice with the left hand also.

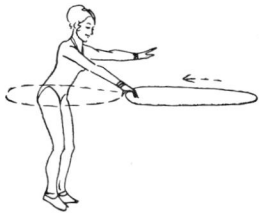

Variations:
a) Do the same movement but circle the hoop in the opposite direction.
b) Do the same movement but change hands in front of the body without interrupting the movement of the hoop.
c) Perform various turns while circling the hoop in the low horizontal plane.

13. Horizontal Circle Overhead
Stand with arms extended to the side and the hoop held horizontally in the right hand with palm facing upward. Swing the hoop over the head and circle it above the head in the horizontal plane. Practice rotating the hoop in both ways—inward and outward.

Variations:
a) Perform a 360° or 720° turn while circling the hoop horizontally above the head.

b) Do a waltz turn or chaîné turn while changing the circling hoop from one hand to the other above the head.

14. Combination of Front and Overhead Circles
Stand with arms extended to the sides and the hoop held horizontally in the right hand with palm downward. Circle the hoop twice horizontally in front of the body as in exercise 12; then swing hoop upward over the head and circle the hoop first around the thumb as you turn your hand upward and place fingers inside the hoop for the second rotation. Immediately swing the hoop downward in front of the body and, without interruption, circle the hoop first around the thumb and then between the thumb and fingers. Continue circling the hoop alternately in front of the body and above the head. Practice with the left hand also. Keep the

movement smooth and continuous and circle the hoop clearly in the horizontal plane.

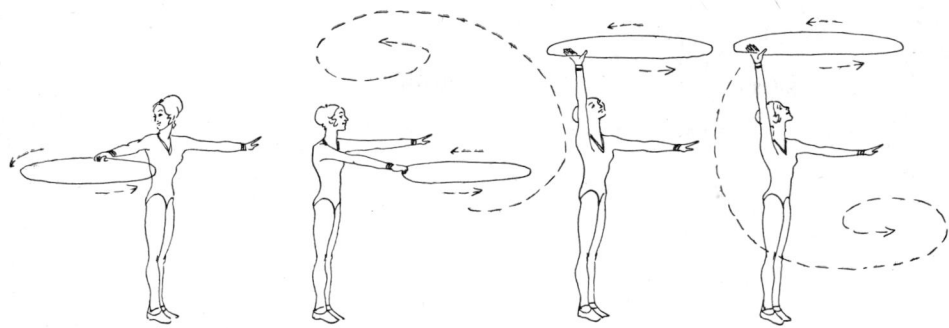

Variations:
a) Do the same movement while moving forward or backward with either walking or dancing steps.
b) Do the same movement performing different kinds of turns, including pirouettes.

15. Poses
Perform the depicted poses while circling the hoop horizontally above the head. Find different ways of going into and coming out of these positions.

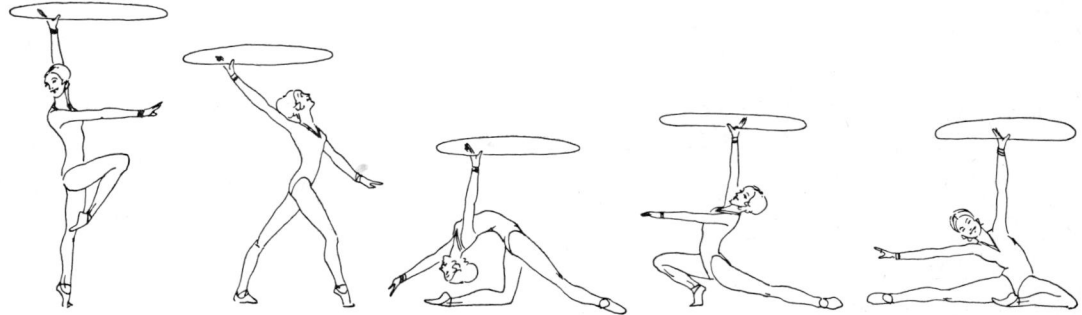

16. Circle Around the Waist *(hula-hooping)*
Stand in a wide straddle with arms extended over the head, and the hoop held in both hands horizontally, with an inside grip. Bend the elbows and bring the hoop downward until it is horizontally around the waist. Spin the hoop around the waist in either clockwise or counterclockwise direction. Remove hands and let hoop circle freely. Catch the hoop before it falls.

Variations:
a) Do the same exercise while moving forward or backward with either walking or dancing steps.
b) Do the same movement performing different kinds of turns or pirouettes.

THROWING AND CATCHING MOVEMENTS

The hoop can be tossed with one hand and caught with the same hand, the other hand or both hands. It can also be tossed with both hands and caught with one hand or both hands. The toss can be started from either the shoulder or the wrist. The hoop should be caught high in the air between the thumb and index finger. The whole body should follow the movement of the descending hoop. Any interruption of the motion of the descending hoop interrupts the continuity and rhythm of the movement and counts as a major fault in competition.

In the beginning, practice with low tosses and later with higher and higher ones. Then combine throwing and catching movements with swinging and circling ones.

1. Two-Handed Throw *(in sagittal plane)*
Stand with the knees slightly bent and the hoop held with both hands in an outside grip at the right side of the body. Swing the arms forward and up and toss the hoop slightly upward. Reach up and catch it with both hands (in an outside grip again) and swing the arms downward and backward to the starting position.

Variations:
a) Do the same movement but catch the hoop with the right hand high and the left hand low, then swing it backward to the left side. Alternate sides.

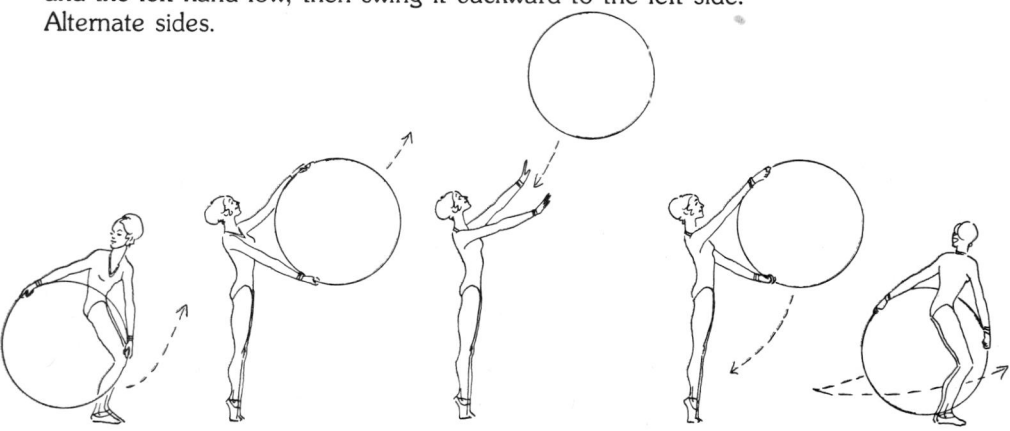

b) Do variation (a) with walking or dancing steps.

185
Hoops

2. One-Handed Throw *(in sagittal plane)*
Stand with the arms at the sides and the hoop in the right hand, the palm of the hand facing inward. Swing the right arm forward and up, and toss the hoop upward in front of the body. Catch the hoop with the right hand. The whole body should follow the up and down motion of the hoop. Repeat several times. Practice with the left hand also.

Variations:
a) Throw the hoop high upward with the right hand, as described above; then do a 360° turn and catch it with the right hand.
b) Throw the hoop up from the right hand and catch it with the left hand; then throw it up from the left hand and catch it with the right. Establish a time pattern of throws with alternating hands.

c) Do the same hoop toss as in (b) while walking or skipping forward.
d) Perform the same throw as in (b) with scissor kicks or cat leaps.

3. Overhead Throw *(in sagittal plane)*
Stand with arms in a front extension, holding the hoop in the right hand with the palm of the hand facing inward. Swing the right arm down and

backward while bending slightly forward. At the top of the backward swing, use wrist action to toss the hoop over the head; catch it in front with the right hand.

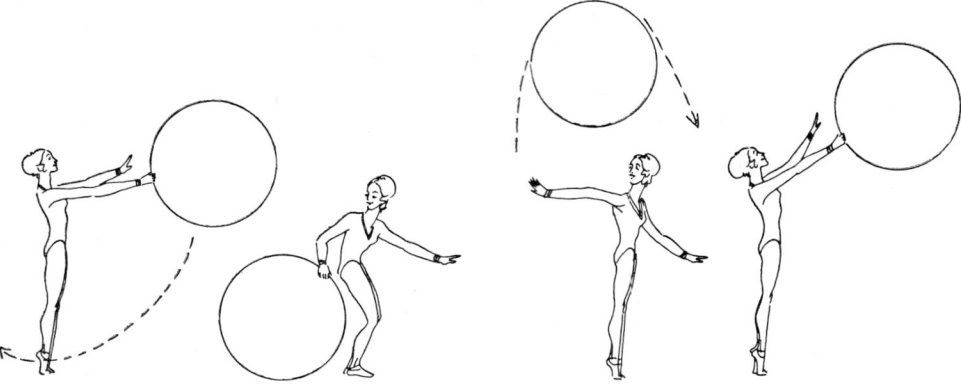

Variations:
a) Catch the hoop with the left hand and repeat the movement with the left hand.

b) Do the same movement while walking or running forward and alternating hands.

4. Overhead Throw *(in frontal plane)*
Stand in a wide straddle with weight on the right foot, extend the arms to the sides, holding the hoop in the right hand with the palm of the

hand facing forward. Throw the hoop over the head and catch it with the left hand as the weight is shifted from the right foot to the left. Repeat the movement with the left hand.

Variations:
a) Do the same movement using a gallop step.

b) Do the same hoop toss while walking or running forward.

5. Circle and Throw Over the Head
Stand in a wide straddle with weight on the right foot, arms extended to the side and the hoop in the right hand, palm facing forward. Start to circle the hoop outward with a wrist action then throw it over the head in the frontal plane. Catch the hoop with the left hand while transferring the weight to the left foot. Repeat with the left hand.

Variations:
a) Circle in back of the head and in front of the body (see circling movement 9) and then toss the hoop over the head.

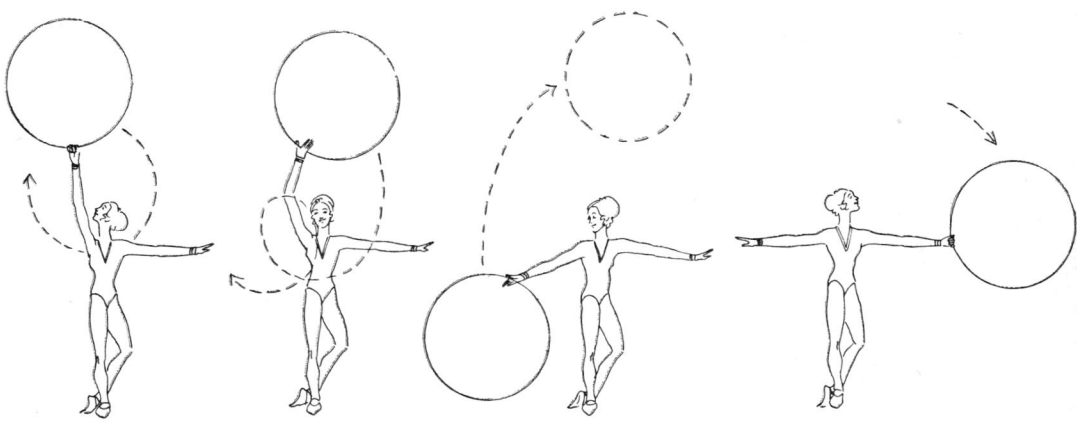

b) Do the same movements with walking or dancing steps.

6. Throw Behind Shoulder

Stand in a wide straddle with weight on the right foot, extend the arms to the sides, holding the hoop in the right hand, with the palm of the hand facing forward. Swing the hoop downward and with a wrist action throw it upward and to the left behind the body. Catch the hoop with the left hand. Repeat the movement with the left hand.

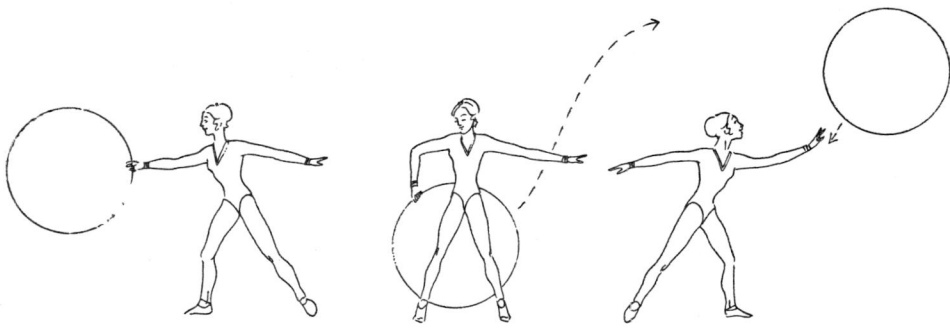

Variations:

a) Do the same movement but catch the hoop with the right hand.

b) First circle the hoop inward in front of the body, then toss it behind the shoulder.

c) Combine this movement with walking or dancing steps.

7. Throw in Horizontal Plane

Stand with the arms extended forward, and the hoop held horizontally with both hands using an outside grip. Throw the hoop horizontally upward. Catch it with both hands. The whole body should follow the up and down movement of the hoop.

Variations:

a) Do the same movement but turn 180° before catching the hoop.

b) Throw the hoop high up so that you will be able to do a 360° turn while the hoop is in the air.

c) Throw the hoop high over the head and let it fall horizontally over the body so you will be inside of the hoop. Catch it with both hands in an overgrip at hip level.

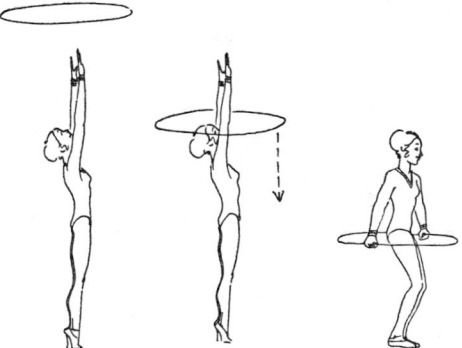

8. Throw with Horizontal Spin

Standing with arms extended forward use an outside grip with both hands to hold the hoop in a horizontal position. Throw the hoop upward with a spin on its horizontal axis. The hoop should turn at least twice in the air before you catch it with both hands.

Variations:
a) Do the same movement but perform a full turn before catching the hoop.

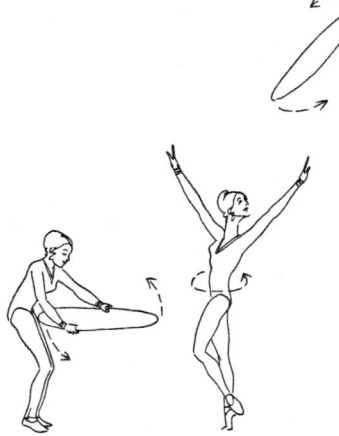

b) Throw the hoop high up so it will rotate at least three times in the air.

9. Throw and Leap

Stand with the arms extended to the side and the hoop held in the right hand, palm facing upward. Circle the hoop backward twice, with a bent arm, in the sagittal plane as you do two running steps forward. Straighten the arm and throw the hoop upward from circling, with a back spin, while you do a leap. Catch the hoop between the thumb and index finger and immediately start circling it backward.

Variations:

a) Throw the hoop far ahead then run, run, and leap to catch it.

b) Throw the circling hoop upward with a jump or leap and catch it in rotation during the second jump or leap.

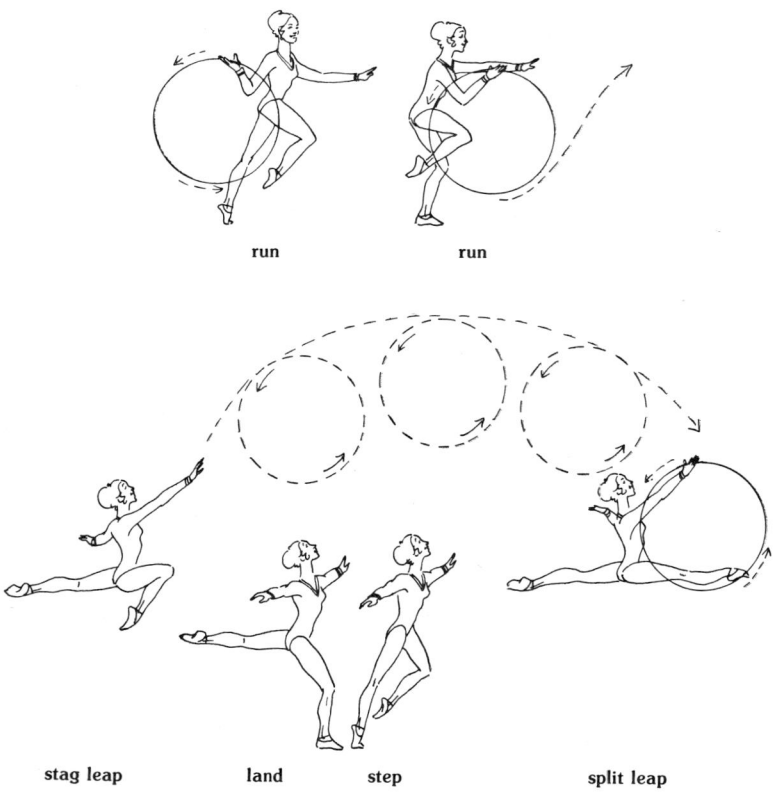

run　　　run

stag leap　　　land　　　step　　　split leap

c) Do the same movement as in (b) but catch the hoop during the third jump or leap.

10. Partner Tossing
Stand facing your partner, holding your hoop in front of your body with your right hand, the palm of the hand facing inward. Swing the hoop backward then forward and toss it in an arc to your partner. Catch your partner's hoop with your left hand. Repeat the movement several times, alternating hands. Try to increase the distance up to fifteen feet.

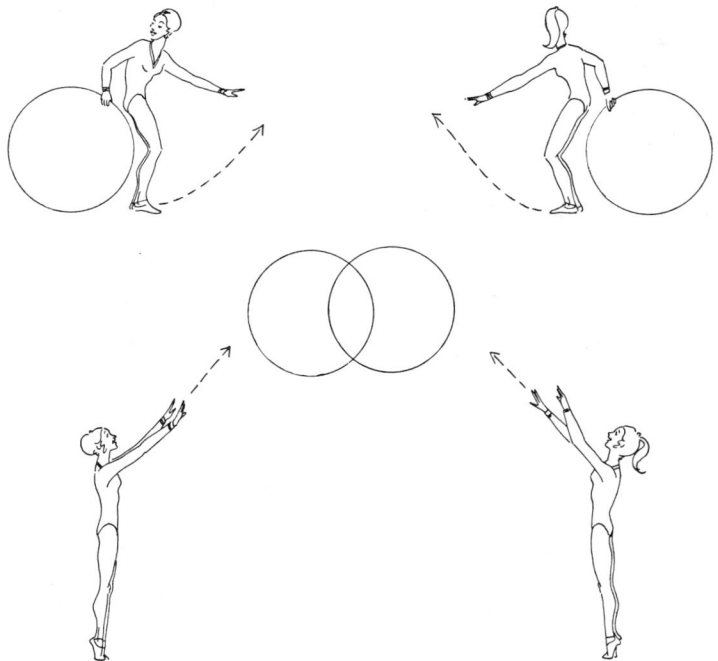

ROLLING MOVEMENTS

The hoop may be rolled on the floor or on the body in various ways. Rolling the hoop without bouncing or vibrating it requires skill. Rolling movements should be performed smoothly with other movements without interrupting the rhythm of the combination.

1. Roll in Frontal Plane
Stand in a wide straddle, with weight on the right foot, arms extended to the side and the hoop in the right hand, palm facing downward. Place the hoop on the floor and roll it along the floor from right to left while shifting weight to the left foot. Stop it with the left hand and

immediately roll the hoop back to the right. Roll hoop with right and left hand alternately in front of the body.

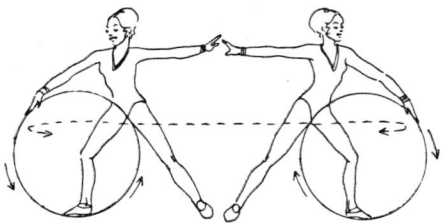

Variation:
Do the same movement with a gallop from side to side.

2. Run with Roll
Stand in a front stride position with arms at the sides, holding the hoop in the right hand, palm facing downward. Roll the hoop across the floor in the sagittal plane and run with it. Push the hoop with the right hand if necessary to keep it rolling straight. Practice with the left hand also.

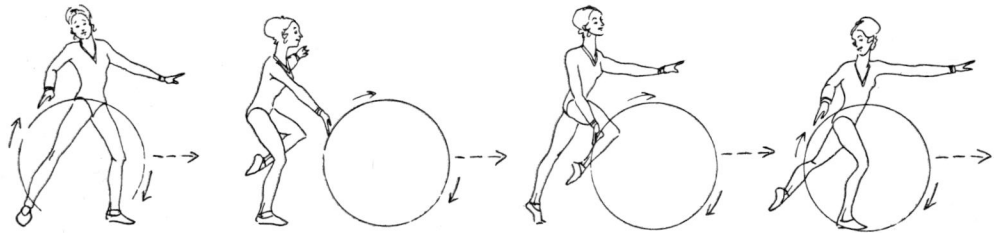

Variations:
a) Do the same movement but run beyond the hoop and turn halfway around to catch it.

b) Run and leap beside the rolling hoop.

3. Jump over Rolling Hoop
Stand in a front stride position, extending the arms to the sides and holding the hoop in the right hand, with the palm of the hand facing

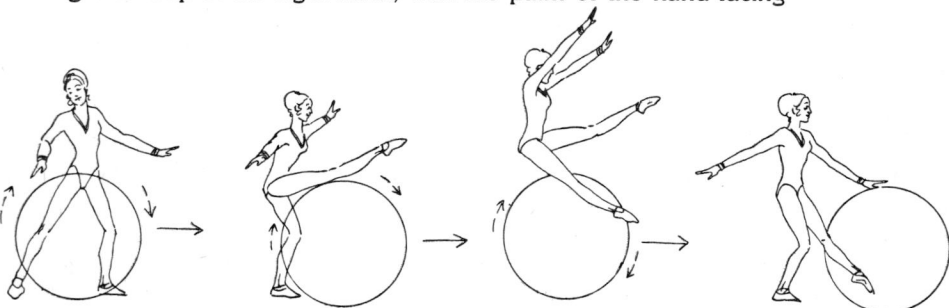

downward. Roll the hoop straight forward, follow it, and scissor jump sideways over it while it is rolling. Catch the hoop with the left hand.

Variations:
a) Scissor jump from the right side over the rolling hoop then do a few running steps forward and scissor jump over it from the left side. Catch the hoop with your right hand.
b) Do cat leaps over the rolling hoop.

4. Tour Jeté over Rolling Hoop
Stand in a front stride position, the arms extended to the side and the hoop held in the left hand with the palm of the hand facing downward. Roll the hoop forward, glissade on the left alongside the hoop and tour jeté to the left over it. Let the hoop roll into the left hand upon the completion of the movement.

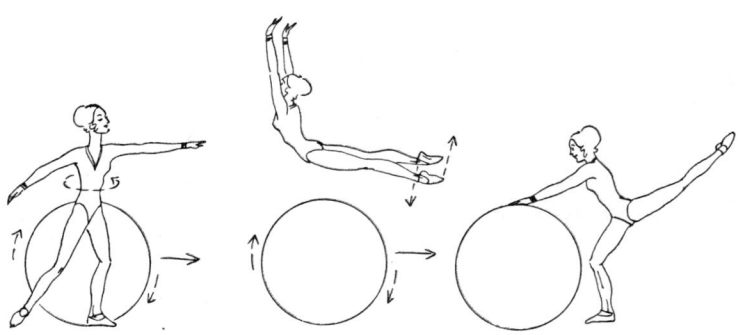

Variation:
Do the same movement but finish the tour jeté in a kneeling position, then catch the hoop as before.

5. Roll with Backspin
Stand in a forward stride position with the arms extended to the side and the hoop in the right hand, the palm of the hand facing downward. Roll the hoop forward with a backspin so it will return to you like a boomerang. This can be achieved only by pulling the wrist downward before you let go of the hoop. Practice this several times with the right hand. Practice with the left hand also.

Variations:
a) Perform the same movement but turn around before catching the hoop.

b) Do the same roll but after a half-turn catch the returning hoop in a deep backbend.

c) Do the same roll but jump over the returning hoop.

6. Roll in a Circle
Stand with the arms extended to the sides and the hoop in the right hand, the palm of the hand facing downward. Roll the hoop in a circle so it will return to you. This can be achieved only by slanting the top of the hoop from the upright position toward you when you release it. The hoop will roll around on its inside edge. Practice this several times with the right hand. Practice this with the left hand also.

Variation:
Roll the hoop as described above. Before it returns execute different types of turns or jumps.

7. Crawl Through Rolling Hoop
Stand with the arms extended to the sides, the hoop held in the left hand, with the palm of the hand facing downward. Roll the hoop forward, follow it, and crawl through the hoop while it is rolling without touching it. Catch it with the right hand. This is a quite difficult movement. A good preliminary exercise for learning this movement is

the following: stand holding the hoop in the sagittal plane on the floor. Release it and pass through the stationary hoop sideways and catch it with the other hand.

8. Roll on Arm and Back
Stand with the arms extended forward and the hoop in the right hand, the palm of the hand facing inward. Give a very slight impetus to the hoop by pulling the wrist upward and let the hoop roll along the right arm, down the right shoulder, and down the rounded back toward the waist. Catch the hoop behind the body with the right hand.

Variations:
a) Do the same movement but catch it with the left hand.

b) Repeat (a) in a lunge position.

9. Roll Along the Arms *(in front)*
Stand with the arms extended to the side and the hoop in the right hand, palm facing forward. Raise the right arm slightly above the horizontal, and give a small impetus to the hoop by pulling the wrist upward. Let the hoop roll along the right arm, across the chest, and down along the left arm into the left hand (palm of the hand facing

forward). Keep the head and chest high during the movement. Repeat with the left hand. NOTE: this exercise is very difficult and needs much practice.

Variation:
Combine the roll with walking or dancing steps.

10. Roll Along Arms *(in back)*
Stand with the arms extended to the side and the hoop in the right hand, palm facing backward. Give a slight impetus to the hoop by pulling the wrist upward and let the hoop roll along the right arm, across the back of the neck and down along the left arm. Catch the hoop with the left hand, palm facing backward. During the movement keep the body bent forward and hold the head slightly tucked. Follow the hoop with your eyes by quickly turning your head and watch it roll down into your left hand. This exercise is very difficult and requires a great deal of practice.

Variation:
Combine the roll with walking or dancing steps.

11. Hoop Rolling to Partner
Stand, facing your partner, with the hoop in your right hand, palm facing downward. Roll the hoop to your partner on your right side and

receive your partner's hoop with your left hand. Then roll the hoop with the left hand to your partner. Repeat several times. Each person rolls her hoop simultaneously. Increase the distance up to twenty feet.

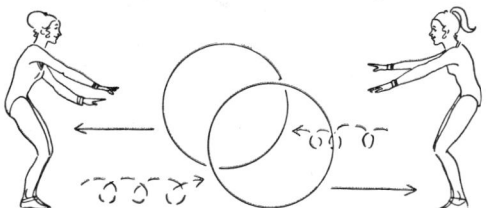

JUMPING MOVEMENTS

Like a jump rope, the hoop may be turned forward, backward or from side to side with one or both hands. If the hoop is swung forward the arms are straight when you jump through it, then the arms must be bent to allow the hoop to pass over your head and at the end of the movement the arms straighten again. The movement is just the reverse when you swing the hoop backwards. Turn the hoop without allowing it to touch the floor or the body.

1. Basic Forward Jump
Stand holding the horizontal hoop with both hands in front of the body, palms facing downward. Swing the hoop downward and jump through it; then swing it upward, overhead, and forward to the starting position. Repeat several times.

Variations:
a) Do the same movement but swing the hoop with one hand.

b) Do the same movement but perform high tuck jumps instead of the basic ones. Repeat several times.

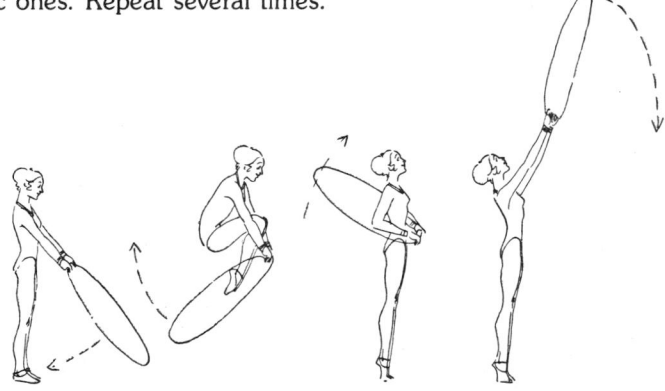

c) Jump over the hoop twice then throw it upward, turning it on its horizontal axis; catch the hoop and do two more basic jumps through it.

2. Basic Backward Jump
Stand holding the horizontal hoop in front of the body with both hands. The hoop may be held either with a regular grip (palms downward) or with a reverse grip (palms upward). Swing the hoop up, overhead, then downward in back of the body and jump over it as in rope jumping.

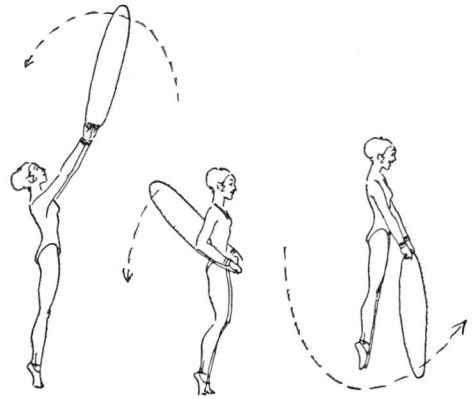

Variation:
Do the same variations as in exercise 1 but turn the hoop backward.

3. Step-Hops
Stand holding the hoop horizontally in front of the body with both hands, palms facing downward. Execute step-hops forward through the hoop. Perform this exercise first in place then across the gymnasium.

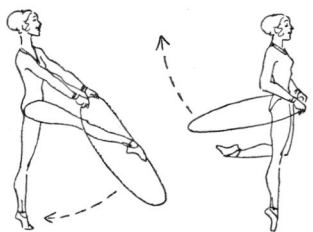

Variations:
a) Do step-hops backward while turning the hoop backward also.

b) Do the same movements extending the free leg either forward or backward.

c) Do schottische steps forward or backward—step, step, step, hop or run, run, run, hop—while turning the hoop either forward or backward. Pass through the hoop on the first and third steps.

d) Do all of the above movements while turning the hoop with one hand.

4. Leaps
Stand holding the hoop overhead with both hands, palms facing forward. Turn the hoop forward and leap through it. Keep the back leg lifted high and bent.

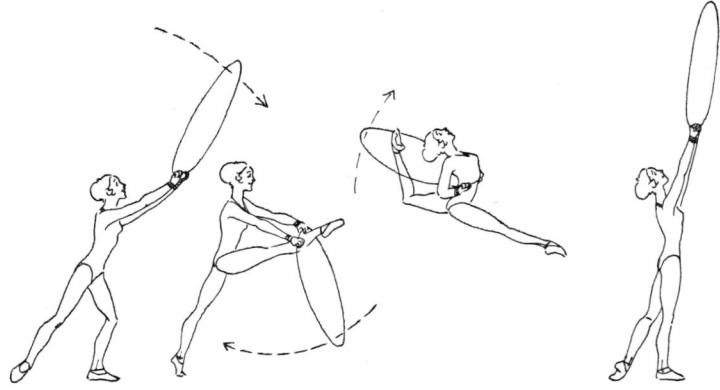

Variations:
a) Do cat leaps through the hoop.

b) Do the above movements while turning the hoop with one hand.

5. Pendulum Swing
Stand with arms extended to the side, hoop in the right hand, palm facing downward. Swing the hoop downward from the side and jump into it, then swing it outward and up as you jump out of it. Repeat several times. Swing the hoop under the feet in a pendulum fashion. Practice with the left hand also.

Variation:
Jump into the hoop and catch it with the left hand. Simultaneously let it go with the right hand and swing the hoop outward with the left hand as you jump out of it.

6. Lateral Turn

Stand with arms extended to the side, the hoop in the right hand, palm facing downward. Swing the hoop downward with one hand, jump into the hoop, and then swing it upward, overhead, and back to the starting position. Repeat the movement several times, then practice it with the left hand also, turning the hoop from left to right.

Variations:
a) Do different kinds of jumps into and out of the hoop while turning it laterally.

b) After jumping into the hoop catch it at waist level with the left hand. Lift the hoop upward overhead with both hands, then let it go with the left hand and swing it back to the starting position with the right hand.

c) Repeat (b) but when the hoop is overhead let it go with the right hand and execute the movement in the opposite direction.

TEACHING SUGGESTIONS

1. Exercises with the hoop require much space. To learn the basic skills the class should be in staggered lines with ample space between gymnasts. When teaching locomotor movements, line the class up at one end of the gymnasium. The first line begins the exercise, then after a few musical bars the next line starts, and so on. These formations will allow the teacher to observe each girl. See the Teaching Suggestions in the chapters on rope jumping and clubs for more ideas.
2. Most of the basic skills should first be taught in a stationary position in order to gain control of the hoop; then have your students repeat them with locomotion movements. As the students learn the various moves, combine them into short sequences with the music so that they get the feeling of arranging movements with a continuous flowing quality on various planes and levels.
3. Let the students create some of their own combinations after they have learned to perform the various movements with accuracy and grace. For creative assignments divide the class into smaller groups of three to six students. Give each group either the same or different movement problems. Walk around and encourage each group while they are working on their projects. At the end of the lesson evaluate each group's short combination. Let the class comment on what they liked or didn't like in the routine. Students benefit very much from the constructive criticism of their fellow gymnasts.
4. Emphasize good posture and natural total body movements with the hoops at all times. Practice alternately with right and left hand from the very first day, so that students immediately get used to working with both hands. The free arm should also participate in the movement.
5. Students should not be afraid of losing the hoop. They should rather lose the hoop, using the right technique, than try to hold on to the hoop by grasping it too tightly. Emphasize light handling of the apparatus.
6. Movements of the hoop must be precisely executed in one of the movement planes. To help the gymnast see and feel her movement, divide the class into twos and have partners judge each other's performance. This will make each gymnast more aware of her own and others' mistakes.
7. Always use music. Waltz rhythm is very suitable for hoop exercises.

COMPETITIVE RULES

The dimensions of the performing area are 12 meters x 12 meters (approximately 40 square feet). When planning the exercise be sure that the entire area will be used.

The routine must be executed to music of the competitor's own choice. The composition must match the music and it must be perfectly timed. The time limit is one minute to one minute and thirty seconds. Shortening or lengthening the time results in deduction from the given score.

The routine, which should be aesthetically pleasing, must be presented with confidence, control, and amplitude and in good rhythm with no faults in execution. Loss of balance, jerky execution, lack of continuity between movements, unpointed toes, bent legs, and any other breaks in form are penalized by the judges.

Common execution faults in handling the hoop for which deductions are made are:

Movements	Faults
all exercises	—hoop used as a decoration; hoop not moving clearly in a specific plane—changing plane.
swinging, turning, and circling	—touching the body with the hoop (except circling around the waist—"hula-hooping"); slight stop during hand changes.
throwing	—during the flight of the hoop, gymnast is not moving; hoop vibrates during the flight; catching the hoop on the forearm or the wrist instead of in the hand; catching the hoop, interrupting its movement; dropping the hoop.
rolling	—the hoop hops or vibrates during the roll; losing the hoop.

EXAMPLES OF DIFFICULTIES

Swinging

Medium difficulties: Scissor jump or cat leap while doing a figure eight in the sagittal plane; swing the hoop horizontally and pass it in front of and behind the body from one hand to the other while performing a pirouette (360°).

Superior difficulties: During any jump pass the hoop in front of and behind the body from one hand to the other; during a split leap pass the hoop under the legs and above the head from one hand to the other.

Turning

Medium difficulties: Turning of the hoop combined with different rhythmical steps; pirouetting while swinging the raised leg above the free spinning hoop.

Superior difficulties: Change the spinning hoop in front of the body from one hand to the other under the leg; any type of jump over the free spinning hoop.

Circling
Medium difficulties: One full turn (360°) on one leg while circling the hoop horizontally above the head; change the circling hoop from one hand to the other while doing any dance step.

Superior difficulties: Double turn (720°) on one leg while circling the hoop horizontally above the head; circle the hoop in any plane while executing a split leap or any other large jump.

Throwing and Catching
Medium difficulties: Throwing the hoop from circling upward with a pirouette (360°) and regrasping it in rotation; throwing the hoop from circling upward with a jump or leap and catching it in rotation during the second jump or leap.

Superior difficulties: Throwing the hoop from circling upward with a pirouette (540° or more) and regrasping it in rotation; throwing the hoop from circling upward with a leap, performing a second leap during the flight of the hoop and regrasping it during the third leap.

Rolling
Medium difficulties: Scissor jump over the rolling hoop; rolling the hoop with a backspin and straddle jump over returning hoop.

Superior difficulties: Crawling through the rolling hoop; rolling the hoop along the arms.

Jumping
Medium difficulties: Cat leap through the hoop; jump twice through the hoop, then toss it upward so it will turn on its horizontal axis, regrasp it and do two more jumps through the hoop.

Superior difficulties: Split leap through the hoop; do several high tuck jumps through the hoop.

COMPOSITION

An optional individual routine should be well thought out and planned to demonstrate your ability. You should not immediately work toward a final competitive routine but rather toward acceptable short compositions by starting to put together a variety of the learned movements. Slowly, as your skill develops, you may add more and more difficulties and better connecting moves to develop an interesting routine.

In your composition you don't have to include all six hoop elements, but your routine must contain circling, throwing, and rolling movements. However, for variety it is best to utilize all phases of hoop technique. You must also combine hoop movements with the following dance movements: dance steps, turns, jumps, balances, body waves, and backbends. In addition judge your composition on the following points: smoothness, grace, poise, rhythm, variety, and ambidexterity.

The possible combinations are infinite. There are unlimited possibilities for combining hoop movements with dance movements. Your imagination and creative capacity are the only limitations. An example of a composition from the skills already presented is given below. Certain skills can be added or eliminated depending upon your ability. Perform your composition with good posture, elegance, and proper technique, and without interruption.

1. Starting pose, then stand up with a body wave to a moderate arabesque.
2. Three running steps forward and leap while circling the hoop with the right hand in the sagittal plane.
3. Four walking steps forward in a curve pattern while performing two figure eights in the sagittal plane.
4. Toss the hoop overhead in the sagittal plane from the backward swing of the last figure-eight loop. Catch the hoop with the left hand and immediately start circling it forward in the sagittal plane.
5. Swing the hoop behind the body and pass it to the right hand while doing a scissor jump.
6. Roll the hoop along the right arm and down the back. Catch it with the right hand. Swing the hoop forward, upward, and backward as you do a body wave into a deep backbend.
7. Do a front and overhead horizontal circle while turning around.
8. Roll the hoop forward with a backspin, and straddle jump over the returning hoop.
9. Raise the hoop overhead and grasp it with the other hand also. Swing the hoop backward and jump over it; then throw it with a horizontal spin upward. Catch it with both hands, palms upward, and do another backward jump through the hoop.

10. Do a quarter turn as you let the hoop go with the left hand. Swing the hoop downward and jump into it. Catch it with the left hand and simultaneously let it go with the right hand. Then swing the hoop outward with the left hand as you jump out of it.

11. Lie down holding the hoop with both hands, palms facing inward. Do a full turn to the left and finish the roll in a V-seat position. Put the legs through the hoop and stand up to a finishing pose.

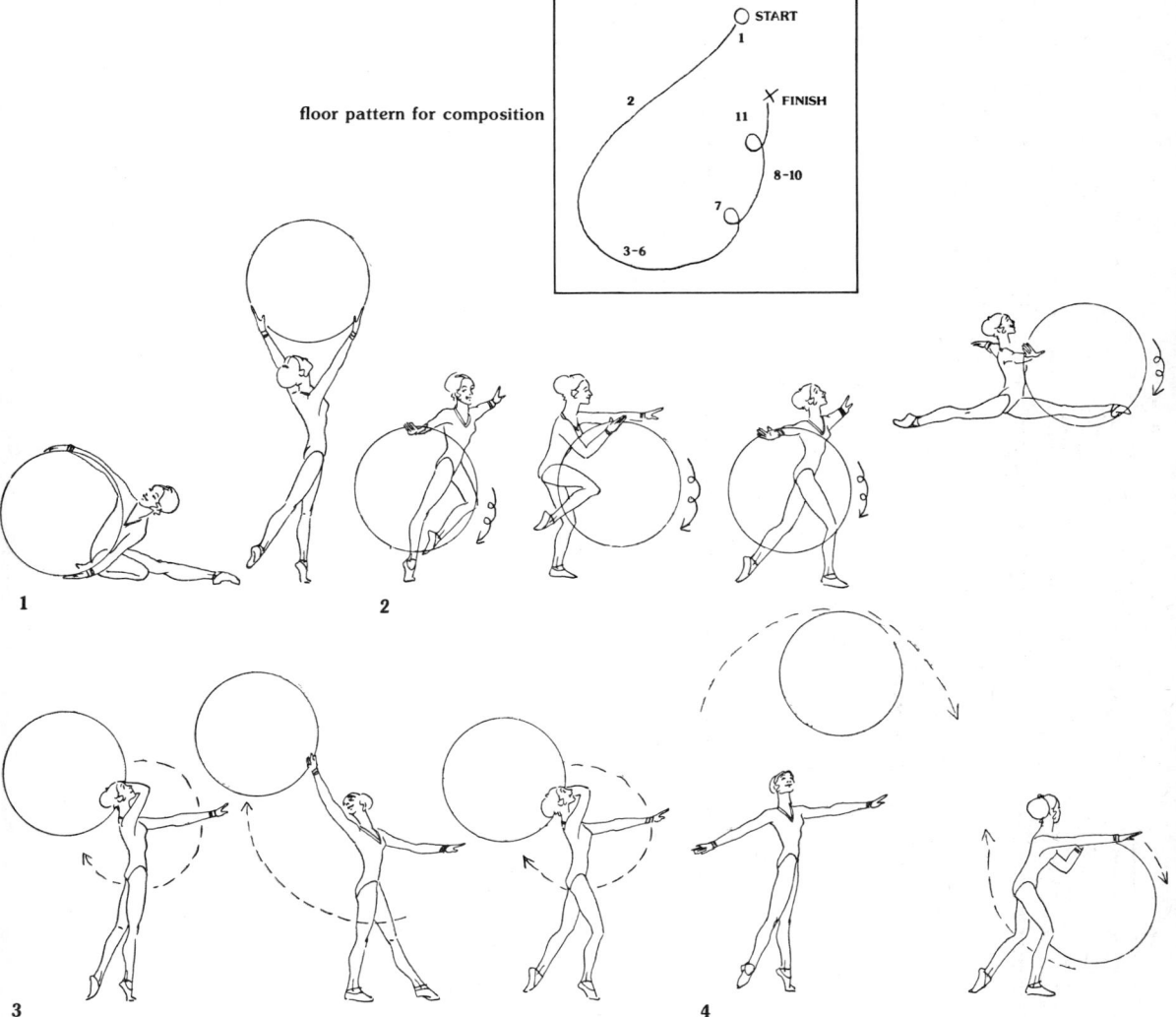

floor pattern for composition

GROUP EXERCISES

Area: 12 x 12 meters (approximately 40 square feet)
Music: one instrument
Time limit: two minutes and thirty seconds to three minutes

The hoop is a commonly used hand apparatus in group exercises. It is also often used in combination with other hand apparatuses. In the third Modern Rhythmic Gymnastics World Championships in Copenhagen, Denmark, the group routine was first introduced with the hoop. In the fifth World Championships in Cuba the hoop was used in combination with the ball. On a team of six members, three girls used hoops and the other three used balls. Since a group exercise using hoops can be very spectacular, hoops can be used effectively by large groups for demonstrations. Whatever the size and purpose of the group, the composition should have a logical sequence of patterns and exchanges of hoops between members of the group. A few suggestions for group formations and exchanges are given below.

FLOOR PATTERN EXAMPLES

1. Form a straight vertical line across the floor. Do step-hops through the hoop while circulating counterclockwise to form the second pattern—a straight horizontal line across the floor. Members 2, 3, and 6 do a half turn while performing the last step-hop.

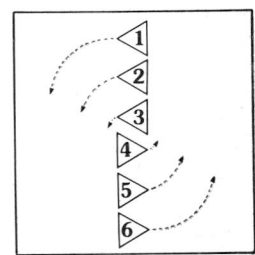

207

2. From the straight horizontal line formation do chaînés turns while turning the hoop horizontally above the head to arrive in the next formation.

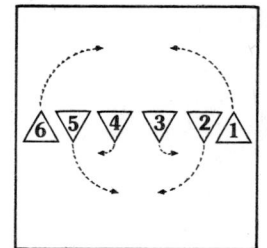

3. Two parallel lines, facing in opposite directions. Both lines move forward with alternate forward and backward scissor jumps while doing figure eights with their hoops in the sagittal plane.

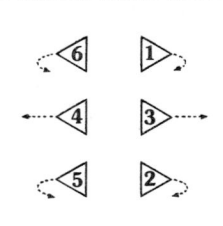

4. Two triangles, facing in opposite directions. Do a quarter turn to the left to face counterclockwise. Perform a waltz run forward to form a circle. Circle the hoop inward in front of the body, then circle it in back of the body and pass it to the other hand with each waltz run.

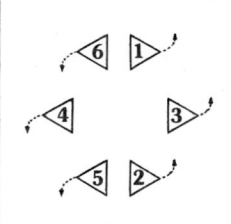

5. Circle formation, everybody facing inward. Roll the hoop into the circle with a backspin and do a pirouette before catching the returning hoop. Then run forward to form the sixth pattern. Toss the hoop high in the sagittal plane from the right hand to the left hand and from the left hand back to the right while running.

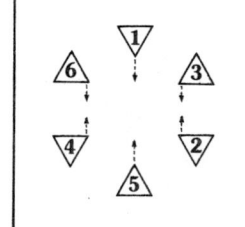

6. Double triangle formation, facing each other. Place the hoop on the floor and spin it around. Do a 360° turn while lifting the raised leg above the spinning hoop. Catch the hoop before it falls.

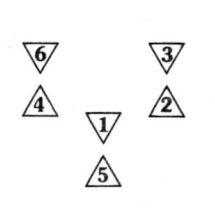

EXCHANGE EXAMPLES

1. Two diagonal lines facing each other, each member with the hoop in her right hand. Partners roll their hoops at the same time, from the right side, each one receiving her partner's hoop with the left hand. They then roll the hoop forward, on the left side, with a backspin and run forward to exchange places with their partners. Each girl catches her partner's returning hoop with the right hand.

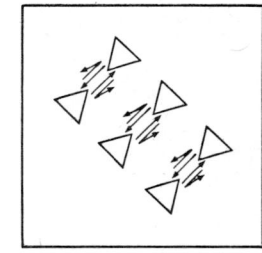

2. Circle formation, facing inward, hoop in the right hand. Circle the hoop twice outward, then throw it over the head in the frontal plane to the next person who catches it with the right hand.

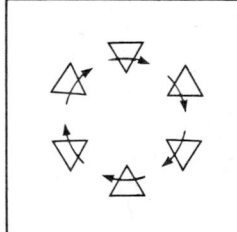

3. Circle formation, facing counterclockwise, hoop in the right hand. All place hoops on floor and spin them around clockwise. Let hoop spin freely and skip forward to catch the spinning hoop of the girl in front.

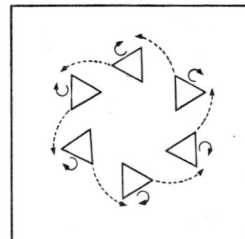

4. Two parallel lines, facing each other, members holding the hoops in front of the body with their right hands. Both lines swing the hoops backward then forward and throw them simultaneously in an arc toward their partner. Members in both lines catch the hoops with their left hands. They then repeat the movement with their left hands.

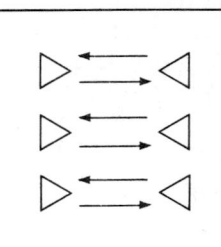

SUGGESTED GROUP ASSIGNMENT

After the basic skills have been developed fairly well the students are ready for a group assignment. Through group assignments a gymnast will learn to synchronize her movements not just with the time structure of the accompaniment but also with other students. Group assignment will also promote creativity.

Problem: There are five patterns illustrated below. Move into these specific formations smoothly and creatively in the given sequence.

210

Modern Rhythmic Gymnastics

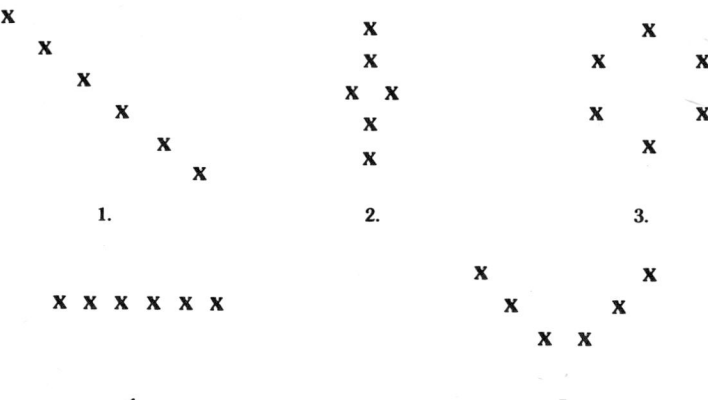

A. Be sure to incorporate at least three of the following six types of movements into the routine.

    swinging   tossing
    spinning   rolling
    circling   jumping

B. Make use of the different planes: frontal, sagittal, and horizontal.

C. Have at least two exchanges of hoops between members of the group.

D. Attempt the use of the hoop on a level other than standing up.

E. Keep the hoop moving at all times.

Music—Waltz Medley—arrangement by Harriet Jones

    Listen for high points or climaxes so that appropriate movements can be planned at those points.

Musical breakdown:
    36 measures
    3/4 meter
        4 measures—introduction, soft, natural waltz rhythm
        8 measures—medium loud, smooth, flowing
        8 measures—soft, smooth (Notice at the sixth bar the melody rises
                to the highest point of this smooth phrase.)
        8 measures—medium loud, faster tempo
        8 measures—very loud, grandiose

Music for Hoop Group Assignment

Ribbons

Chapter 6

The words *ribbon* and *streamer* are used interchangeably in gymnastics literature, but the official modern rhythmic gymnastics term is *ribbon*. The ribbon is one of the most spectacular hand apparatus; it is also difficult to use. The ribbon was first used in team competition by the Hungarians in the 1956 Olympic games. Its use was first introduced in an individual compulsory routine in the Fifth Modern Rhythmic Gymnastics Championships, in Cuba, in 1971. It was again employed in 1973 in Holland during the Sixth Championships as part of an individual optional routine with compulsory elements. It was included again in the 1975 World Championships, in Spain.

The ribbon can be used very effectively in small or large demonstrations. In the Soviet Union it is often used in big gymnastics exhibitions. An evening demonstration in which fluorescent ribbons are used is spectacular. The luminating circles, spirals, and other patterns formed with the ribbon make the exercise very interesting and beautiful.

Movements made with ribbons should be large, smooth, and flowing, with arm, leg, and body movements coordinated with the movement of the ribbon. Unless there is a high degree of coordination, many loops and knots will occur in the ribbon or it will entangle the gymnast.

EQUIPMENT

The length and width of the ribbon can vary; the longer the ribbon, the greater the amount of skill required to work with it.

The official standards for ribbons used in the Modern Rhythmic Gymnastics World Championships are:

Ribbon: any material (heavy satin is recommended because of its flowing character)

Length of ribbon: 6 meters (19′8¼″). Note that at the end of the stick, the ribbon is doubled along a length of 1 meter (3′3⅜″), thus the total length of the ribbon is: 7m (22′11⅜″)

Width of ribbon: 4–6cm (1⅝″–2⅜″)

Weight of ribbon: minimum of 35 g (approximately 1¼ ounces) excluding the stick

Stick: wood or bamboo (bamboo is recommended because of its flexibility). The part of the stick held in the hand may be covered by a thin layer of anti-slip material

Length of stick: 50–60cm (19⅝″–23⅝″)

Diameter of stick: maximum 1cm (⅜″)

Attachment of the ribbon to the stick: the ribbon is attached to the end of the stick with a very strong thread (fish line) which passes through a hole in the stick, or by any other system which allows for a high degree of mobility of the ribbon. The string attaching the ribbon to the stick should not exceed a maximum length of 7cm (2¾″)

For juniors and beginners the ribbon should be 5 meters (16′4⅞″) long and the stick 50cm (19⅝″).

If two ribbons are used each one should also be only 5 meters (16′4⅞″) long.

In Germany and in some other European countries, children use two ribbons attached to a single bamboo stick in preparation for use of the long ribbon. The length of these ribbons varies from 1 to 2 meters (3′3⅜″ to 6′6¾″).

Gymnastics clubs and schools sometimes use shorter and wider ribbons (4.50 meters or 14′9⅛″ long and 30–50cm or 11¾–19⅝″ wide) for demonstration purposes. The material for this wider ribbon should be silk or any material with the same light, flowing character which is so important for a ribbon routine.

HOW TO MAKE RIBBONS

Ribbons used for modern rhythmic gymnastics competition or for demonstrations may be made by the gymnast or teacher. You will need the following materials: (1) the proper width and length of satin or china silk in the color desired; (2) a dowel or bamboo stick about ⅜ inch in diameter and about 20″–23½″ in length; (3) three to four inches of fish line; and (4) a spool of silk or nylon thread in a color that matches the fabric.

For competition the proper width (2 inches) of ribbon may be purchased but if you are using wider ribbons for demonstration purposes you must sew your own. When cutting out the ribbon, cut the fabric to measure ½″ longer and wider than you want the finished ribbon to be. Hem the ribbon on all four sides by folding the material over ⅛″ and then ⅛″ again and then stitching it. The ribbon should now be the correct size. Double the ribbon along one end about 1 yard and 3 inches for double thickness. A piece of stiffening approximately one inch wide should be inserted in this doubled end to which the fish line is attached. This will protect the fabric. Drill a small hole through one end of the dowel or bamboo stick about ¼″ from the end, and pass the fish line through the hole and tie it to attach the ribbon to the stick. A more efficient way is to drive an eye bolt into the end of the stick. With a snap swivel attach the ribbon to the eye bolt.

TECHNIQUES

Movements with the ribbon can be performed with the stick held in one or both hands. The stick is held lightly between the thumb and middle finger and with the index finger softly extended. The fourth and fifth fingers just rest on the stick. There are two kinds of grips used with the ribbon depending upon the plane in which it is being moved.

1. The regular grip, with the palm of the hand down.

2. The reverse grip, with the palm of the hand up.

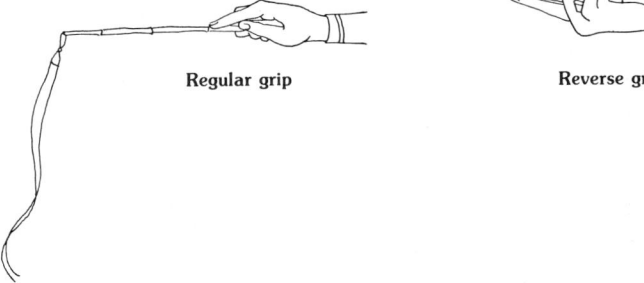

Regular grip   Reverse grip

Play with the ribbon, swinging and circling it to the music. This will give you a feeling for how much force you must apply to the movement. If too much force is applied the ribbon will snap and crack; too little force will cause it to wrap around the body.

Movements with the ribbon should be performed with a relaxed wrist and clearly done in the movement planes in which they are started. The exercises must be perfectly executed to show the preciseness and beauty of the circles, ovals, spirals, waves, and other figures. These figures can be in various movement planes and at different levels of elevation. The rhythmic flow of the movement should continue to the end of the ribbon. The end of the ribbon should not be motionless at any time.

Emphasize the light, flowing quality of movement with total body involvement to avoid tangling and snapping of the ribbon. The focus should be on the ribbon so that the movement of the body follows the direction of the streamer. The free arm should also participate to bring out the character of the movement.

To facilitate the continuous flow of ribbon movement and avoid tangling the ribbon, when changing planes or connecting exercises be sure the momentum gained in one movement will be utilized in the next one. Therefore, the direction of the ribbon and body movement at the end of a move should determine what the next move will be.

The ribbon should not touch any part of the body except during movements in which the end is caught when it may touch the hand.

Large swings, circles, figure eights, and the like, are performed with a straight arm, and the movement starts from the shoulder. Medium size movements will start from the elbow and small ones from the wrist. The bamboo stick should always be a straight continuation of the arm.

MOVEMENTS

Exercises with the ribbon require much space.

In order to develop balanced handling of the apparatus, all movements with the ribbon should be practiced with both the right and left hand from the beginning.

As each new exercise is learned, it should be combined with other skills immediately. This will help you gain an early understanding of the relationships of different movements to each other.

Exercises with two ribbons should be attempted only by gymnasts who are capable of performing one ribbon exercise with good technical skills.

Experiment with different qualities of movement. For example:

(1) start the movement with a burst of energy and end it slowly;

(2) start the exercise either fast or slow and continue with the same force evenly until its completion.

The exercises should be performed with music at all times. The music must be chosen carefully. Not all music is suitable for a ribbon routine. It should have a flowing quality and a medium tempo. Too fast music will not allow the gymnasts to perform the movements to their fullest possible range. Waltz rhythm is very good to get the relaxed flowing and swinging quality of the movements; however, 6/8, 2/4 or 4/4 meter music works just as well, as long as the speed is correct. Choose music with interesting phrasing, nuances in dynamics and which could be harmonized with the movements of the body and ribbon.

Movements with the ribbon are divided into the following categories: swings, circles, figure eights, serpentines, spirals, and throws. The ribbon can be held with one or both hands. The movements are initiated from the shoulders, the elbows, or the wrists. Variations of combinations of arm, lower arm, and wrist circles are limitless. The ribbon may be swung in the frontal, sagittal, and horizontal planes. The movement of the ribbon should be followed by the entire body. Vertical movements are performed in front and in back of the body or head in the frontal plane. Lateral movements can be done on either side of the body in the sagittal plane and horizontal moves are executed above the head, around the body, below the legs and on the floor in the horizontal plane.

SWINGING MOVEMENTS

All swinging movements must be accompanied by body waves. There is a total flow of the body in the sense that every part of the body is coordinated with the swinging motion.

1. Swing Forward and Backward

Stand with the left arm extended forward and the right arm backward, with the ribbon in the right hand. Swing the right arm forward and backward on the right side twice. At the end of the second swing, pass the ribbon to the left hand behind the body and continue the swing with the left hand. The arm moves like a pendulum: it swings forward until it reaches its highest point, then swings backward to reach the highest opposite point. This motion will assure smooth and flowing ribbon movements.

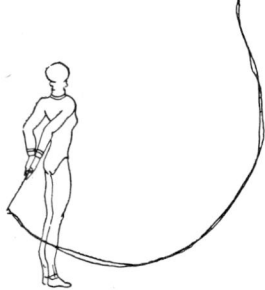

back view

Variations:
a) Do the same movement but change hands in front of the body.

b) Do the same movement in a forward stride position, shifting the weight forward and backward with the motion of the ribbon.

c) Repeat the movement while walking in a waltz rhythm. Walk forward (1-2-3) during the forward swing and walk backward (4-5-6) on the backward swing.

2. Swing Across the Body

Stand in a wide straddle with weight on the right foot, the arms extended to the sides and the ribbon in the right hand. Swing the right arm downward across the body to the left, back to the right, and then down to the left again and transfer the ribbon into the left hand. Repeat with the left hand. Transfer the weight from side to side while swinging the ribbon.

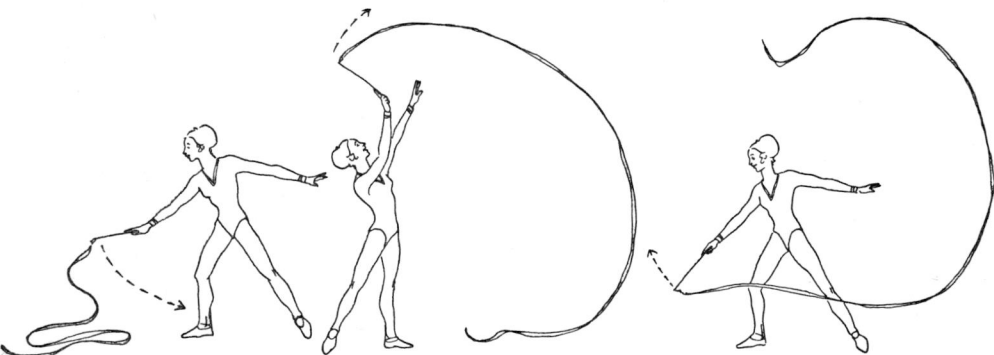

Variation:
Do the same movement while walking or running forward or backward.

3. Swing Overhead
Stand with feet in a wide straddle, arms extended to the side and the ribbon in the right hand. Swing the ribbon in a large motion over the head from right to left and, when it is on the left side, pass it to the left hand as the weight is shifted from the right foot to the left. Swing the ribbon back over the head to the right. Repeat the movement.

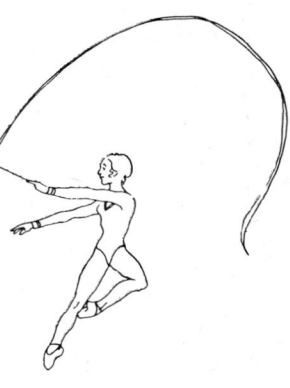

Variations:
a) Do the same movement using a gallop step.
b) Do the same swing while walking forward or backward.
c) Perform the same ribbon swing with various jumps.

4. Swing Forward and Overhead
Hold the ribbon in either hand. Try to perform the movements depicted below while moving the ribbon in a big swing forward, upward, over the head and to the rear. Find different ways of going into and coming out of these swinging movements.

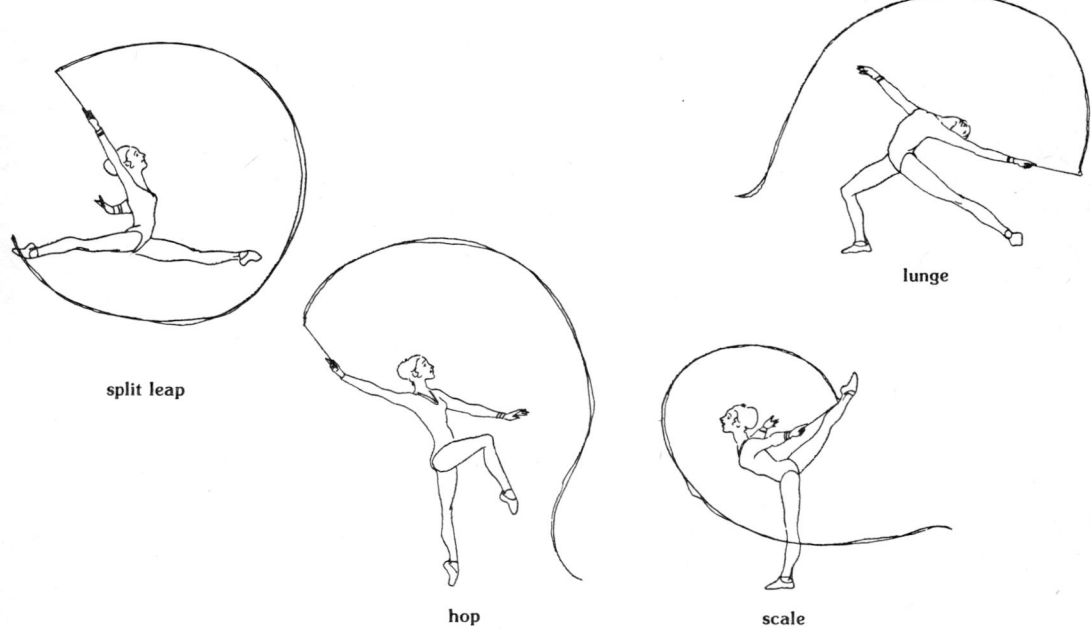

split leap   hop   scale   lunge

5. Swing Under the Leg

Stand holding the ribbon in the left hand, out to the left side. Run forward and do three low swings back and forth in front of the body. After the third swing execute a big swing in which the ribbon moves from right to left on the floor. Leap over the ribbon as it moves across the floor. Repeat the movement. Practice this exercise with the right hand also.

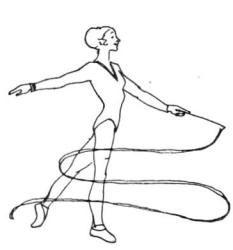

Variations:
a) Same movement but perform small running steps over the ribbon during the frontal swings before the leap.
b) Do the same movement but perform leaps or jumps over the ribbon.

6. Swing and Catch

Stand holding the ribbon in the right hand. Run forward as you swing the ribbon upward, overhead and backward. Catch the ribbon close to the end with the left hand and swing it behind you. Repeat several times, then practice the movement with the left hand also.

7. Swing Around the Body

Stand with arms extended to the right, the stick in one hand and the end of the ribbon in the other. Swing the ribbon to the left in front of the body and continue swinging it toward the rear by arching the trunk backward then around to the right finishing in the original position. The ribbon completes a full horizontal swing around the body. Also practice this movement toward the opposite side.

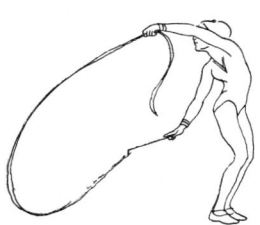 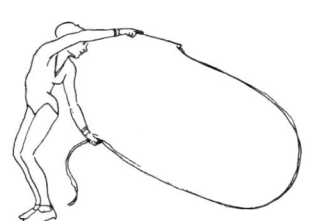 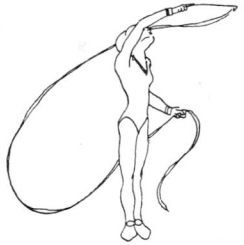

8. Swing with Two Ribbons

Some of the above exercises can be performed with two ribbons also. For example, you can easily perform the forward and backward swings and the swing forward and over head.

Perform large swings so the ribbons will not tangle. If both sticks are held in one hand the technique is identical to that for swings with one ribbon.

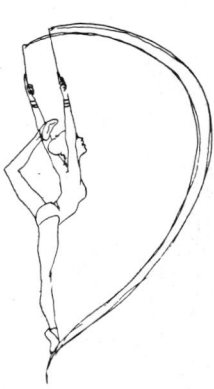

CIRCLING MOVEMENTS

When performing circling movements, the entire circle must be performed from beginning to end with an equal amount of force. This will cause the ribbon to design a precise circle without any wave-like movements. Large circles are executed by the entire arm, small circles by the wrist. Vary the size of the circles to make interesting patterns with the ribbon.

1. Circle in the Frontal Plane

Stand with the arms extended to the sides and the ribbon held in the right hand. Swing the right arm downward, upward over the head, and then downward again toward the left side, making one and one-half circles in the frontal plane. Transfer the ribbon to the left hand and make one and one-half circles in the opposite direction. The whole body should follow the movement of the ribbon.

Variations:
a) Do the same movement with a gallop from side to side.

b) Make a large circle and then a small one in front of the body before passing the ribbon to the other hand.

c) Perform the above movements while circling the ribbon in the opposite direction.

d) Perform the above movements while holding the bamboo stick with both hands.

2. Circling in the Sagittal Plane

Stand holding the ribbon in front of you in the right hand. Swing the ribbon forward in a circle on the right side of the body. Repeat several times and then alternate sides.

Variations:
a) Do the same movement while circling the ribbon backward.

b) Do a body wave while circling the ribbon.

c) All the above movements may be done while walking or dancing forward or backward.

3. Horizontal Circles
Stand, holding the ribbon in the right hand. Perform horizontal circles inward overhead. Repeat with the left hand.

Variations:
a) Perform a horizontal circle outward overhead.

b) Do the same movement while walking or dancing forward or backward.

c) Do the same movement while performing different kinds of turns or pirouettes.

d) Do an inward horizontal circle over the head with the right arm. Without stopping, lower the right arm to the front and make a horizontal circle with the ribbon on the floor. Repeat the movement.

e) Perform chaînés turns to the left while circling the ribbon horizontally around you at waist level, by changing hands.

4. Circle Under the Leg
Stand holding the ribbon in the right hand, out to the side. Swing the ribbon low inward, jump over it, and continue the circle. Repeat with the left hand.

Variation:
Do a few running steps and then leap or jump as the ribbon passes under the legs.

5. Circles over the Head and Under the Leg
Stand with the arms extended to the sides and the ribbon held in the right hand. Circle the ribbon inward above the head then swing the right arm down and circle the ribbon in the same direction slightly above the floor level, passing over it with a jump. Practice this with the left hand also.

Variation:
Do a few running steps while circling the ribbon above the head then leap or jump as the ribbon is circled under the legs.

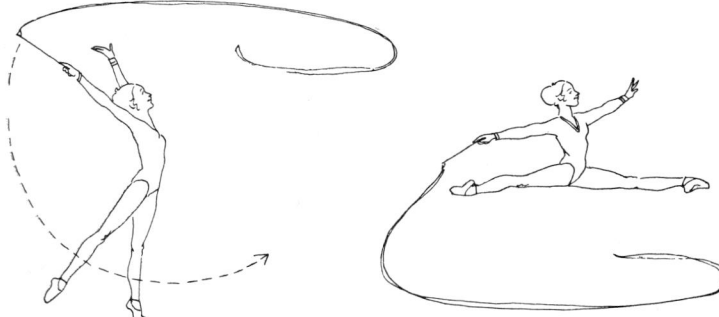

6. Circle with Two Ribbons
Stand with the right arm over head and the left arm to the side. Circle the right arm forward and simultaneously circle the left arm backward.

Variations:
a) Do the same movement while walking forward.
b) Do the same movement with the arms while performing a waltz-turn step.
c) Do the same circles, but circle the arms backward (as in a swimming backstroke).

FIGURE-EIGHT MOVEMENTS

Figure eights can be performed in the frontal, sagittal, and horizontal planes. Large figure eights are made using the entire arm with the movement starting from the shoulder. Medium figure eights are performed using the lower arm with the movement originating from the elbow. Small figure eights are performed using only wrist action. The two loops that make up the figure eight must be equal in size and must be made on the same movement level. Figure eights can be performed with the stick held in one or both hands. While sketching the figure eight pattern, the hand should turn smoothly, moving from a regular grip to a reverse grip.

1. Figure Eight in Frontal Plane

Stand in a wide straddle with the arms extended to the right side and the ribbon in both hands. Make a figure eight starting from the right, moving the ribbon toward the left, and then moving it back toward the right to form the figure eight. The whole body follows the ribbon, transferring the weight and pushing the hips from side to side with the swinging ribbon. Keep the center of the eight in front of you and make both loops the same size. Repeat the movement several times.

Variations:
a) Perform the same movement with either the right or the left arm. The arm and hand rotate inward and outward in a continuous successive motion.

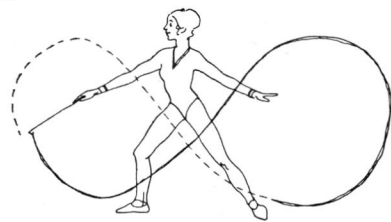

b) Do the same variation as in (a) while walking or dancing backward. Make small figure eights using wrist and elbow action.

2. Vertical Figure Eight
Stand with arms extended to the side and the ribbon in the right hand. Make a vertical figure eight (with one loop on top of the other) in front of the body with the ribbon. The center of the eight should be at waist height. The trunk should follow the movement of the arm.

Variation:
Do the same movement using both hands.

3. Figure Eight in the Sagittal Plane
Stand with arms extended to the side and the ribbon in the right hand. Swing the right arm across to the left over the horizontal left arm and swing the right arm downward, backward and around making the first loop of the figure eight at the left side. When the right arm is overhead, switch the ribbon to reverse grip (palm upward) and swing it downward, backward and upward to sketch the second loop of the movement on the right side of the body. To be able to do this exercise smoothly the trunk must rotate with the movement of the arm and the arm must pass through the sagittal plane. Practice with the left hand also.

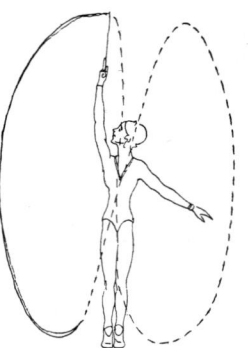

Variations:
a) Do the same movement while walking or dancing forward or backward.

b) Do the same exercise but swing the ribbon in the opposite direction.

c) Do body waves while executing the figure eight.

d) All of the above movements may be performed holding the ribbon in both hands.

4. Figure Eight in the Horizontal Plane

Stand with the arms extended to the sides and the ribbon in the right hand. Sketch a figure eight with the ribbon on the floor in front of you. Make the entire movement large by keeping the arm straight.

Variations:
a) Do the same movement, holding the ribbon in both hands.

b) Do the same movement while walking or dancing backward. The walking or dancing should be in a rhythm different from that of the smooth movement of the figure eights.

c) Do the same movement but step in each loop of the figure eight while moving forward.

d) Describe a figure eight above the head.

5. Leap over the Ribbon

Perform a figure eight in the sagittal plane as described in exercise 3. As you swing the right arm downward and backward at the right side to make the second loop, cat leap sideward over the ribbon.

Variation:
Do a forward or backward scissor kick over the ribbon.

6. Figure Eight Front and Back

Stand holding the ribbon in the right hand. Circle the ribbon inward in front of you, toward the left, and overhead; then bend the elbows so the palm of the hand is up and circle the ribbon inward in back of the body. Repeat this several times and then practice it with the left hand.

Variations:

a) Repeat the movement while walking or dancing sideward, forward, or backward.

b) Repeat the movement but jump or leap over the ribbon while making the circles. For example: Perform a scissor jump forward over the ribbon when making the front circle and do a scissor jump backward while making the back circle.

SERPENTINE MOVEMENTS

Serpentines may be executed in the air or on the floor. They may be made in front of, behind, around, and above the body. Serpents may be performed vertically and horizontally on various levels. Vertical serpentines are done with even, continuous up-and-down hand movements; horizontal ones are executed either with left-to-right or right-to-left hand movements. The arm must be relaxed and the elbows slightly bent. The movement of a ribbon should be the result of wrist action and the wave-like serpentine pattern should continue to the end of the ribbon.

1. Vertical Serpentines

Stand with arms extended to the sides and the ribbon in the right hand. Perform vertical serpents on the floor in front of the body while walking backward. Practice this with the left hand also.

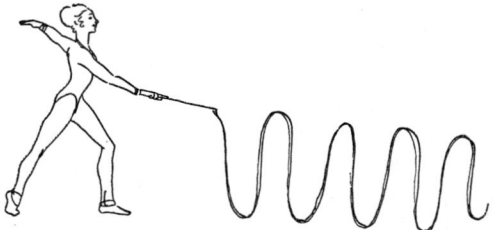

Variations:
a) Perform vertical serpents either on the left or right side of the body while moving forward.
b) Do vertical waves at different levels (i.e., chest height or above the head).
c) Perform an arabesque while doing a vertical wave.
d) Do vertical waves from left to right or right to left in front of the body.
e) Do the same movement as in (d) and leap or jump over the vertical waves.

2. Turns with Vertical Serpents

Stand holding the ribbon out to the side in the right hand. Perform a turn or pirouette, simultaneously making the ribbon serpentine around you. Practice with the left hand also.

Variations:
a) Make serpentines around you, alternating levels (high and low) while performing turns. For example, execute an arabesque turn to the right on the right foot with the left leg in air as you make serpents at chest height. Then bring the left foot forward, across the right one and do a squat turn to the right while making serpentines on the floor.

b) Do a knee turn (kneel on the right knee, bring the left knee across in front of the right knee, place your weight on it as you turn to the right. Step on the right foot, then on the left) while performing vertical serpents around you.

3. Horizontal Serpentines *(in the air)*
Horizontal serpentines in the air may move either downward or upward. They may be performed in place or while walking or dancing. Move the hand evenly from side to side in order to sketch a perfect wave.

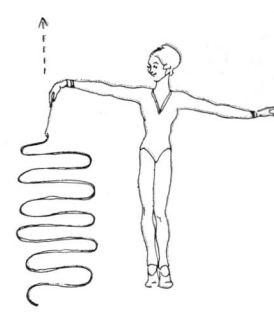

4. Horizontal Serpentines *(on the floor)*
Stand holding the ribbon out to the side, in the left hand. Perform horizontal serpents on the floor in front of the body while walking or running backward. Practice with the right hand also.

Variations:
a) Do the same movement but walk or run forward and with each step, step over the ribbon.

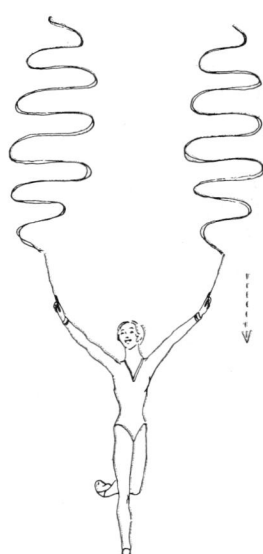

b) Run backward and step over the ribbon with each step while performing horizontal waves behind the body.

5. Serpentines with Two Ribbons
All of the above movements can be performed with two ribbons. For example, run backward with small steps while executing horizontal serpentines downward with both hands.

SPIRAL MOVEMENTS

Series of circles to the end of the ribbon are called *spirals*. The circles in a spiral must be of the same size or of gradually increasing or decreasing diameters. The whole ribbon must participate in the design. Spirals are performed by even, continuous circling of the lower arm and wrist—either from left to right or from right to left.

1. Vertical Spirals on the Floor

Stand with arms extended to the side and the ribbon in the right hand. Perform vertical spirals in front of you on the floor while running backward. Practice this with the left hand also.

Variations:
a) Do the same movement as you perform an arabesque.

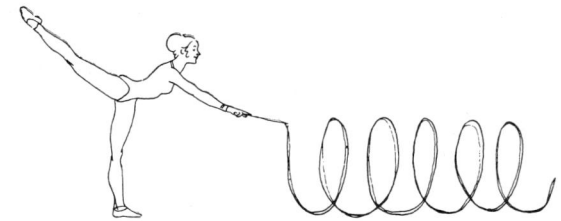

b) Perform vertical spirals on the floor from left to right in front of the body. Practice this from right to left with the left hand also.

c) Do the movement described in (b) but jump or leap over the vertical spiral.

d) Do vertical spirals on the floor on either the left or the right side of the body.

2. Vertical Spirals in the Air

Stand with arms extended to the side and the ribbon in the right hand. Run backward while performing vertical spirals in front of you at waist level. Practice this with the left hand also.

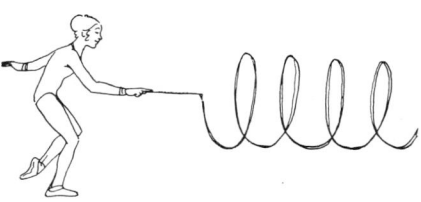

Variations:
a) Do the same movement from left to right in front of the body. Also practice this movement from right to left with the left hand.

b) Repeat (a), with a gallop sideward.

c) Do vertical spirals in the air on either the left or the right side of the body.

3. Vertical Spiral Overhead

Stand with the arms extended to the sides and the ribbon in the right hand. Perform vertical spirals from left to right above the head. Reverse the movement, using the left hand.

Variation:
Do the same movement while performing a turn under the spiral.

4. Frontal Circle with Spiral

Stand with the arms extended to the sides and the ribbon in the right hand. Perform a 360° turn to the right (cross the left foot in front of the right) with a slight backbend while executing a series of spirals progressing from the left side to the right in the form of a large frontal circle. Repeat with the left hand.

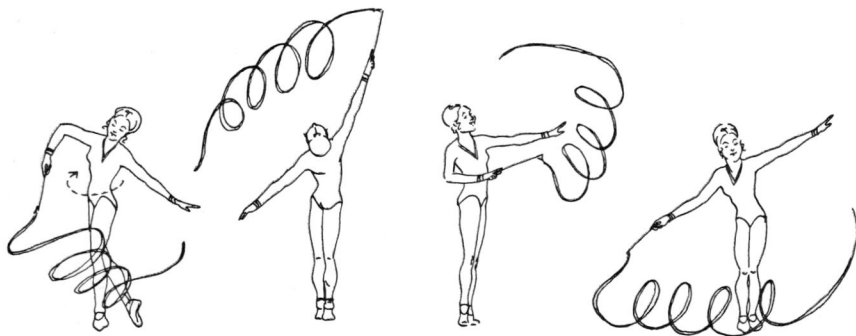

5. Spirals with Increasing Circles

Stand with arms extended to the sides and the ribbon in the right hand. Run backward while enlarging the frontal circle of the ribbon. The first couple of circles are executed from the wrist, the medium size ones from the elbow and the large ones from the shoulder.

Variation:
Perform horizontal circles downward and gradually increase the size of the circles.

6. Spirals with Decreasing Circles
Stand with arms extended to the sides and the ribbon in the right hand. Do a large frontal circle inward and continue with decreasing frontal circles. Each circle should be smaller than the previous one.

Variation:
Do the same movement, moving downward in the horizontal plane. For example, do four fast horizontal circles consecutively above the head (the first one is the largest, the last one is the smallest). Then swing the arm to the side. Repeat with other hand.

7. Horizontal Spirals
Stand with arms extended to the sides and the ribbon in the right hand. Do horizontal spirals moving upward in front of the body.

Variations:
a) Do the same movement behind the body.

b) Do the same movement moving downward.

c) Do horizontal spirals on either the left or the right side of the body.

d) Repeat all the above exercises while moving forward or backward with either walking or dancing steps.

8. Spirals with Two Ribbons
Spirals may be performed with two ribbons, one in each hand. Here is an example of horizontal spirals upward performed with two ribbons.

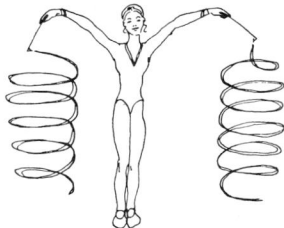

THROWING AND CATCHING MOVEMENTS

Throwing and catching are the most difficult movements to perform with ribbons. These movements can be performed in both the frontal and sagittal planes. The ribbon may be tossed by one hand and caught with the same hand or with the other hand. Throwing and catching skills are usually combined with swinging, circling, and figure-eight movements.

The ribbon must be tossed high with a good follow through so that it will stay in the air long enough to project a good parabolic curve. The ribbon should not touch the floor or collapse during the flight. The trajectory, or path, of the ribbon should be long.

1. Swing Toss Overhead
Stand in a wide straddle with the weight on the right foot, the arms extended to the sides and the ribbon in the right hand. Swing the ribbon

downward across the body to the left, back to the right, and toss it high over the head. Catch it with the left hand while shifting the weight from the right foot to the left. Repeat with the left hand.

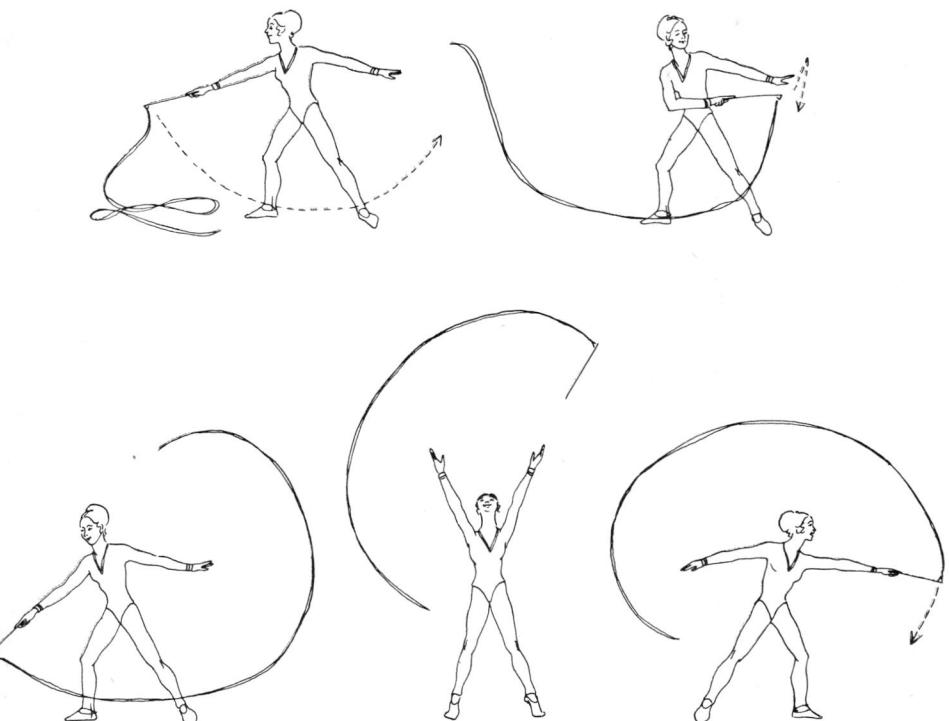

Variations:
a) Do the same movement using a side gallop step. When the ribbon is in the right hand gallop to the left and vice versa.

b) Do the same movement while walking or running forward or backward.

2. Overhead Throw *(in frontal plane)*
Stand with the arms extended to the sides and the ribbon in the right hand. Swing the right arm upward, over the head, and downward toward the right side, making a circle in the frontal plane. Then throw

the ribbon overhead as in number 1 and catch it with the left hand. Practice with the left hand also.

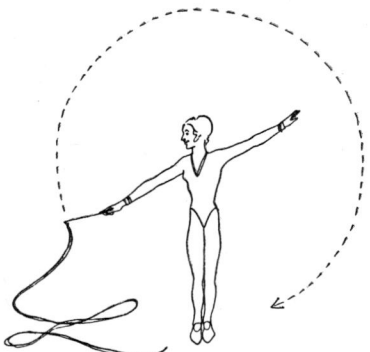  

Variations:

a) Do the same movement with a gallop.

b) Perform the above movement while walking or running forward or backward.

3. Overhead Throw *(in sagittal plane)*

Stand holding the ribbon in the right hand at the right side. Swing the right arm forward, then backward. At the top of the backward swing, throw the ribbon over the head and catch it in front with the left hand. Repeat with the left hand.

Variations:

a) Do the same movement from a figure eight.

b) Do the same toss while walking or running forward.

4. Throw Two Ribbons

Stand with the arms extended to the sides. Throw the ribbons upward and forward simultaneously with both hands, and catch them with the same hands.

TEACHING SUGGESTIONS

1. Exercises with the ribbon require much space. To learn the basic skills the class should be in staggered lines with ample space between gymnasts so they will not get entangled in each other's ribbons. If all gymnasts face the same direction, analysis of skills learned will be easier for the teacher.
2. When teaching locomotion movements, line the class up in twos or fours across one end of the gymnasium. The first line starts the exercise and moves forward, the next line follows when a new musical phrase starts, and so on. See teaching suggestions in the chapters on ropes and clubs for more ideas.
3. Allow the class to play with their ribbons, swinging and circling them to the music. This will help students to learn how much force they must apply to movements. If too much force is applied the ribbons will snap and crack, too little force will cause them to wrap around the body.
4. Let the class experiment with different qualities of movement. For example;
   a) start the movement with a burst of energy and end it slowly
   b) start the exercise either fast or slow and continue with the same force evenly until its completion.
5. Emphasize the light and flowing quality of movement with total body involvement to avoid tangling and snapping of the ribbon. The focus should be on the ribbon so that the movement of the body follows the direction of the streamer. The free arm should also participate to bring out the character of the movement. Stress relaxation of the head and shoulders. Most beginners will tend to hunch their shoulders.
6. Emphasize good ribbon handling techniques. Tangling, snapping, twisting,

and knotting of the ribbon reveals poor execution and lack of total body movements.
7. The ribbon should not touch any part of body except the hand in movements in which the end of the ribbon is caught.
8. As each new exercise is learned, it should be combined with other skills immediately. This will help the gymnast gain an early understanding of the relationship between different movements.
9. Students should be given an opportunity to create new sequences. This will help them discover the endless possibilities for making even the simplest movement demonstrative and exciting.
10. From the beginning all movements should be practiced with both the right and the left hand in order to develop balanced handling of the apparatus.
11. Exercises with two ribbons should be attempted only by gymnasts who are capable of performing one-ribbon exercises with good technical skills.
12. Exercises should always be performed with music. Music must be chosen carefully. Not all music is suitable for a ribbon routine. It should have a flowing quality and a medium tempo. Music that is too fast will not allow gymnasts to perform the movements to their fullest possible range. Waltz rhythm is very good to get the relaxed flowing and swinging quality of the movements; however, 6/8, 2/4 or 4/4 meter music works just as well, as long as the speed is correct. Choose music with interesting phrasing and nuances in dynamics, and which could be harmonized with the movements of the body and ribbon.

COMPETITIVE RULES

Area: 39⅓ square feet (12 x 12 meters)
Music: one instrument
Length of individual routine: one minute to one minute and thirty seconds.

Floor space should be used effectively in a pleasing choreographic design. The exercise must be executed with the accompaniment of music; the music should inspire a gay mood in the gymnast which she should project to the audience. The movements must correspond to the rhythm and mood of the music. The music should allow for a variety of rhythms including slow and fast passages. Avoid music that sounds sad and/or monotonous. Monotony and lack of coordination of music and movements are penalized.

The routine should include elements of all movement groups: serpentines, figure eights, spiral swinging, and circling. Throwing and catching movements do not have to be included in the composition. It is a compositional error if the exercise is composed of elements of only two or three groups (for example: swinging, circling, and serpentines, without using elements from the other groups). The routine must contain movements involving both the right and left hand. Elements of difficulty should be executed by both hands. Usually if a gymnast executes easy elements with the left hand, this signifies that the composition is not balanced or harmonious and consequently it will be penalized.

Good form, fluency, and faultless execution are very important when performing the exercise. Common faults in execution are: touching the body with the ribbon; twisting the ribbon; snapping the ribbon; tangling the ribbon around the body or a leg; the end of the ribbon not participating in the design of the movement; in throwing, end of ribbon touches floor; end of ribbon touches outside border of area; dropping ribbon and stick.

EXAMPLES OF DIFFICULTIES

Swinging and Circling
Medium difficulties: One full turn (360°) on one leg while swinging or circling the ribbon; performing different balances on one leg (with the free leg bent or held straight forward, sideward, or backward) while swinging or circling the ribbon.

Superior difficulties: Double turn (720°) on one leg while swinging or circling the ribbon; performing different balances on toes on one leg (with the free leg bent or held straight forward, sideward, or backward) while swinging or circling the ribbon—balance must be held for at least two seconds.

Figure Eight
Medium difficulties: Make figure eights with the ribbon front and back while moving forward, sideward, or backward with dancing steps; make horizontal figure eights sketched on floor while moving backward with dancing steps.

Superior difficulties: Make a figure eight in front and back-jump over the ribbon during the circles with a scissor jump or cat leap; horizontal figure eight sketched on floor—stepping into each figure-eight loop while moving forward with dancing steps.

Serpentine
Medium difficulties: Serpentines coordinated with different rhythmical steps; make horizontal waves on the floor in front of the body and with each running step, step over the ribbon (at least four running steps forward).

Superior difficulties: Leap over a vertical wave; horizontal waves on floor behind the body and with each running step, step over it (at least four running steps backward).

Spirals

Medium difficulties: Spirals coordinated with different rhythmical steps; make a horizontal spiral on floor and jump into it.

Superior difficulties: Leap over a vertical spiral; make a horizontal spiral on the floor, jump into it, and continue the spiral in the same direction above the head.

Throwing and Catching

Medium difficulties: All small tosses, for example: overhead throw in sagittal plane.

Superior difficulties: All large throws, for example: throw the ribbon upward with a large leap and catch it with the second leap.

COMPOSITION

When composing a ribbon exercise, plan an interesting ribbon design using different movement levels and a variety of movements. The ribbon should sketch various lines, shapes, and forms in the air. The patterns can be straight, curved, wavy, and circular. To make the exercise more exciting, alternate the pattern by increasing or decreasing the sizes of the design. Map out your ribbon design in your floor area. This way you can avoid monotony in the routine. You may use the following notations:

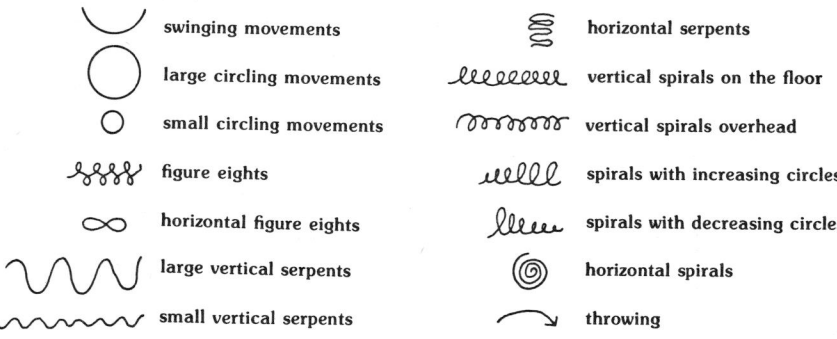

∪	swinging movements	≋	horizontal serpents
○	large circling movements	llllllll	vertical spirals on the floor
○	small circling movements	∽∽∽∽	vertical spirals overhead
∞∞	figure eights	ulll	spirals with increasing circles
∞	horizontal figure eights	lllu	spirals with decreasing circles
∿∿∿	large vertical serpents	◎	horizontal spirals
∼∼∼∼	small vertical serpents	↷	throwing

Make up short combinations before attempting to create a competitive routine. Below is an example of a combination:

1. Sketch two large circles in the sagittal plane while performing a backbend with leg lift.
2. Do a 360° moderate arabesque turn to the right while performing vertical waves from left to right in front of the body.
3. Do figure eights in the sagittal plane while dancing forward.
4. Throw the ribbon overhead at the top of the backward swing on the right side. Catch the ribbon with the left hand.
5. Grapevine step to the left as you do a large circle in front of the body and a small one behind the head.
6. Run backward and spiral the ribbon in the air in front of the body.
7. Throw ribbon overhead in the frontal plane and catch it with the right hand.
8. Run forward and swing ribbon from right to left and back to the right on floor and leap over it.
9. Spiral the ribbon overhead from left to right.
10. Do a knee turn while performing vertical serpentines around you at waist level.
11. Take two running steps forward while performing an inward overhead circle then swing the arm down and circle the ribbon in the same direction slightly above the floor passing over it with a cat leap. Repeat.
12. Spiral the ribbon in decreasing horizontal circles above the head while doing a step-hop and finish the combination in a kneeling position.

floor pattern for composition

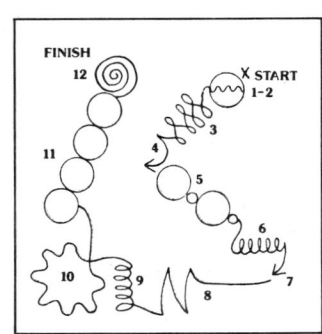

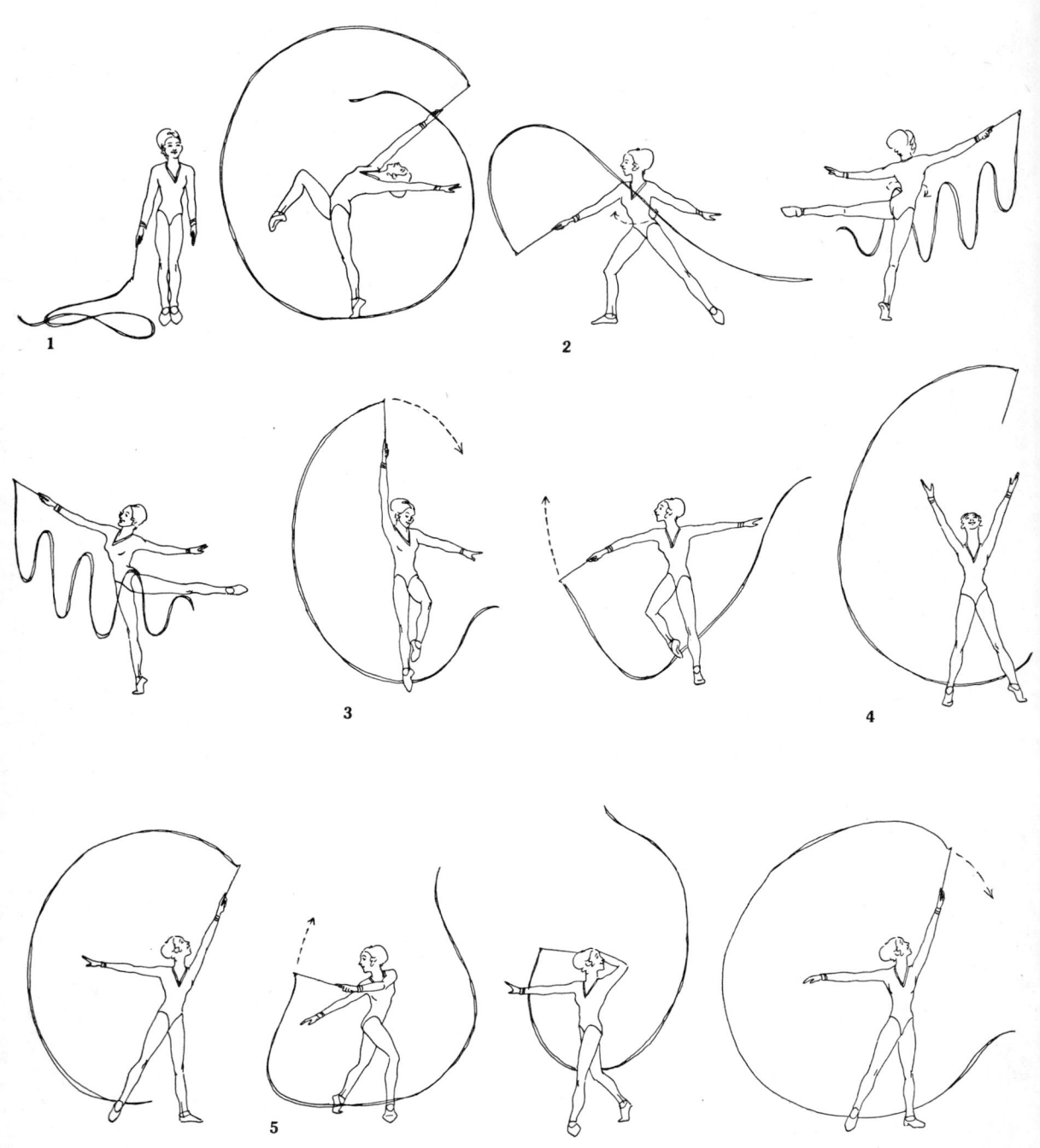

Ribbons

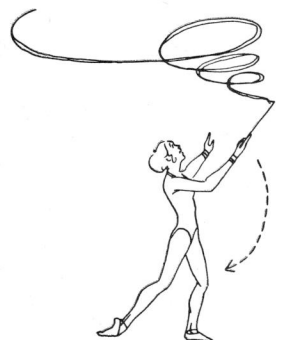

~~~~~~
GROUP EXERCISES
~~~~~~

Area: 12 x 12 meters (approximately 40 x 40 feet)
Music: one instrument
Time requirement: two minutes and thirty seconds to three minutes

Ribbon exercises are very spectacular and can be used very effectively with large groups for school exhibitions. In group competition there must be six gymnasts. All six must have the same kind of ribbon; only the colors may vary. The examples presented here are for a group of six girls. They can easily be adapted to larger groups.

FLOOR PATTERN EXAMPLES

1. Form a straight line, holding the ribbon in the right hand. Run forward in counterclockwise direction, following the leader (number 1) while doing figure eights with the ribbon. Continue until a circle is formed.

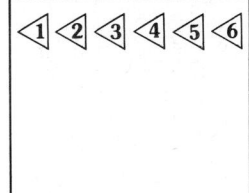

2. Circle formation, everybody facing inward. Glissade into the center of the circle, circling the ribbon on the right side. Spiral the ribbon above the head in decreasing circles while in the center, then toss the ribbon overhead and catch it with the left hand. Glissade out to the edge of the circle, circling the ribbon on the side. Face counterclockwise in circle formation.

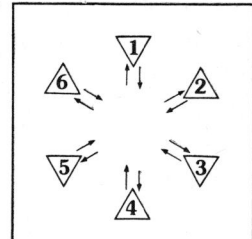

3. Circle formation, everyone faces counterclockwise. Run backward while performing vertical spirals in front of you on the floor. Pairs (numbers 5 and 6 and numbers 2 and 3) move to opposite corners, while the two single girls (numbers 1 and 4) move into the remaining corners. Pass the ribbon to the right hand in front of the body.

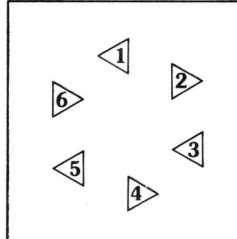

4. The two pairs run forward and with each step, step over the ribbon while doing horizontal waves on floor. Simultaneously, the two single girls change places with a forward run and split leap over the ribbon.

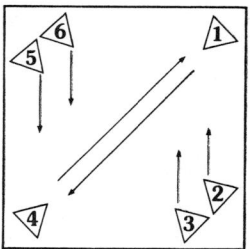

5. Two diagonal lines, facing in opposite directions. Both lines move forward doing circles over their heads and under their legs; but one of the lines forms a triangle.

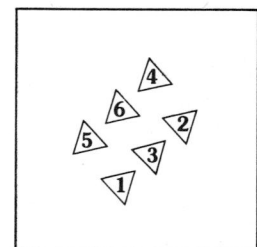

6. An asymmetrical floor pattern, which can be combined with an asymmetrical work pattern. The triangle group performs a vertical wave at waist level while performing a 360° moderate arabesque turn to the right, simultaneously the diagonal line executes a squat turn to the right performing vertical waves on the floor. Then the triangle performs a squat turn while the diagonal line does a moderate arabesque turn.

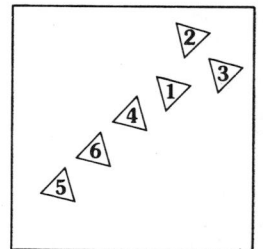

EXCHANGE EXAMPLES

Since group routines with the ribbon have not been included in any Modern Rhythmic Gymnastics Championships, rules regarding the exchange of ribbons have not yet been clarified. However, it is unlikely that long distance changeovers will be required.

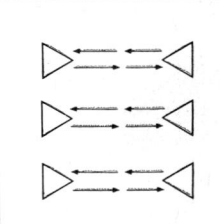

1. Two-line formation, lines facing each other. The lines run toward each other while circling the ribbon forward on the right side of the body with the right hand. When partners meet, they smoothly exchange ribbons and run back to their original places while circling the ribbon backward on the left side of the body with the left hand. (The exchange is made with a smooth, slight toss so as not to break the rhythm and the pattern of the ribbon.)

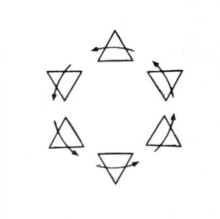

2. Circle formation, facing outward, holding the ribbon in the right hand. Swing and toss the ribbon overhead toward the left to the next person. The person on the left catches the ribbon with the right hand.

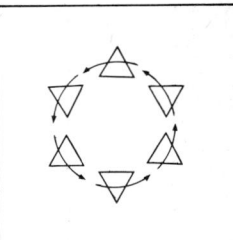

3. Two parallel lines facing each other, holding the ribbon in the right hand. Do a body wave while making a figure eight in the sagittal plane. At the top of the backward swing of the second loop, throw the ribbon overhead in the sagittal plane to your partner. Catch your partner's ribbon in your left hand.

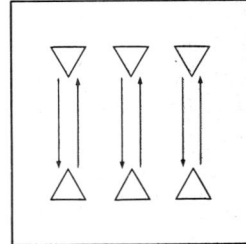

4. Two diagonal lines moving from opposite corners, facing each other. There is an exchange of ribbons between pairs while lines change places. Number 1 exchanges ribbons with number 2, number 3 with number 4, and number 5 with number 6. The lines move forward with locomotion patterns and partners pass each other with left shoulder while throwing the ribbon in an arc overhead in the frontal plane. Ribbon is tossed to your partner from the right side with the right hand and your partner's ribbon is caught with the left hand on the left side.

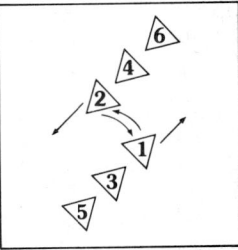

SUGGESTED GROUP ASSIGNMENT

248

Modern Rhythmic Gymnastics

Creative assignments should be a natural extension of preparatory work. The transition from the teacher-directed activity to a group project and to an individual task is very important in teaching modern rhythmic gymnastics. At first, choreographic assignments should be structural so that the students have something to help them. However, the structure should be set in such a way that it will stimulate creative and imaginative responses.

Problem: Work out the following formations. Be inventive when working out transitions from one formation to another.

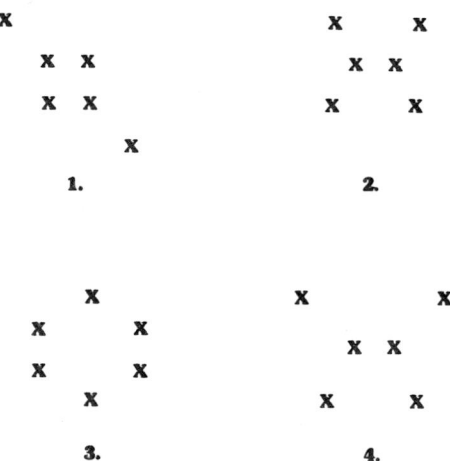

A. Include swinging, circling, figure eights, serpentines, and spirals with the ribbon.

B. In the routine there must be at least one exchange of ribbons between members of the group.

C. Explore different levels and qualities of movement. Look for something new. Invent new movements, new combinations.

D. Use your whole body to follow the movement of the ribbon. Try to make the various movements flow together. Change the tempo and the intensity of the routine as the music changes.

E. *Music*—Chopin "Valse"—arrangement by Harriet Jones.

This music is very suitable for a ribbon routine because it has a lively flowing quality.

Musical breakdown:
    34 measures
    3/4 meter
        8 bars—soft, smooth, medium slow
        8 bars—medium loud, dynamic, staccato
        8 bars—soft, smooth, medium slow
      10 bars—loud, medium fast, grandiose

Music for Ribbon Group Assignment

250

Clubs

Chapter 7

Clubs, which are the oldest of the hand apparatuses, were first used only by men gymnasts. But after a long period of development they have become a hand apparatus primarily used by women. At the beginning, much heavier and thicker clubs were used than today, therefore the skills performed were generally limited to swinging and circling movements. Today, in modern rhythmic gymnastics, much lighter, thinner clubs are used and they allow for greater variety of performance. But even these lighter clubs should only be introduced to girls who are in the fifth grade or older.

The club is one of the most difficult of hand apparatus to use. It requires a great deal of practice to become proficient. To master the use of the club one must be equally skillful with both hands. In addition, it takes a great deal of skill to synchronize body movements with the club movements. The club movements should follow the natural movements of the body.

The club is an excellent teaching aid for learning the natural swinging movements. Its use also helps develop good posture and rhythm as well as strength in the arms and the shoulder girdle which are usually weak areas of a girl's body. Swinging movements with the club also help to loosen and stretch tight, contracted chest muscles.

Clubs can be very effectively used for school demonstrations. An evening demonstration in which lighted clubs are used can be truly spectacular. (A wire can be put through the club with a small battery in the club and a light on the end which is controlled by the hand.) The clubs may also be painted with phosphorescent paint. The variations of swings, circles, and the like, performed with the clubs glowing in the dark are both interesting and beautiful. For the best effect start the exercise with the lights on so that the audience can see the exercise, then turn off the lights in order to obtain a luminous effect.

The clubs were first introduced in gymnastic demonstrations by the Sokol in Czechoslovakia. They were first used in competition in Hungary in 1928. In the second Women's Gymnastics World Championships in Prague 1938, the clubs were first included as a group event. The Czechoslovakian team won and since that time the Czechs are leaders in the development of new movements with the clubs. The clubs were first introduced in an individual compulsory routine in the Sixth Modern Rhythmic Gymnastics Championship, in Holland, in 1973. They were employed again in the Seventh Modern Rhythmic Gymnastics Championships in an individual optional routine with compulsory elements in Spain, in 1975.

EQUIPMENT

Clubs are bottle shaped and generally made of hard, light-colored wood that will not split or break and will make a pleasant sound when two clubs are struck together. They can also be made from plastic material. The clubs are usually polished natural wood; they may also be painted, and if they are, they are usually red, white, or black. Today there are many types of clubs available, but for competition long, slender, lightweight clubs are used. The longer, lighter club can be put into motion and kept in motion more easily which makes it easier to perform many of the new skills.

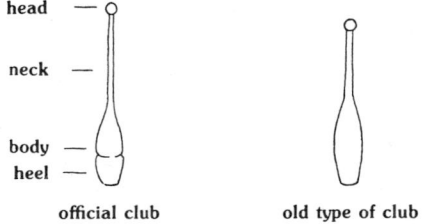

The specific parts of the club should have the following dimensions:

The *head* of the club may have a maximum diameter of 3 cm (1⅛ inches). The head may take the form of either a small ball or a widening of the end of the neck.

The *neck* is the thinnest part of the club. The minimum diameter of the part of the neck nearest the head is 2.2 cm (approximately ¾ inch). (The diameter of the body of the club has not been officially specified.)

The *heel* or base of the club, which is a little thinner than the body, has a minimum diameter of 2½ cm (1 inch).

The *length* of the club should be 40–50 cm (approximately 16–18 inches).

The *weight* of the club should be a minimum of 150 g (approximately 5¼ ounces). In the World Championship most girls used 7 or 8 ounce clubs.

A jumping rope may be used in practice as a substitute for the club. Fold the rope twice and make a knot close to the open ends. Hold the quadrupled rope by the unknotted end. The knotted end will have enough weight to give the students a feeling of swinging and circling movements as they are done with the club.

TECHNIQUES

Movements with the clubs should be light, playful, and natural and should be clearly performed in the movement plane in which they are started.

The whole body should be involved in every exercise. When the club is down, bend the knees, when the club is up, straighten the knees, so that the club movement is coordinated with the body movement. The movements must flow through the entire body and be performed rhythmically with alternating phases of tension (contraction) and relaxation of the muscles involved.

Movements with the clubs include swinging, circling, clapping, throwing, and catching. Other movements, such as dropping and kipping, may be included in a routine to make it interesting but are not typical of this hand apparatus.

During swinging exercises the club should always be held so that it is a straight continuation of the arm. Movements come from the shoulders with the arms straight. There are two types of grips for swinging movements:

a) Regular grip, with hand in pronation (palm down). The head of the club is placed in the palm of the hand; the neck is held between the thumb and middle finger, just below the head; and the index finger is extended on the neck. The fourth and fifth fingers rest on the head.

regular grip—swinging

b) Reverse grip, with the hand in supination (palm upward). Grasping the club as is noted in the regular grip but the club will be supported by the index finger underneath the club.

reverse grip—swinging

In *circling* movements the club should be held with the thumb and index finger forming a loose ring around the neck, just below the head, so that it can circle freely. Circling movement should start from a slightly flexed elbow and be done with a relaxed wrist. Circling of the club is aided by its weight. Grips for circling movements are also of two kinds, depending upon the plane of the circle:

a) regular or over grip;

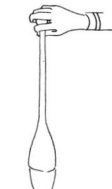

regular grip—circling
front view

b) reverse or under grip.

reverse grip—circling
rear view

When *clapping* with the clubs the club is generally grasped either by the body or by the neck in the same manner as one would grasp a hammer (hammer grip). The sketch shows the club held with a hammer grip at its body.

hammer grip

The clubs can also be held horizontally with both hands, one hand at each end. See illustrations below.

one club

two clubs

Throwing exercises are done with total body movement and with a good follow through. When *catching* the club the body should again follow the movement of the falling club and absorb the weight of the club with the catch. The club should be caught softly and silently either at its body or head but never at the neck.

MOVEMENTS

Allow plenty of time to practice movements with clubs. Good club technique requires refined muscular coordination and therefore demands careful, patient practice. Only after much practice will you be able to handle the clubs lightly, gracefully, and in rhythm.

When the basic technique has been learned, combine the exercises with leg and trunk movements. Try putting movements into sequences or combinations as soon as a few skills have been learned.

Club exercises should always be performed with music. 6/8, 3/4, and 4/4 meter music are usually used for club routines.

The weight and the bottle shape of the club determine the type of movements that are characteristic of club gymnastics. The most commonly used movements with the clubs are:

1. Large swinging and circling movements in which the club is held as an extension of the arm itself. These types of movements are initiated from the shoulders and performed by the entire arm.

2. Medium circling movements which originate from the elbow.

3. Small circling movements which originate from the wrist.

4. Throwing and catching movements in which one or both clubs are tossed in the air in various directions.

5. Rhythmic clapping or tapping of clubs against the floor or against each other.

Other movements such as kipping and dropping will make a routine interesting but are not typical of this hand apparatus. In competition a gymnast must work with two clubs because, according to the F.I.G. rules, the two clubs are considered one implement. However, club exercises should be learned first with the right hand alone and then with the left hand before two clubs are used simultaneously.

SWINGING MOVEMENTS

Clubs may be swung in the frontal, sagittal, diagonal, or horizontal plane. The movements can be done forward or backward, inward or outward, or to the left or the right. All swings and large circles are initiated from the shoulders and should be performed with the arms straight and the club moving as a continuation of the arm. If the arm is swung properly, the club will feel heavy at the bottom of the swing and light at the top. The movements should be made very large by keeping the arms and trunk long and following the club with the entire body.

1. Forward and Backward Swing
Stand with the arms extended horizontally forward and the clubs held in a regular grip. Swing both clubs downward and backward to the right side then down and forward back to the original position. Reverse the movement to the opposite side. Keep the arms parallel during the swings and follow the clubs with your eyes while turning the body slightly when the arms are moving backward.

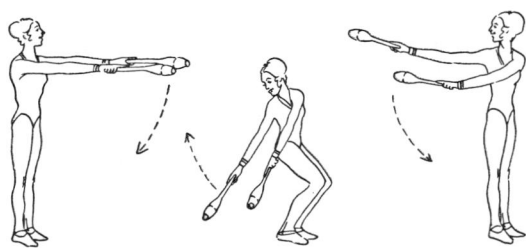

Variations:
a) Swing the clubs back and forth at the side of the body.

b) Do the same movement in a forward stride position, shifting the weight forward and backward with the movement of the clubs.

c) Perform the same movement with waltz steps forward. Use three counts for each backward swing and three for each forward swing.

2. Alternate Forward and Backward Swings
Stand with the arms at the side with the clubs held in a regular grip. Do alternate arm swings forward and backward.

Variations:
a) Do the same movement with walking steps forward or backward. Arms move in opposition.

b) Perform the same movement with a step-hop forward or backward, but swing the arm in the front slightly above shoulder level.

3. Forward and Backward Mill Swing
Stand with the arms extended horizontally forward, clubs held in a regular grip. Swing the right arm backward then the left arm; then swing the right arm forward upward followed by the left arm. The arms follow each other in the forward and backward swings. Perform a forward body wave while the arms swing forward and a backward body wave when they swing backward. The entire body follows the movement of the clubs.

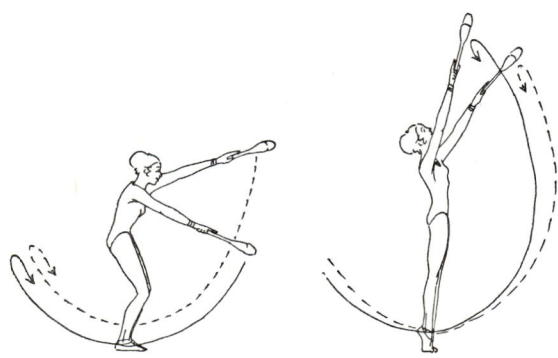

Variations:
a) Do the same movement with walking steps.

b) Perform the mill swing swinging the clubs first to the right side then to the left side.

4. Large Circle in Sagittal Plane *(forward)*
Stand with the arms extended backward, clubs held in a regular grip.

Swing the arms in a complete circle downward, forward, upward, and backward. Repeat the movement several times.

Variations:
a) Both clubs are first circled on the right side then on left side of body (this makes a figure-eight pattern).
b) Do the same movement while moving forward with either walking or dancing steps.

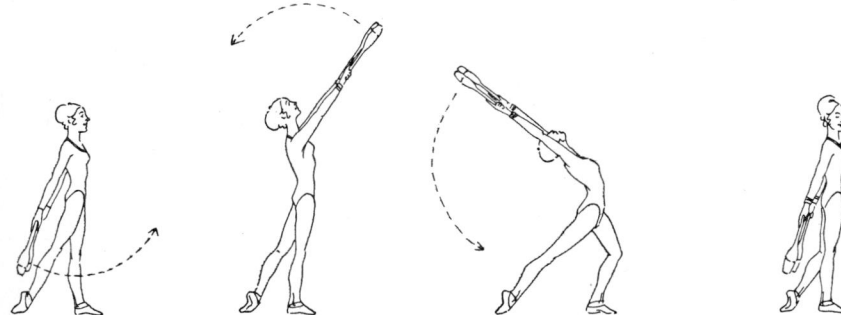

5. Jump with a Circle
Stand with the arms extended backward, clubs held in a regular grip. Swing the arms in a complete circle moving them downward, forward, upward, and backward while doing a tuck jump.

Variations:
Perform different kinds of jumps instead of the tuck jump.

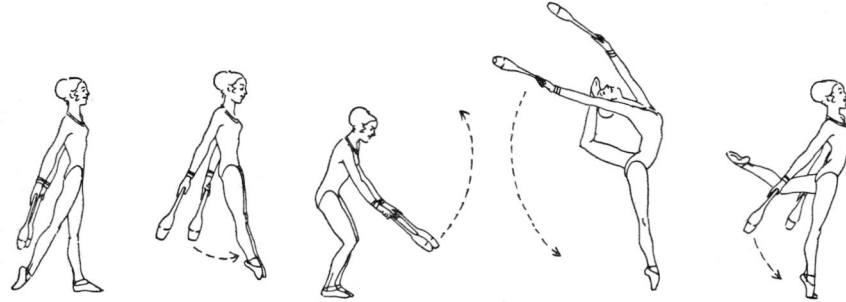

6. Large Circle in Sagittal Plane *(backward)*
Stand with the arms extended forward, clubs held in a regular grip. Swing the arms downward to the back, upward over the head, and downward to the front.

Variations:
a) Circle both clubs to the right side then to the left side of the body.
b) Take two walking steps forward or backward with each circle.
c) Glissade forward or backward with each circle.
d) All the above movements may be performed with a body wave.

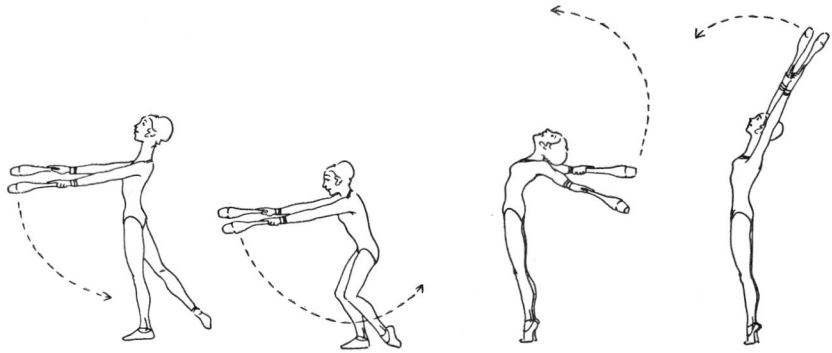

7. Mill Circle Forward
This movement is similar to the swimming front-crawl arm movement. Stand with the right arm overhead and the left arm down to the side. Circle the right arm forward and simultaneously circle the left arm backward. To facilitate the circling movement twist the trunk from side to side at the moment each arm is passing the body backward. Keep the arms a half-circle apart during the movement.

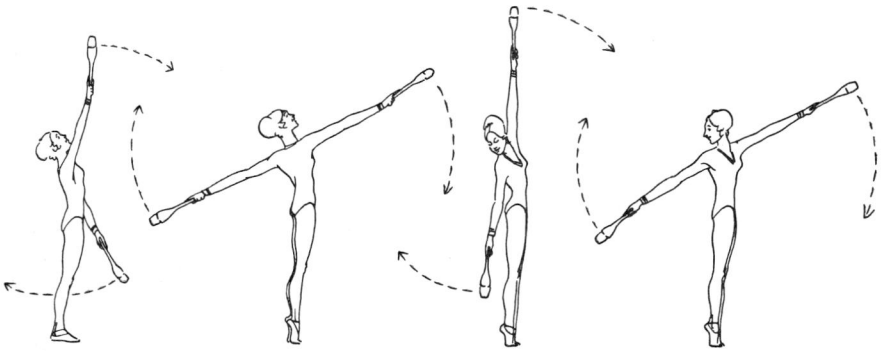

Variations:
a) Do the same movements while moving forward or backward with either walking or dancing steps.
b) Do the same arm movements while performing a turn or a pirouette.

8. Mill Circle Backward
Do the same exercises as described in exercise 7 but circle the arms in the opposite direction. Arms circle backward as in a back crawl.

9. Mill Circle with Front Cross
Stand holding the clubs in a regular grip with the arms extended forward. Circle the left arm outside the right shoulder downward, backward and upward as the right arm swings backward. Circle the left arm under the right arm pit in the same direction while the right arm swings upward and forward to the starting position. Repeat the movement to the opposite side. Continue the above pattern first crossing the left arm then the right arm.

Variation:
Do the above movement while moving forward with either walking or dancing steps.

10. Alternate Forward and Backward Circle
Stand on the balls of the feet, holding the clubs in a regular grip with the arms extended overhead. Circle the right arm forward and simultaneously circle the left arm backward. Turn the body 90° from side to side in the direction of the backward arm. The clubs bypass each other above the head.

Variations:
a) Do the same movement while performing a split or stag leap.

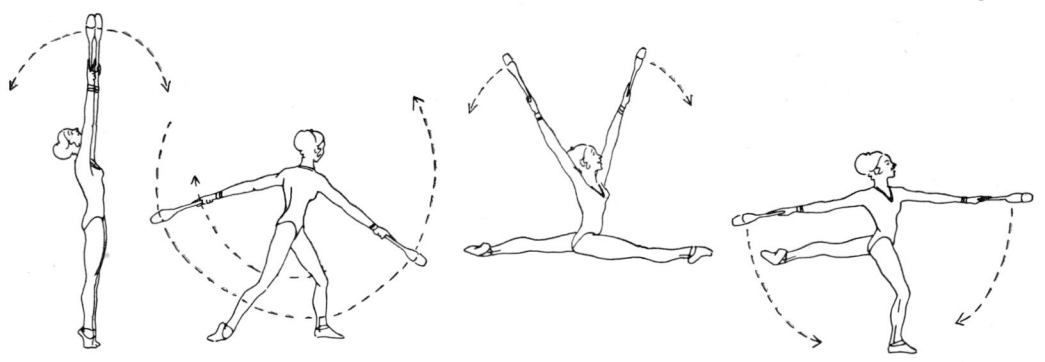

b) Reverse the movement—circle the left arm forward as the right arm circles backward.

11. Swing Across the Body
Stand in a wide straddle with weight on the right foot, the arms extended to the right side and the clubs held in a regular grip. Swing the clubs downward in front of the body to the left then back across the body to the right side. Transfer the weight from side to side while swinging the clubs.

Variations:
a) Do the same movement while performing step-hops forward or backward.

b) Do the same movement with a gallop from side to side.

c) Do side body waves while performing swings across the body.

12. Simultaneous Front and Back Swing

Stand in a wide straddle with weight on the right foot, the arms extended to the right side and the clubs held in a regular grip. Swing the right arm downward across the body to the left, simultaneously swing the left arm behind the head to the left side. Reverse the movement to the opposite side.

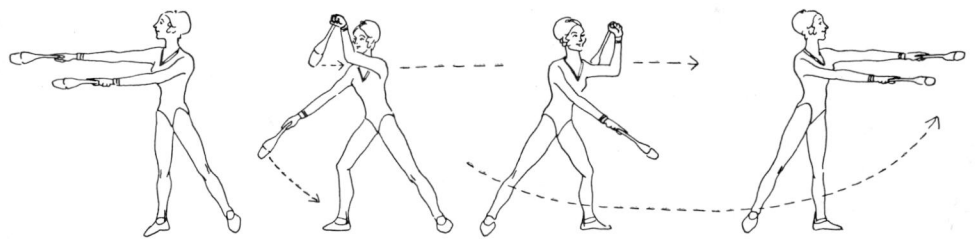

Variations:

a) Stand in the same starting position. Swing the left arm downward and over to the left side and simultaneously swing the right club behind the head, both ending on the left side. Reverse the action toward the opposite side.

b) Do the above movements while walking forward or backward.

c) Do the same movements with a gallop or balancé from side to side.

13. Large Circle in Frontal Plane

Stand in a wide straddle position with the arms extended to the right side clubs held in a regular grip. Swing the arms downward, upward over the head, and downward again to the left side, making one and a half circles in the frontal plane. Repeat toward the right side. Shift your weight from side to side while circling the clubs in front of the body.

Variations:

a) Perform the above movement but circle the clubs in the opposite direction—upward, over the head, downward, and upward again over the head to the left side.

b) Perform two side gallops to the left, turn 180° to the left, then do two side gallops to the right and turn 180° to the right, etc. Do one frontal circle with each gallop step.

c) Do a full turn (360°) as the clubs circle in the frontal plane.

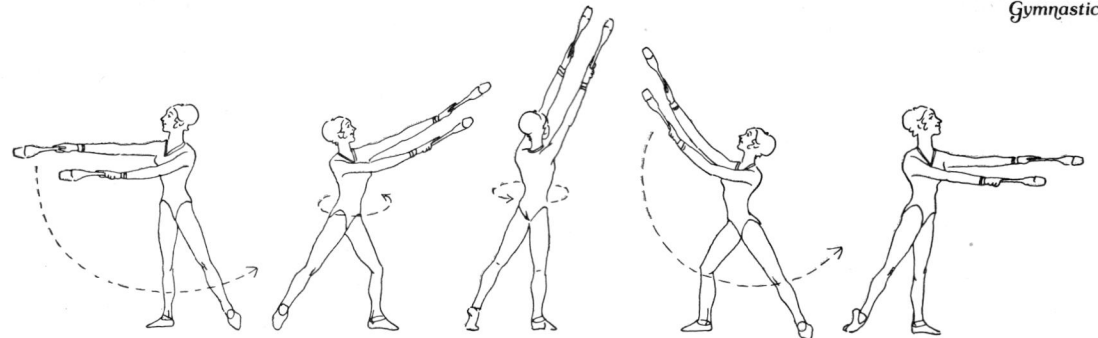

14. Opposite Cross Swing
Stand in a wide straddle with weight on the right foot, arms at side with the clubs held in regular grip. Move to the left with a grapevine step (step to the left with the left foot, cross the right foot in front of left, step to the side with left foot again and cross with right foot in back of left, and so on). Swing the arms out when stepping with the left foot to the side, and cross them in front when stepping across with the right foot. Clubs move in and out in the frontal plane. Alternate right and left arm in front of the swing. Repeat the exercise going in the opposite direction.

Variation:
Do the same exercise but cross arms alternately in front of and in back of body.

15. Large Opposite Cross Circle
Stand with the arms extended to the side, clubs held in a regular grip. Swing both arms downward, cross in front of the body, upward and

complete a big circle overhead. Swing with sufficient vigor so that the feet are almost lifted from the floor as the arm circle is made. Practice crossing with the right arm in front, then with the left arm in front.

Variations:
a) Circle the arms in the opposite direction—upward, cross overhead, and downward to the side. Start the movement holding the clubs in a reverse grip.

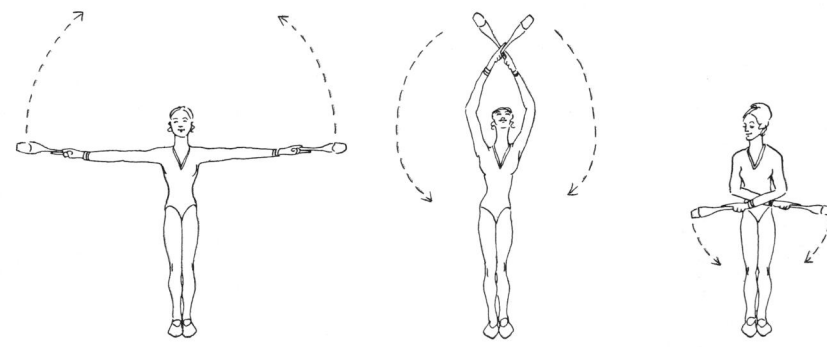

b) Perform the above movements with sideward gallop steps. Do one large cross circle with each gallop step.

16. Mill Circle in Frontal Plane
Stand with right arm overhead, the left arm at the side, and the clubs held in a regular grip. Rotate the trunk toward the left and circle the right arm forward while you simultaneously circle the left arm backward. The entire body follows the movement of the clubs by rotating the trunk to the left and forward.

Variations:
a) Do the same movement but circle the arms in the opposite direction.
b) Reverse the above exercises to the opposite side.
c) Combine a forward mill circle with a backward mill circle by rotating the trunk to the left, forward, to the right and forward again. The movement is done in the following sequence:
   1. Rotate the trunk 90° to the left, start circling the right arm forward as the left arm goes backward.

2. After half a circle, rotate the trunk forward, swing the left arm downward as the right arm swings upward, finishing a complete mill circle forward.

3. Twist the trunk 90° to the right and start circling the right arm backward simultaneously bringing the left arm forward.

4. After half a circle, twist the trunk forward and swing the right arm upward as the left arm moves downward completing a backward mill circle.

Circle the arms in the frontal plane with a smooth continuous movement by twisting the trunk from side to side.

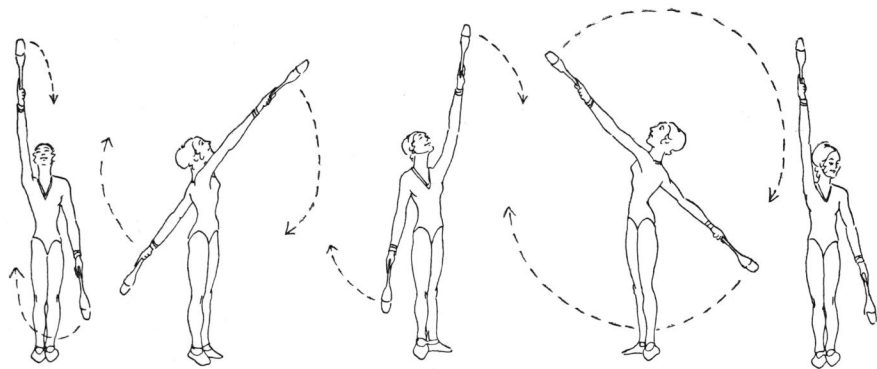

17. Alternate Front and Back Circle *(frontal plane)*
Stand holding the clubs in a regular grip with the arms extended overhead. Turn the body 90° to the left and circle the right arm forward as the left arm circles backward. Follow the movement of the clubs by rotating the trunk to the left and forward. Repeat the movement several times, the clubs will bypass each other above the head. Practice also to the opposite side by reversing the movement. Swing the arms with sufficient vigor so that they will make a complete frontal circle.

Variation:
Combine alternate front and back circles to the left and right side:

1. turn the body 90° to the left and circle the arms as described above, then

2. rotate the trunk 90° to the right and reverse the movement—left arm circles forward simultaneously, right arm backward.

Facilitate the movement by twisting the trunk smoothly from side to side in the direction of the arm in the back.

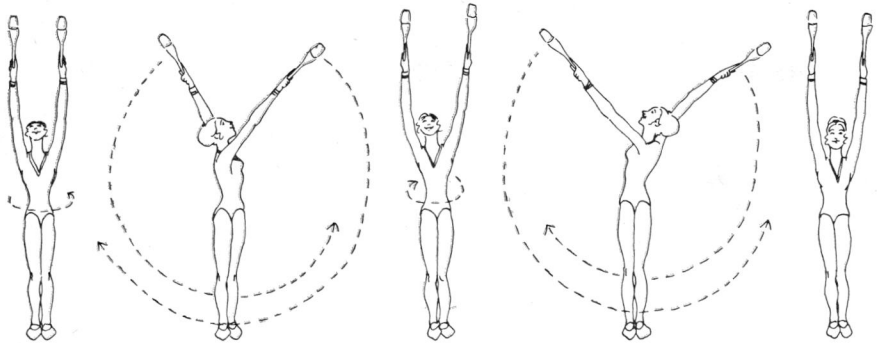

18. Swing Overhead
Stand in a wide straddle with weight on the right foot, the arms extended to the right side and the clubs held in regular grip. Perform horizontal circles inward overhead—swinging the clubs forward, to the left, backward, and back to the right side. Repeat from left to right side.

Variations:

a) Perform horizontal circles outward overhead.

b) Do the same movement while moving forward or backward, with either walking or dancing steps.

c) Do the same movement performing different kinds of turns including pirouettes.

19. Figure Eight in the Sagittal Plane
Stand with the arms extended horizontally forward and the clubs held in regular grip. Swing both clubs to the left side downward, backward and around, making the first loop of the figure eight, then swing the clubs to the right side downward, backward and around to make the second loop. In order to perform this exercise smoothly the trunk must rotate

with the movement of the arms and the hands must turn from a regular to a reverse grip in a continuous successive motion.

Variations:
a) Do the same movement while moving forward or backward with either walking or dancing steps.

b) Do the same exercise but swing the clubs in the opposite direction.

c) Perform body waves while doing the figure eight.

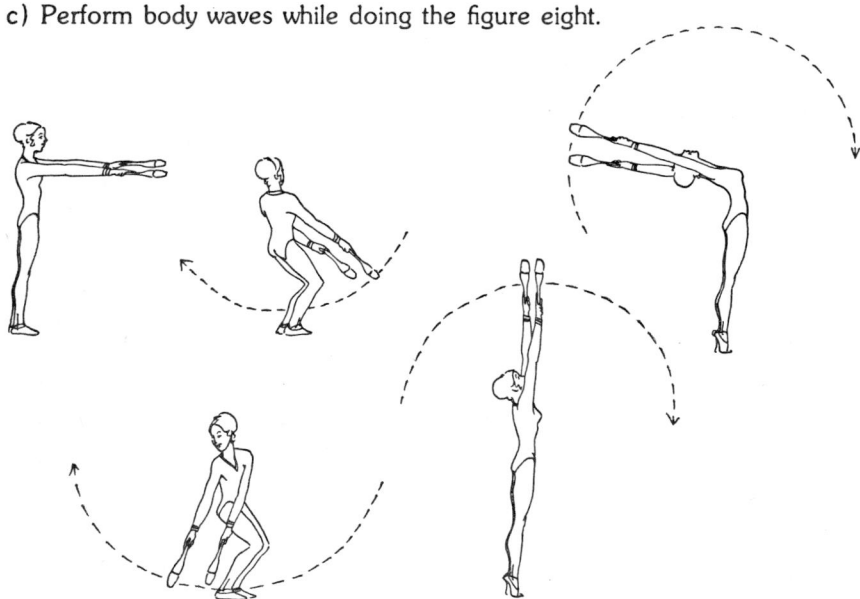

20. Figure Eight in the Frontal Plane
Stand in a wide straddle position with the arms extended to the right side and the clubs held in a regular grip. Circle the arms inward in front of you toward the left, overhead, then bend elbows and circle the clubs inward in back of the body. Repeat several times, then practice the movement to the opposite side.

Variations:
a) Do the same movement while moving sideward, forward, or backward with either walking or dancing steps.

b) Combine the above movement with a mill circle in the frontal plane. NOTE: the clubs must always be a half circle apart; therefore, start the exercise with the right arm overhead, left arm at the side.

Clubs

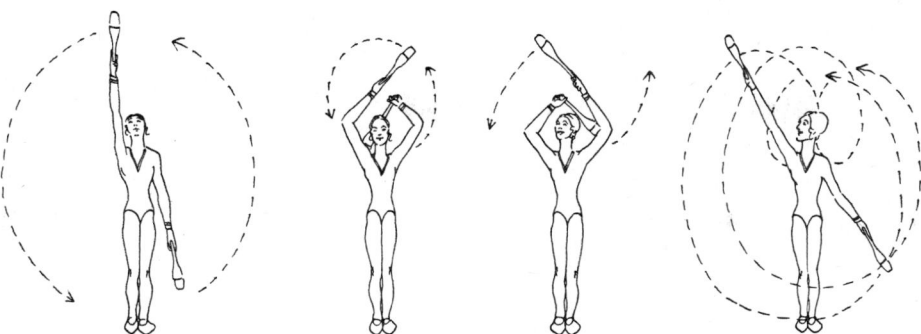

CIRCLING MOVEMENTS

The clubs may be circled in the frontal, sagittal, or horizontal planes. Hold the clubs loosely so that they rotate freely in the hands. Concentrate on relaxing the arms and shoulders. Circle the clubs with total body movement and with sufficient force so that they move around smoothly. Perform the movement with a lively rhythm. Do the slower circles to a quarter musical note and the faster ones to an eighth note. Continue the circling movements with various swinging movements.

1. Preliminary Exercise
The following sequence of movements will help you to learn the circling movements:

a) Stand with arms extended to the side, club in the right hand, held in a regular grip. Let the club drop by its weight and change the grip immediately to a circling grip (the club held loosely with thumb and index finger around the neck, just below the head). Swing it back to the horizontal position and support the club again with the index finger.

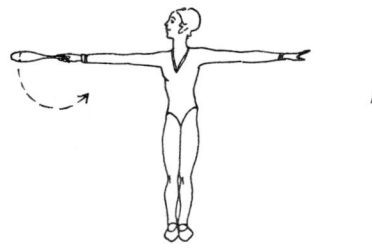 

b) Give a push with the index finger when the club is dropped. Experiment to find out how much force it takes to obtain sufficient momentum so that the club makes a complete circle in front of the arm. At the end of the circle, once again support the club with the index finger.

c) Do two or three circles in a continuous manner before stopping the club.

d) Perform exercises *a–c* with the left hand.

e) Now try to circle the clubs with both hands simultaneously.

f) Practice the above sequence with a reverse grip, circling the club in back of the forearm. Here, when starting the circle, just bend your supporting index finger around the neck of the club.

2. Circle in Front of Arms

Stand with arms extended to the side, clubs held in a regular grip. Make a small circle downward, inward toward the body, and finish the circle in a regular grip.

Variations:

a) Perform the same movement but circle the clubs in the opposite direction, upward and outward.

b) Do the same movement with a gallop or a balancé from side to side.

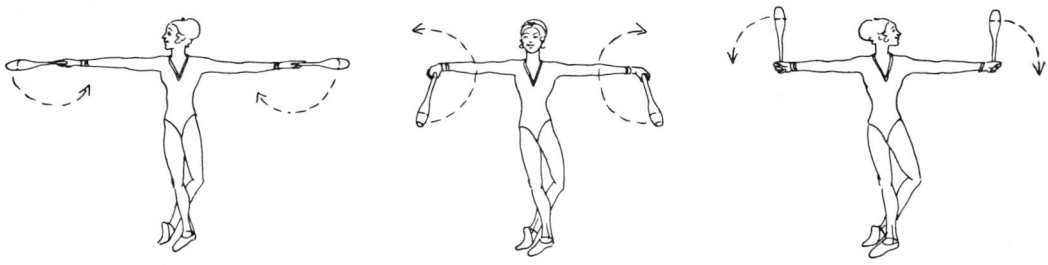

3. Circle in Back of the Arms

Stand with arms extended to the side, clubs held in a reverse grip. Make a small circle inward, in back of the forearms, with slightly bent elbows and end the movement in reverse grip.

Variations:
a) Do the same circle in the opposite direction. Start the movement outward and upward.

b) Do the same arm movement while moving sideways with dance steps.

4. Combination of Front and Back Arm Circles
Stand in a wide straddle position with weight on the right foot, the arms extended to the side and the clubs held in regular grip. Make a small inward circle in front of the arms, as in exercise 2, but end the circle in a reverse circling grip. Then make a small inward circle in back of the arms as in exercise 3. Repeat several times.

Variations:
a) Do the same exercise but circle the clubs in the opposite direction.

b) Move to the left with a grapevine step while circling the clubs in front and back of the arms. Do one circle for each step.

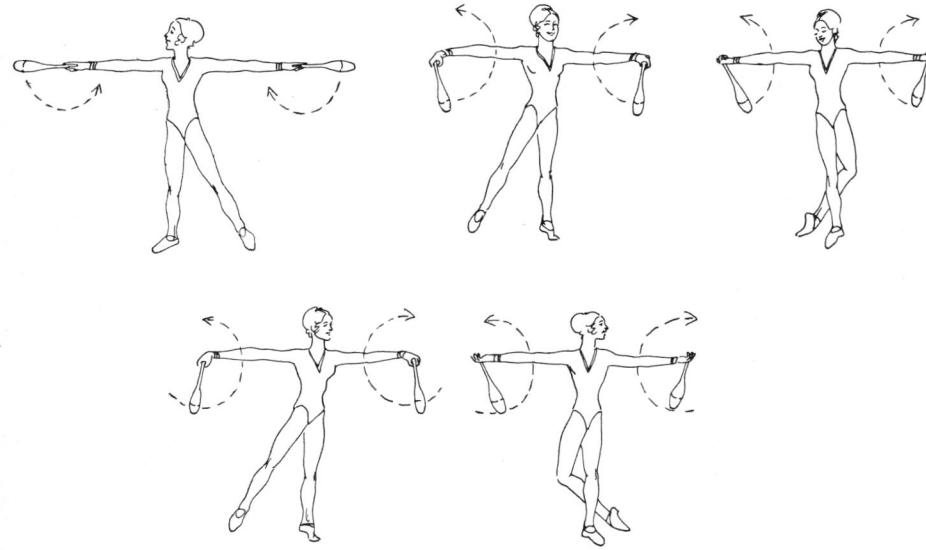

5. Circle in Front of the Body
Stand in a wide straddle with weight on the right foot, the arms extended to the right side and the clubs held in a regular grip. Swing the clubs downward and make an inward circle with both clubs in front of the body and then swing them to the left side. Repeat the movement

from left to right side. Transfer the weight from side to side while the entire body follows the movements of the clubs.

Variations:
a) Do the above movement while either walking or dancing forward or backward.
b) Do the same movement with a gallop from side to side.
c) Do a side body wave while circling the clubs in front of the body.
d) Circle the clubs twice in front of the body while doing the above movements.

6. Circle in Back of the Body
Stand with arms extended to the side, clubs held in a regular grip. Swing the right club downward to the side, push with the index finger and circle the club inward in the back of the body. Bring the club in front of the body and swing it to the left, then back to the right side. Reverse the movement with the left hand.

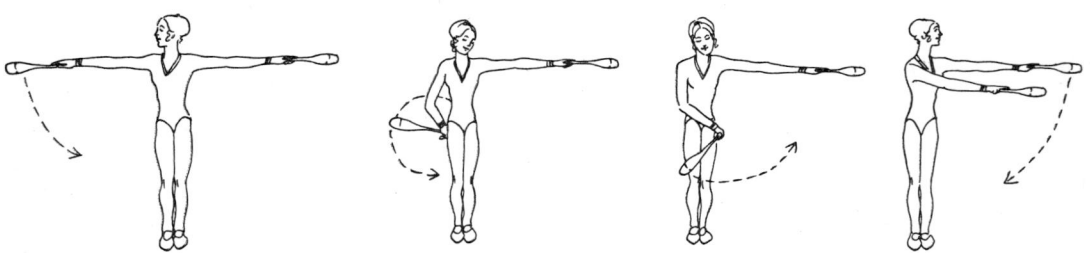

Variation:
Do the same movement but circle the club outward.

7. Simultaneous Front and Back Circles
Stand with arms extended to the right side, clubs held in regular grip. Swing the left arm downward and circle the club in front of the body, simultaneously the right arm makes a circle in the rear. Both arms then swing to the left side, ending in a side horizontal position. Repeat the movement toward the opposite side.

Variations:
a) Start in the same position, swing the arms downward in front of the body and make an inward circle with both clubs; continue circling the clubs outward with the right arm making the club circle in the front of the body, while at the same time the left arm makes its club circle in the back of the body. Finish the movement with the arms extended to the left side. Reverse the exercise to the opposite side.

   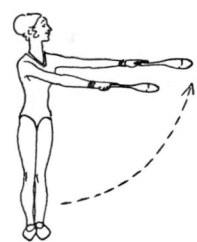

b) Do the above movements while dancing or walking sideward, backward or forward.

8. Circle in Front of the Head
Stand holding the clubs in a regular grip with the arms extended overhead. Bend the elbows slightly and circle the clubs downward to the right and back to the original position. Repeat several times. Also, practice circling the clubs to the left.

9. Opposite Cross Circle in Front of the Head
Stand holding the clubs in a regular grip with the arms extended overhead. Circle the right club downward to the right and simultaneously circle the left club downward to the left so that the clubs cross in front of the head. Practice crossing with the right club in front, then with the left club in front.

Variation:
Circle the clubs in the opposite direction: Cross the clubs overhead, swing them downward, uncross them in front of the head and swing them back upward to the original position.

10. Circle in Back of the Head
Stand with arms stretched overhead, the clubs held in a reverse grip. Bend the elbows slightly and circle the clubs downward to the right in back of the head. Repeat several times. Practice circling the clubs to the left also.

Variation:
Perform opposite cross circles in back of the head in both directions—downward and upward. This movement is performed similar to the opposite cross circles in front of the head (exercise 9).

11. Combination of Circles in Front and in Back of the Head
Stand with arms stretched overhead, with clubs held in a regular grip. Circle the clubs downward to the right in front of the head, as in exercise 8, but end the circle in a reverse circling grip. Then circle the clubs downward to the right in back of the head as in exercise 10, and finish the movement in a regular grip. This is like a figure eight, the first loop sketched in front of the head, the second in back of the head. Repeat the exercise several times in a smooth continuous manner.

Variations:

a) Do the same movement but circle the clubs in the opposite direction.

b) Combine opposite front and back head circles.

c) Combine large opposite cross circle (see club swinging exercise 15) with small opposite cross circle in back of the head.

d) Do the above movements while walking or dancing sideward, forward or backward.

275

Clubs

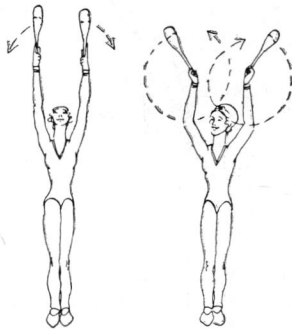

12. Alternate Circles in Front and in Back of the Head
Stand with arms extended overhead, clubs held in regular grip. Circle the left club to the left in front of the head at the same time as you circle the right club to the right in back of the head.

Variations:

a) Reverse the movement by circling the clubs in the opposite direction.

b) Circle with the right hand first in front and then in back of the head, simultaneously circle with the left hand in back and then in front of the head. Repeat circling in opposition several times.

13. Alternate Front and Back Continuous Circles
Stand with arms extended to the side, clubs held in a regular grip. The following movements should be done smoothly and continuously to 4/4 music. Both clubs circle simultaneously, moving as indicated below:

Right hand 1. Swing down and circle the club in front of the body
2. Circle the club in back of the body
3. Circle the club in front of the head
4. Circle the club in back of the head

Left hand 1. Swing down and circle the club in back of the body
2. Circle the club in front of the body
3. Circle the club in back of the head
4. Circle the club in front of the head

Variation:
Do the same movement while moving sideward, forward or backward with either walking or dancing steps.

14. Lateral Circle Inside of the Arms
Stand with arms extended horizontally forward, clubs held in a regular grip. Circle the clubs downward inside of the arms with slightly bent elbows.

Variations:
a) Circle the clubs in the opposite direction

b) Do two downward circles then two upward circles. Repeat several times.

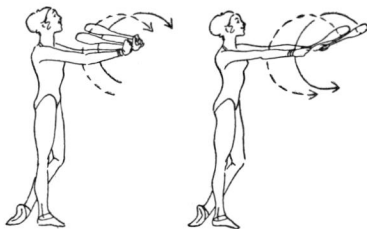

15. Lateral Circle Outside of the Arms
Stand with the arms extended horizontally forward and the clubs held in reverse grip. Circle the clubs downward outside of the arms with slightly bent elbows. Repeat several times.

Variations:
a) Circle the clubs in the opposite direction.

b) Perform two downward circles then two upward circles.

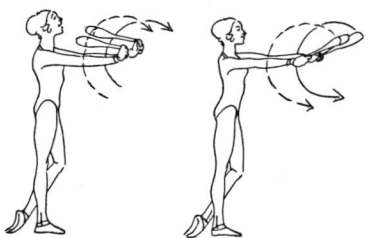

16. Combination of Inside and Outside Lateral Circles
Stand with the arms extended horizontally forward and the clubs held in a regular grip. Execute a lateral circle inside of the arms as in exercise

14 then perform a lateral circle outside of the arms as in exercise 15. Practice circling the clubs both downward and upward.

Variations:
a) Make an outside circle with the club in the right hand while at the same time making an inside circle with the club in the left hand. Alternate sides. Repeat this several times until you can circle the clubs smoothly and continuously.

b) Perform the above movements while either walking or dancing forward or backward.

17. Mill Circle in Sagittal Plane
Stand with arms extended horizontally forward and the clubs held in a regular grip. Do a half circle downward inside of the arm with the right hand and then start to circle the left hand in the same direction. Continue circling the clubs 180° apart.

Variations:
a) Do the same movement but circle the clubs with a reverse grip outside the arms.

b) Start in the same position but cross the arms in front with right arm on top. Start to circle with the left hand downward outside the right arm then circle with the right hand downward outside of the left arm. Uncross the arms and change to reverse grip and circle the left club downward outside the left arm then circle the right club in the same direction outside the right arm. Repeat the movement. Keep the clubs a half circle apart.

c) Repeat all the above movements but circle the clubs in the opposite direction.

d) Perform the same movements while walking or dancing forward or backward.

18. Lateral Circles at Sides
Stand with the arms extended horizontally forward, clubs held in a regular grip. Swing both clubs down and near the hips, make a lateral circle, then swing the clubs as far to the back as possible. Reverse the movement and return to the original position.

Variations:
a) Swing both clubs to the right side and circle near to the right hip. Reverse the circle and return to the original position. Perform the movement on the left side. Keep the arms parallel during the circles and follow the clubs with your eyes while turning the body slightly when the arms are moving backward.

b) Do the same movements with a forward stride, shifting weight backward and forward with the clubs.

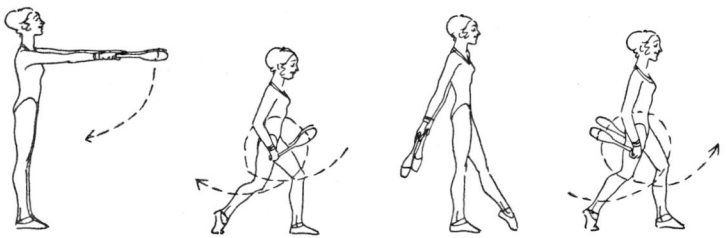

c) Perform the same movements while walking or dancing forward or backward.

19. Opposite Lateral Circles
Stand with the arms at the sides, with the clubs held in a regular grip. Circle the right club backward and simultaneously circle the left club forward. After the circle, the right arm swings backward as the left swings forward. Reverse the movement.

Variation:
Do the same movement with a dance step forward or backward.

20. Horizontal Circles on the Floor
This is a good preliminary exercise for learning to make horizontal circles with clubs. Kneel with arms extended to the right side. Hold the clubs in a regular grip. The bodies of the clubs touch the floor. Circle the clubs forward and inward several times, moving the circling clubs in a semicircle in front of the body. Repeat the movement from left to right, returning to the original position.

Variation:
Do the same exercise but circle the clubs in the opposite direction backward and outward.

21. Horizontal Circle Above the Arms
Stand with arms extended to the sides with the clubs held in a regular grip. Circle the clubs forward and inward above the arms several times.

Variations:
a) Do the same exercise with arms extended in front horizontal position.

b) Perform variation *a* while moving sideward, forward or backward with walking or dancing steps.

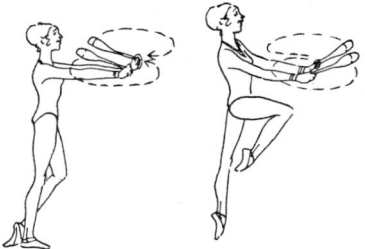

c) All the above movements may be performed by holding the clubs in reverse grip and circling the clubs outward over the arms.

d) Circle the clubs forward and inward from the right side to the left and back across the body.

e) Same exercise as variation d but circle the clubs in the opposite direction.

22. Horizontal Circle Below the Arms
Stand with arms extended to the side, clubs held in a regular grip. Circle the clubs forward and inward underneath the arms several times.

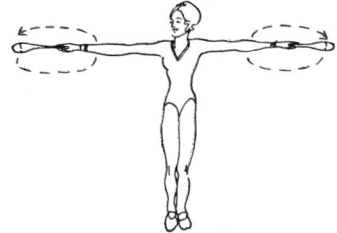

Variations:
Do the same variations as in exercise 21 circling the clubs below the arms. NOTE, even the outward circles are done with a regular grip.

23. Combination of Circles Above and Below the Arm
Stand with arms extended to the side, clubs held in a regular grip. Make a circle forward and inward above the arms as in exercise 21, then make a circle inward below the arms as in exercise 22. Repeat several times. The clubs sketch a figure eight in the air.

Variations:
a) Do the same exercise but circle the clubs in the opposite direction.

b) Circle the right club forward and inward above the arm while at the same time circling the left club in the same direction below the arm. Continue by circling the right club under the arm as the left club circles over the arm. Repeat several times.

24. Figure Eight in the Horizontal Plane
Stand with the arms extended to the right side with clubs held in a regular grip. Swing the arm inward in a horizontal circle above the head

then swing the arms down and circle the clubs in the same direction in front of the body. Also practice circling outward.

Variations:
a) Do the same movement while moving forward or backward with walking steps.
b) Do the same movement performing different kinds of turns or pirouettes.

25. Asymmetrical Circles
To coordinate different asymmetrical movements of the arms is quite difficult. For example, one arm does a large swinging movement while the other performs small circling movements as in the following exercise: Stand with arms extended to the right side, clubs held in a regular grip. Do a large horizontal circle above the head with the left arm as the right club circles above and below the right arm. Try the same movement while doing walking or dancing steps.

THROWING AND CATCHING MOVEMENTS

Throwing movements are usually connected with swinging movements. The club is tossed in the air by simply swinging it upward and releasing it at a 45° angle. To minimize the impact of the catch, the club should be caught above the horizontal with a downward motion of the arm. (A dead catch will make an awkward break in the rhythm and will probably sting the hand.) The club may be caught either with a regular or a reverse grip depending on what movement will follow the catch.

1. Drop and Catch
Stand with the arms extended forward and the clubs held in a regular grip. Lift the arms slightly upward and release the clubs. Bend the knees quickly to catch them from above. Repeat several times.

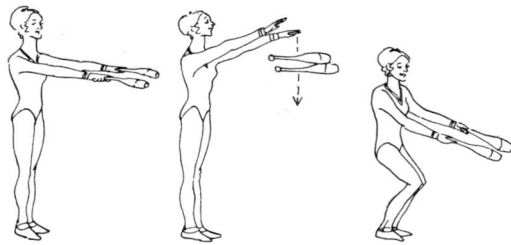

Variation:
Also practice with a reverse grip.

2. Throw in Sagittal Plane
Stand with the arms at the sides and the clubs held in a regular grip. Swing the arms forward and up and toss the clubs slightly upward. Catch them and swing the arms downward and backward. The whole body should follow the up and down motion of the club. Repeat several times.

Variations:
a) Do the same movement but throw the clubs so that they rotate 180° in the air. Catch them at the body. Repeat and catch them at the head, and so on.

b) Do the same toss but give more impetus with the index finger so that the clubs rotate backward and make a full 360° turn in the air.

c) Walk forward while tossing the clubs either alternately with the left and right hand or with both hands simultaneously.

3. Throw in the Frontal Plane
Stand in a wide straddle with the arms extended to the sides, the clubs held in a regular grip. Swing the right arm downward toward the left side and toss the right club upward in front of the body. The club should make a 180° turn in the air. Repeat several times. Catch the

club alternately by the body and then by the head with a regular grip. Practice this also with the left hand. In the beginning practice with low tosses, then later with higher and higher ones.

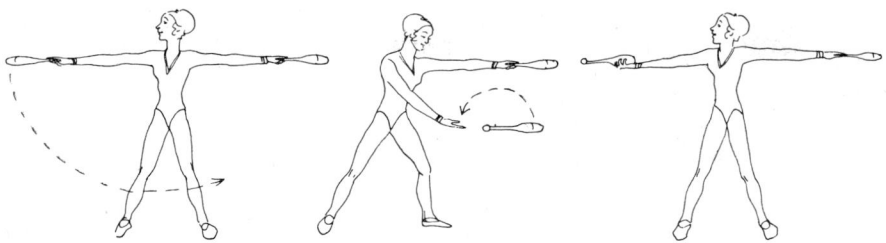

Variations:
a) Throw the club up so that it will make a full 360° turn in the air.

b) Do the same movements while doing walking or dancing steps.

4. Throw Behind the Shoulder
Stand in a wide straddle with the arms extended to the sides and the clubs held in a regular grip. Shift your weight to the right foot, bend to the right as you swing the right club downward and to the back and throw it up behind the left shoulder. After it has made a full circle, catch the club with the right hand and swing it down in front of the body and back to the side. Repeat this movement with the left hand. The club can be caught either above the opposite shoulder or over the shoulder from which it was tossed in the air.

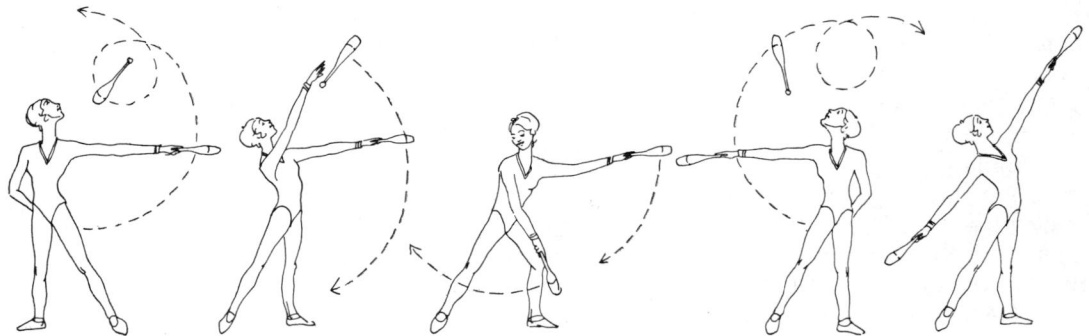

5. Partner Tossing
Stand facing your partner, each of you holding one club in front of the body in a regular grip with the right hand. Swing the club backward then forward and toss it to your partner. The club should do either a half or a full turn in the air. Catch your partner's club with your left hand.

Repeat the movement several times, alternating hands. Try to increase the distance between you up to fifteen feet.

Variations:
a) Only one partner holds two clubs, the other partner catches both.

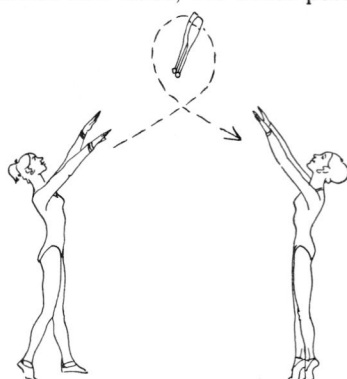

b) Each partner holds two clubs and both pairs of clubs are exchanged at the same time. To keep the clubs from colliding, each partner throws her clubs slightly to the right and catches her partner's slightly on the left.

CLAPPING MOVEMENTS

The clubs may be hit against the floor or against each other. The sound quality of the clubs cannot be varied to a great extent, but different rhythmic patterns and the different accents made by hard and soft strokes can be made audible. Usually the body, rather than the head or neck of the club, is used for clapping. Perform clapping exercises with a quick, sharp motion. The following exercises should help you learn to emphasize the movements.

1. Clapping in Rhythm
Strike the clubs together in varying dynamic and time patterns. Stand holding the clubs in a regular grip in front of the body. Clap out different rhythms with the clubs. Do one clap on each whole, half, or quarter note and a double clap on each eighth note.

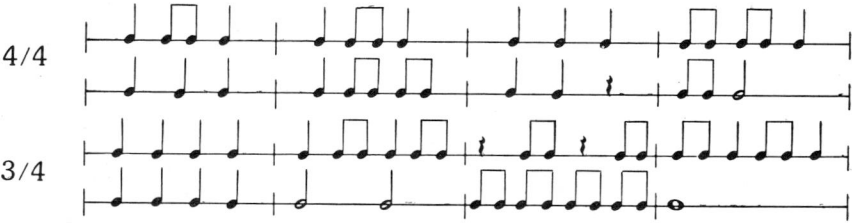

2. Clapping Against the Floor
You may strike the body of the clubs against the floor,

the head of the clubs against the floor, or

the base of the clubs against the floor.

The grip on the clubs may be changed smoothly by sliding the hands from the head to the body and vice versa by using the weight of the clubs as an aid. Clap the clubs against the floor in the same rhythms as described in the previous exercise.

3. Clapping the Clubs Together
Clap the clubs together while performing the following movements:

a) Swing the clubs backward and forward (see swinging movement 1) and clap them in front of the body.

b) Perform different kinds of jumps. Swing the arms up and clap the clubs overhead during the highest point of the jump. (See swinging movement 5.)

c) Do large opposite cross circles (see swinging movement 15) and clap the clubs together above the head.

d) Execute alternate forward and backward circles (see swinging movement 10) and clap the clubs together above the head.

e) Swing the arms across the body (see swinging movement 11) from the right side to the left and clap the clubs together twice on the left side. Repeat to the right.

f) Circle the clubs in front of the body (see circling movement 5) and clap the clubs together at the end of the swing.

g) Perform lateral circles at the sides (see circling movement 18) and clap in back and in front at the end of each swing. Vary the movement by clapping the clubs together three times during the front swing. Make each clap louder than the previous one.

4. Clapping Alternately in the Air and on the Floor
Stand with the arms at the sides and the clubs held in a regular grip. Swing both clubs forward and upward and clap them together at the top of the swing, then squat down and clap them on the floor. Clap alternately in the air and on the floor.

Variation:
Vary the rhythmic patterns; for example, clap the clubs on the floor three times and then stand up and clap the clubs together once.

5. Locomotion
Execute the following locomotor movements while clapping the clubs together:

a) Waltz forward and emphasize the first beat of the waltz rhythm by hitting the clubs together.

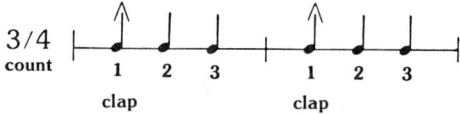

b) Skip forward or backward and clap the clubs in rhythm in front of the body.

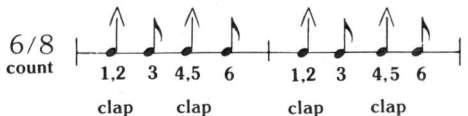

c) Gallop forward clapping out each note. Watch for the rhythmic beat which is strong and uneven in the gallop.

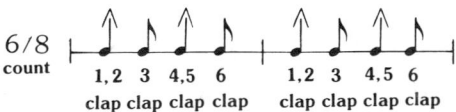

d) Gallop sideways with a 180° turn. Do three side gallops, to the left, hop-turn 180° to the left, then perform three side gallops to the right and hop-turn 180° to the right. Continue this pattern. Do a large frontal circle for each gallop and clap above the head during the hop-turn.

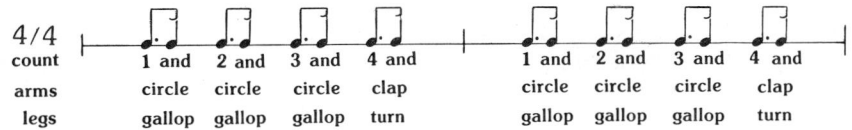

e) Do a glissade and tour jeté. Swing arms upward and clap above the head during the highest point of the tour jeté.

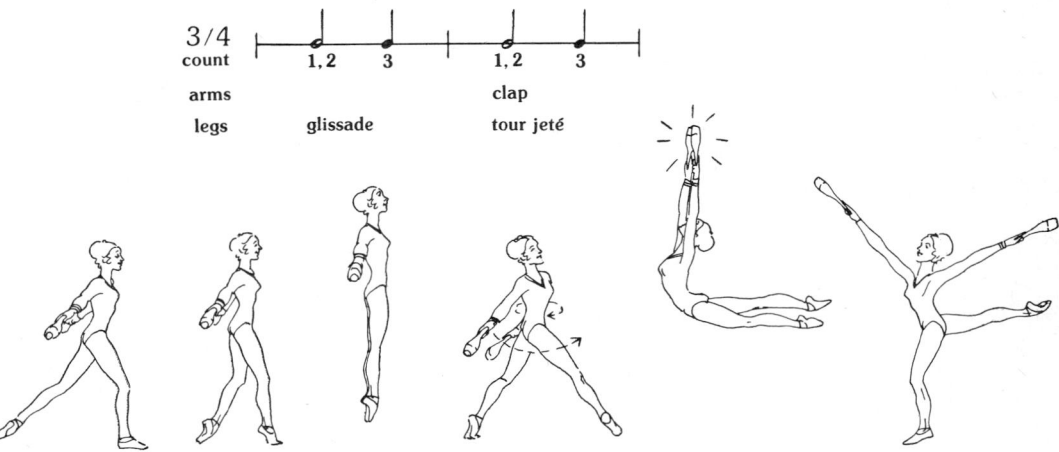

6. Clap with Partner

Stand facing your partner slightly more than two arm lengths apart. The arms are at the sides with clubs held in a regular grip. Each girl swings the right club forward and claps her partner's club as the left arm swings backward. Alternate arm swings forward and backward and clap out different rhythms on each other's clubs.

Variation:
Swing both clubs back and forth simultaneously. Behind the body, clap your clubs together and in front clap on your partner's clubs.

DROPPING AND KIPPING MOVEMENTS

Dropping and kipping exercises are not typical club gymnastics movements; however, they can be used as connecting elements in a routine.

1. Drop Clubs onto the Forearms

Stand with the arms stretched overhead and clubs held in a regular grip. Drop the clubs onto the forearms as the arms are brought down to first position, then swing them downward, forward and upward back to the original position.

Variations:
a) Do the same movement but swing the clubs to a side extension.

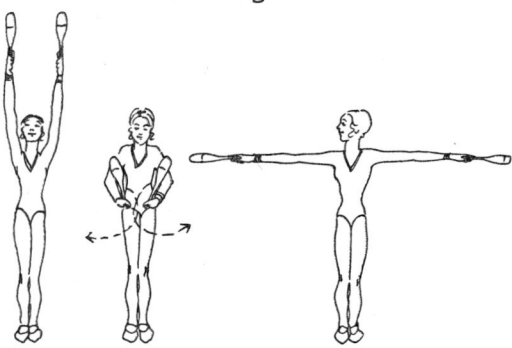

b) Perform the same movements while walking or dancing.

2. Drop the Clubs Behind the Shoulders
Stand with arms extended backward, the clubs held in a regular grip. Swing the arms forward and upward over the head, then bend the elbows and drop the clubs back of the shoulders. Immediately extend the elbows and swing the clubs upward, forward, and downward, ending in the original position.

Variation:
Do the same movement while doing walking or dancing steps.

3. Drop with Grapevine Steps
Stand in a wide straddle, weight on the left foot, arms extended to the side and the clubs held in a regular grip. Cross the right foot in front of the left as the clubs drop onto the forearms, then step with the left foot to the left and simultaneously swing arms back to a side extension. Repeat several times.

4. Drop with Leap
Stand with clubs resting on top of the forearms. Perform a step and leap, swinging the right club downward and outward to side extension

while at the same time swinging the left club downward and forward to a front horizontal position. Repeat several times. Also practice leaping with the other foot.

5. Drop with Turn
Do different types of turns while dropping the clubs onto the forearms and swinging them out to side extension.

6. Half Kip
Stand with arms extended to the sides, clubs in a regular grip. Push with the index fingers and flip the clubs downward and upward parallel in front of the forearms. Then bend the elbows and bring the lower arms down. Immediately raise the forearms over the shoulders and let the clubs drop back of the arms. Swing the clubs upward and outward back to their original position.

Variations:
a) Perform the same movement but start it from overhead or from a front horizontal position.

b) Do the same movement but swing the clubs out over the head or to a front horizontal position at the end.

c) Do the above movements with walking or dancing steps.

7. Kip

Stand with the arms extended to the sides and the clubs held in a regular grip. Kip the clubs up outside of the forearms, then bend both elbows and bring the arms down. Immediately straighten the arms outward to the sides while rolling the clubs over the forearms to the inside. Continue with a half kip (see exercise 6). Do this movement in a quick, smooth, continuous manner.

Variations:
a) Perform the same movement but start from overhead or from a front horizontal position.
b) Do the same movement but swing the clubs out to different positions.
c) Do the above movements while performing walking or dancing steps.

TEACHING SUGGESTIONS

1. When learning the basic skills the class should be in staggered lines to allow plenty of room for movement and to avoid accidents.
2. When teaching locomotion movements it is best to work diagonally across the floor.

If you have a large group work in threes or fours. The gymnasts move diagonally across the floor then walk across the end of the room, and repeat the locomotion pattern on the opposite diagonal path and walk back to the starting position. With this method the teacher has a good opportunity to observe each individual and correct her mistakes.

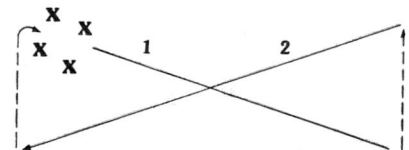

When a rest period between movements is not necessary the whole class can move together in a circle formation, or across the floor. See the teaching suggestions in the chapter on rope jumping for other ideas.
3. Emphasize good club-handling techniques. Allow plenty of time to practice the basic skills. Correct students' mistakes right at the beginning so they are not carried over to more advanced skills. It is easier in the long run to make good habits than it is to break bad ones.
4. The whole body should be involved in every exercise so that the club movement is coordinated with the body movement —when the club is down, bend the knees, when the club is up, straighten the knees.
5. Movements should be learned first with the right and then with the left hand before students attempt to perform with two clubs simultaneously. Next, the gymnast is ready to learn alternating movements in which both clubs are moving at the same time in different directions. Ambidexterity must be attained in order to handle the clubs smoothly and naturally.
6. When the basic technique has been learned, combine the exercises with leg and trunk movements. Sequences or combinations should be taught as soon as a few skills have been learned.
7. After students have acquired the basic skills for a club exercise, let them create their own combinations.
8. Club exercises should always be performed with music. 6/8, 3/4, and 4/4 meter music are usually used for club routines.
9. Allow plenty of time to practice. Good club technique requires refined muscular coordination and, therefore, demands careful, patient practice. Only after much practice will the gymnast be able to handle clubs lightly, gracefully, and in rhythm.
10. A jumping rope may be used in practice as a substitute for the club. Fold the rope twice and make a knot close to the open ends. Hold the quadrupled rope by the unknotted end. The knotted end will have enough weight to give students the feeling of swinging and circling movements as they are done with the club.

COMPETITIVE RULES

Area: 39⅓ square feet (12 x 12 meters)
Music: one instrument
Time Limit: 1:00 to 1:30 minutes

A perfect routine is one that is performed in a smooth, graceful, elegant, flowing manner, with no faults in execution. The entire routine should be interesting and should contain variety. Common faults in execution are: poor coordination between body movements and movements of the clubs, lack of continuity, lack of smoothness, and poor body form and style during the exercise. Specific penalties found in execution are: in swinging movements, the clubs are not an extension of the arms; in circling movements, clubs are clasped in the hands instead of being held loosely, and circles are not parallel to the arms or to the floor; in throwing movements, clubs are caught at the neck instead of at the head or body; and dropping the clubs. Clubs are considered as one implement and therefore if the gymnast drops one club she should pick it up as soon as possible because her routine is not judged during the time in which she has just one club in her hand. In such a case she will also be penalized for loss of rhythm.

EXAMPLES OF DIFFICULTIES

The various exercises and movement combinations are rated according to their difficulty. An individual optional routine must have 8 difficulties. Two of these are to be superior difficulties. The following examples are given only as guidelines:

Medium Difficulties:
1. Do three running steps and a split leap while performing two alternate forward and backward large circles in the sagittal plane. (See swinging movement 10.)
2. Do three fast running steps while circling the clubs in front of the body then perform a cabriole to the right side and simultaneously do front and back circles. Repeat the movement to the opposite side. (See circling movements 5 and 7).
3. Do at least four mill circle combinations with backward walking steps (one possible combination: left club circles under and outside of the right arm, right club over and outside left arm, left club outside left arm, and right club outside right arm). (See circling movement 17.)
4. Throw the clubs forward and upward, arms parallel, while doing dancing steps. Catch them with the same hands, arms remaining parallel.
5. Glissade, tour jeté with a clap above the head during the highest point of the jump. (See clapping movement 5.)
6. Do a backward and forward mill swing and immediately drop clubs onto the shoulders then extend the arms forcefully upward. Combine the above movement with forward walking steps. (See swinging movement 3 and dropping movement 2.)

Superior Difficulties:
1. Perform horizontal asymmetrical circles with a 360° turn on one foot. (See circling movement 25.)
2. Throw the right club behind the left shoulder so that it will make a full 360° turn in the air. Catch it with the right hand. Repeat with the left hand. Combine this movement with walking or dancing steps. (See throwing movement 4.)

COMPOSITION

One of the goals of modern rhythmic gymnastics training is to accomplish a competitive routine that shows a variety of skills and is perfect in execution. However, before attempting to make a competitive routine, it is best to put together a few short combinations. After you have developed the basic skills fairly well, start to create short routines. This will give you an opportunity to demonstrate individuality and creativity.

In your routines, always include circling, throwing, and catching movements. Then select at least one more type of movement from among the following categories: swinging, clapping, dropping, and kipping. Arrange your movements in a variety of curved and straight lines, shaping an interesting floor pattern.

Plan an exercise that fits your ability. Don't include unperfected movements in your combination. Your aim is to flow smoothly from one movement to the next without interruption. Perform your routine with expression, poise, and confidence.

An example of a short composition is given below. A few of the movement sequences are from the 1973 international compulsory routine. You may replace some of the suggested moves with easier or more difficult ones, according to your ability.

1. Pose, then step forward while performing lateral circles at the sides of the body. Continue with a hop and simultaneously swing the arms forward and upward and clap the clubs above the head. Repeat.

2. Execute a lateral circle inside of the arms, then swing the clubs downward and backward at the right side of the body and clap the two clubs together. Immediately swing the clubs forward and make a lateral circle at the right side of the body; then swing the clubs overhead and clap again.

3. Take three running steps forward and leap, while performing two alternate forward and backward arm circles.

4. Do three running steps forward and a hop with the knee lifted high in front and simultaneously perform a horizontal circle above the arms.

5. Walking steps forward while swinging the arms to a pose.

6. Do three mill circle combinations with backward walking steps in a curved pattern.

7. Perform one more mill circle combination and finish the movement with a backbend.

8. Execute a backward and forward mill swing; turn 180° and drop clubs onto the shoulders. Then extend the arms and swing the clubs downward. Squat down and clap the clubs on the floor.

9. Do four walking steps forward in a curved pattern while doing a lateral circle inside of the arms then a large circle at the left side of the body. Repeat to the opposite side.

10. Do Grapevine steps to the left as you do two alternate front and back continuous circle combinations.

11. Hop, knee turn while swinging the clubs around you at shoulder level.

12. Stand up and step, simultaneously swing the arms forward and up and throw the clubs upward so that they make a full 360° turn in the air. Catch the clubs and step back to a finishing pose.

Floor pattern for composition

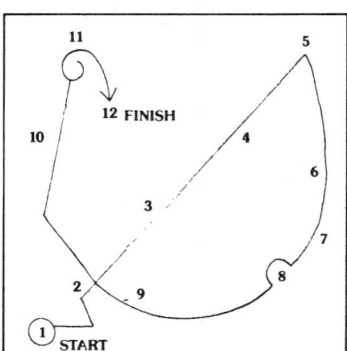

GROUP EXERCISES

The area (12 x 12 meters) should be covered in its entirety. The routine should be accompanied by music played by one instrument. The time limit is from two minutes 30 seconds to three minutes. The composition should have logical sequences of patterns and a few exchanges of clubs between members of the group. The following are suggestions for group formations and exchanges.

FLOOR PATTERN EXAMPLES

1. Six girls form a pyramid. Then, doing two walking steps forward and a moderate arabesque turn while performing asymmetrical horizontal circles, they end in the second formation.

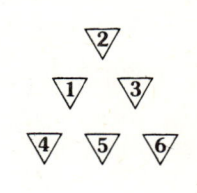

2. Step-hop with alternate forward and backward swings. End in the third formation.

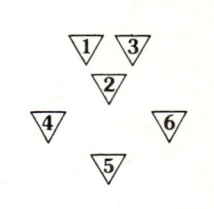

3. Double line facing in the same direction. Gymnasts 1, 2, and 3 move to the left, while performers 4, 5, and 6 go to the right with grapevine steps as clubs drop onto the forearms and swing back to horizontal position.

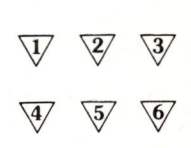

4. Do grapevine steps to the opposite direction with alternate front and back continuous circles. End with a zig zag double line facing each other. Gymnasts 4, 5, and 6 turn 180° during the last step of the grapevine pattern.

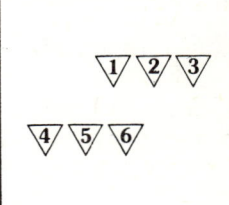

5. Swing both clubs backward then forward and clap them in front on your partner's clubs. Waltz turn, while doing a large forward mill circle, into the sixth formation.

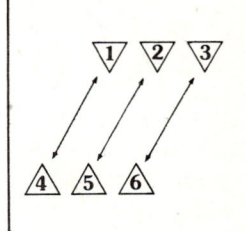

6. H-formation. Circle the clubs from right to left in front of the body and clap the clubs together at the end of the swing. Repeat in the opposite direction.

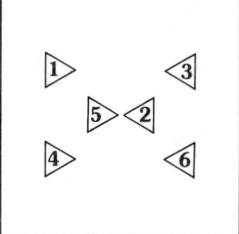

EXCHANGE EXAMPLES

Group routines with clubs have not been included in any Modern Rhythmic Gymnastics Championships; consequently, rules regarding group composition have not yet been clarified. Most likely, long distance changeovers will not be required.

1. Double line formation, facing each other. Stand with the arms extended forward and clubs held in regular grip. Gymnasts 1, 3, and 5 swing their left arms backward and forward while gymnasts 2, 4, and 6 swing their right arms backward and forward. At the top of the forward swing throw the swinging club with a half turn in the sagittal plane to your partner. Catch your partner's club and swing your arm backward and forward again. Then repeat the movement with the other hand. After catching the club, step two steps to the left while swinging the club back and forth. End in a zig zag double line formation.

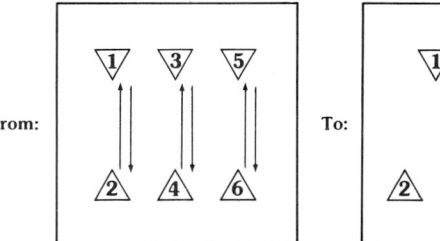

2. Circle formation, facing outward. Stand with the arms extended to the sides, and the clubs held in a regular grip. Swing the right arm downward toward the left side and toss the right club with a sideward and upward movement in the frontal plane to the next person. The club should make a 540° (one and a half) turn in the air. After catching the club with the right hand do a 180° turn to the left, to face inward. Repeat the movement with the left hand.

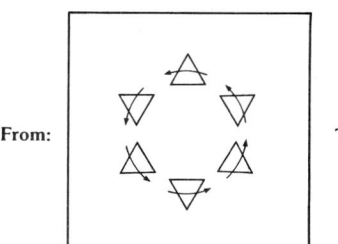

3. Pairs move to the center with forward step-hops while swinging both arms forward and backward. In the center there is an exchange of clubs between pairs (1 with 2, and 3 with 4), while the two single gymnasts do step-hops in place and throw and catch their own clubs. Then pairs step-hop backward while 5 and 6 step-hop forward to the center, forming two diagonal lines facing each other. Next, all gymnasts exchange their clubs simultaneously.

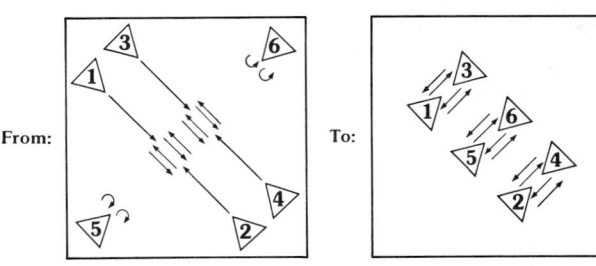

4. Partners facing each other, holding the clubs in forward extension with a regular grip. Gymnast 1 exchanges clubs with gymnast 2, 3 with 4, and 5 with 6 in the following movement. Swing the clubs backward while doing a lateral circle at the side of the body. Then circle the clubs forward and throw both clubs simultaneously at the top of the forward swing. Thus four clubs will be thrown and caught at the same time. After catching the clubs, swing the clubs backward with a lateral circle at the side as you turn to face a new partner. Repeat the movement with your new partner.

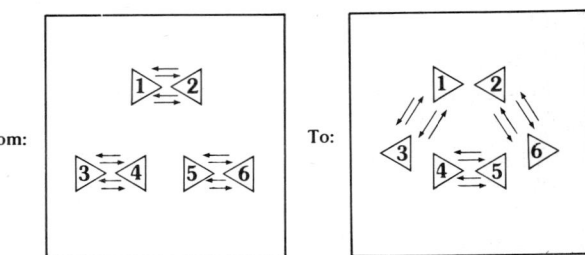

SUGGESTED GROUP ASSIGNMENT

The fact that a great deal of learning takes place through problem solving has been long accepted by educators. The method of creative solving of problems encourages creativity, self-direction, orienting oneself with a group so that the routine proceeds smoothly, choosing movements that fit best into the composition and eliminating those that are unsuitable, and moving in unison with a partner or with the group.

Problem: There are five formations illustrated below. Use your creativity and originality to develop smooth and logical transitions.

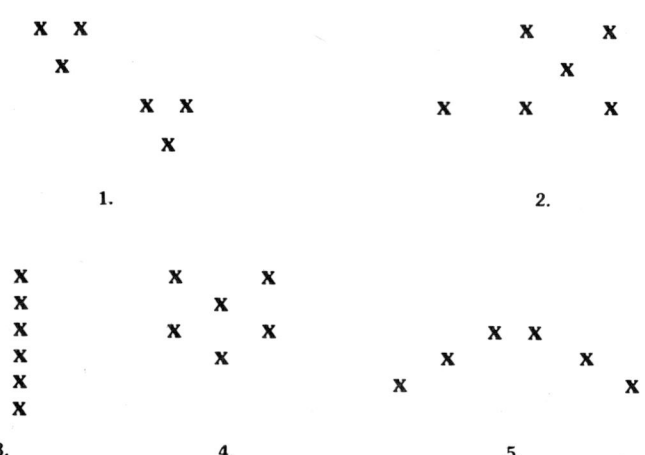

A. Be sure to include various swings, circles, and throwing and catching movements.

B. Make use of different planes: sagittal, frontal, and horizontal.

C. Experiment with asymmetrical arrangements of movements; for example, do a movement twice to one side and only once to the other.

D. Include one exchange of clubs with a partner.

E. Strive for coordination, precision, and grace. Make the various movements flow and change as the tempo and intensity of the music changes.

Music—Rimsky-Korsakov "Schéhérazade" arrangement for clubs by H. Jones.

Musical breakdown:
    26 measures
      2 measures 3/8—slow, loud introduction
      8 measures 3/8—light, soft, staccato
      8 measures 6/8—smooth, major theme of Schéhérazade.
      8 measures 3/8—loud, fast waltz style.

Music for Club Group Assignment

304

Wands, Flags, and Scarves

Chapter 8

Wands, flags, and scarves are included among the apparatus used in competitive rhythmic gymnastics for girls. In international competition only the five F.I.G. accepted hand apparatus—balls, ropes, hoops, ribbons and clubs—are used. However, in gymnastic demonstrations or exhibitions one often sees wand, flag, and scarf routines. This is because they help to develop natural body movements, good rhythm, agility, coordination, quick reaction, ambidexterity and good posture in the same way as routines using the official hand apparatus.

Wands, flags, and scarves lend themselves well to large group demonstrations. An excellent demonstration can be put on by students of just average ability from physical education classes using these light hand apparatuses. Exhibitions give the students a goal in perfecting their skills and an opportunity to show their improvement to others.

WANDS

Wands are usually made of beechwood, although any hardwood doweling may be used. They should be about 70 to 100 cm (27⅝"–39⅜") in length and 1 to 2 cm (⅜"–¾") in diameter. The wand may be enameled in various bright colors to make it attractive.

The wand may be held with both hands at the ends, in the middle or at one end. It may also be held in one hand in the middle or at the end. Hold the wand either with the straight index finger supporting it and the thumb and other fingers around it or simply with the thumb and fingers encircling it. There are three kinds of grips used with the wand movements:

The *regular or overgrip* in which the wand is held in one or both hands with the palm(s) of the hand(s) facing downward.

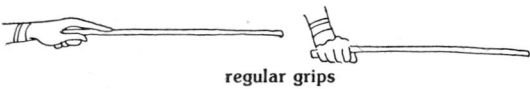
regular grips

The *reverse or undergrip* in which the wand is held in one or both hands, with the palm(s) of the hand(s) facing upward.

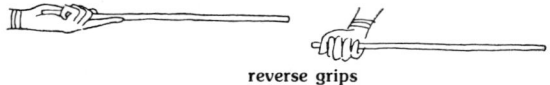
reverse grips

The *mixed or combined grip* in which one hand holds the wand with an overgrip while the other holds it with an undergrip.

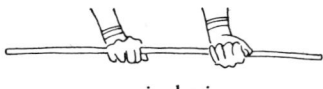
mixed grip

The position of the wand relative to the body may be specified according to the plane (frontal, sagittal, and horizontal) and levels of elevation (hip level, chest level, overhead, and so on) on which it moves.

Wand exercises should be taught in a large area allowing ample space between students. The exercises should be performed to music. Lively folk dance melodies or other 2/4 or 4/4 meter music are the most suitable for wand gymnastics.

The most commonly used movements with wands are: swinging, circling, throwing and catching, turning, and jumping over the wand. All the wand movements must be coordinated with the movement of the body.

SWINGING MOVEMENTS

Swinging movements with the wand should be performed by bending and stretching the arm during the swing so that the wand will not touch the floor. At the beginning of the movement the arm is straight, in the middle the arm is bent, and at the end the arm is straight again. The wand should be held as an extension of the arm itself. When swinging the wand horizontally, the arm is usually kept straight.

1. Swing Across the Body
Stand in a wide straddle with weight on the right foot, the arms extended to the side and the wand in the right hand with a regular grip. Swing the wand downward across the body to the left, back to the right,

and to the left again; then transfer the wand to the left hand. Repeat with the left hand. Transfer the weight from side to side while swinging the wand.

Variations:
a) Swing the wand downward across the body to the left, upward over the head, and downward again across the body to the left before transferring it to the left hand.

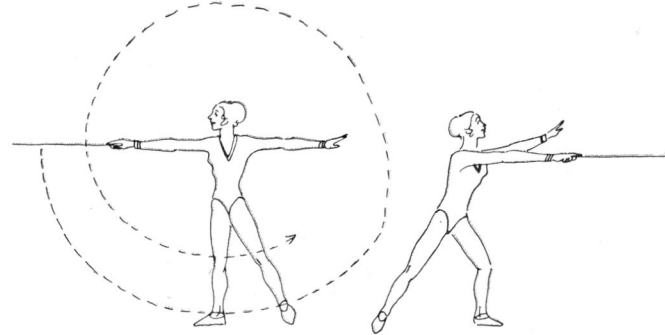

b) Do the above movements while doing walking or dancing steps.

2. Swing Behind Body

Stand in a wide straddle with weight on the left foot, with the arms extended to the sides, and the wand held in the left hand with the palm of the hand facing down. Swing the wand downward and upward to the right in back of the body; grasp the other end of the wand with the right hand (the palm of the hand facing backward) and swing the wand downward and upward to the right side. Repeat to the opposite side. Shift weight from side to side with the wand swing.

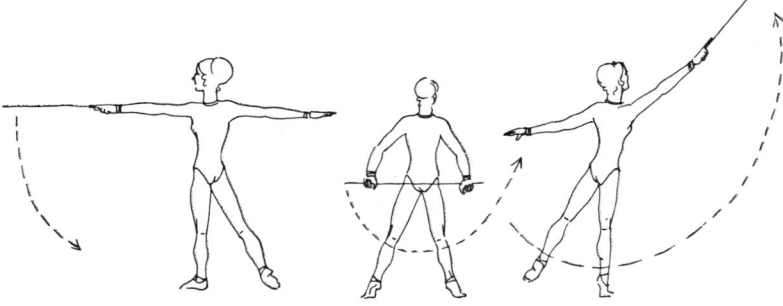

Variation:
Do the same movement with various walking or dancing steps.

3. Swing Forward and Backward

Stand with the left arm extended forward and the right arm backward with the wand in the right hand, the palm of the hand facing down. Swing the right arm forward and backward and pass the wand to the left hand behind the body. Continue the swing with the left hand.

Variations:
a) Do the same movement but change hands in front of the body.
b) Do the same movement with a forward stride, shifting weight forward and backward with the wand.

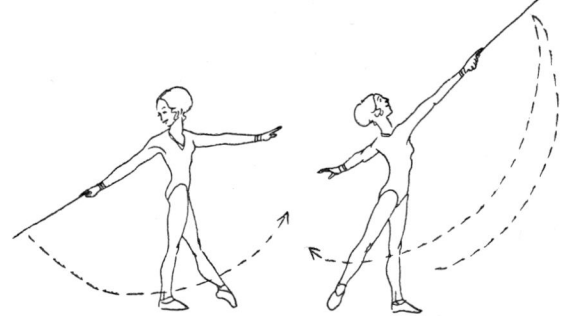

c) Repeat the movement with either walking or dancing steps.

4. Swing and Drop Behind Body

Stand with the arms extended backward with the wand held in the right hand and the palm of the hand facing down. Swing the wand forward and upward over the head; then bend the elbow and drop the wand behind the body. Immediately extend the elbow and swing the wand upward, forward and downward, ending in the original position. Practice this several times, then repeat the movement with the left hand.

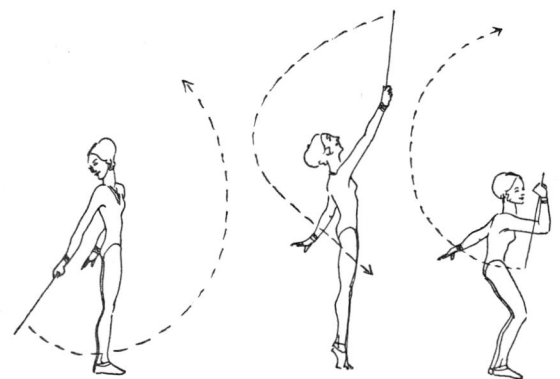

Variation:
Do the same movement while doing walking or dancing steps.

5. Swing Overhead
Stand with the arms extended to the sides, holding the wand in the right hand with the palm of the hand facing down. Perform horizontal circles inward overhead. Repeat with the left hand.

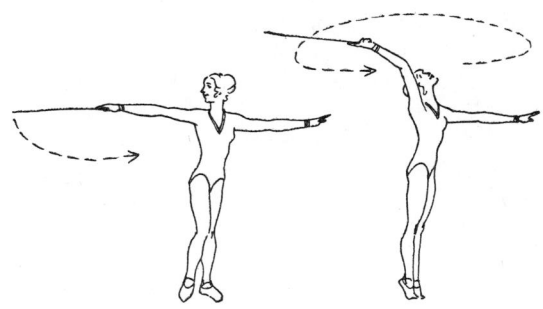

Variations:
a) Perform horizontal circles outward overhead.

b) Do the same movement while walking or dancing forward or backward.

c) Do the same movement while performing different kinds of turns or pirouettes.

6. Swing Under the Leg
Stand with arms extended to the side, holding the wand in the right hand, with the palm of the hand facing down. Swing the wand low inward, jump over it, and continue the circle with the wand. Repeat, holding the wand with the left hand.

Variations:
a) Make a horizontal circle overhead as in number 5 then swing the wand down and circle it slightly above the floor, passing over it with a jump.

b) Do the same movement as (a) but perform a 360° turn with the jump.

7. Figure Eight in the Sagittal Plane
Stand with arms extended forward, holding the wand in the right hand with the palm of the hand facing down. Move the right arm across to the left side over the horizontal left arm and swing the wand downward, backward and around, making the first loop of the figure eight on the left side. When the right arm is overhead switch the hand to a reverse grip (palm upward) and swing the wand downward, backward and upward to sketch the second loop of the figure eight on the right side of the body. Practice with the left hand also. The aim is to sketch two perfect loops, one on each side of the body.

Variations:
a) Do body waves while executing the figure eight.

b) Do the same movement while moving forward or backward with either walking or dancing steps.

c) Do the same movement but swing the wand in the opposite direction.

d) Do all the above movements holding the wand in the middle.

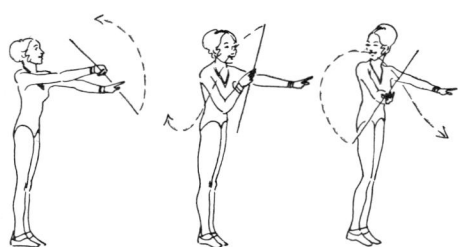

8. Figure Eight Front and Back
Stand holding the wand in the right hand, palm facing downward. Circle the wand inward in front of you, toward the left, overhead, then bend the elbows (palm facing upward) and circle the wand inward in back of

the body. Repeat several times and then practice it with the left hand also.

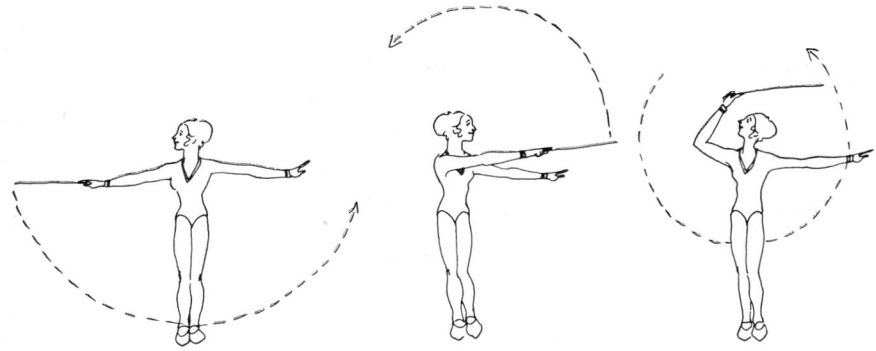

Variation:
Do the same movement while moving sideward, forward or backward with either walking or dancing steps.

CIRCLING MOVEMENTS

Most of the skills listed under "Circling Movements" in the chapter on clubs can be done with the wand, holding the wand at one end with one hand. See pages 269–281 for these exercises.

THROWING AND CATCHING MOVEMENTS

The wand may be tossed by one hand and caught with the same hand, the other hand, or both hands. It can also be tossed with both hands and caught with one or both hands. In high throwing movements the wand may also rotate in the air. To help minimize the impact of the catch, the wand should be caught above the horizontal with a downward motion of the arm.

In the beginning, practice with low tosses and later with higher and higher ones. The following are some of the more common throwing exercises.

1. Two-Handed Throw
Stand with the knees slightly bent, holding the wand in front of the body in both hands with the palms of the hands facing down. Toss the wand upward, attaining complete body extension. Catch the wand from above

in both hands with the palms of the hands facing down, while absorbing the force of the falling wand by bending the hips and knees.

Variations:
a) Practice throwing and catching the wand with both hands, holding the palms of the hands up.

b) Clap twice before catching the wand.

c) Throw the wand up and make a half or full turn before catching it.

d) Do one low toss and one high one. Alternate low and high throws.

e) Catch the wand in a deep squat position.

f) Perform the same movement while doing walking or dancing steps.

2. Overhead Throw *(wand horizontal)*

Stand with the feet in a wide straddle, arms extended to the side and the wand held horizontal in the right hand, palm facing downward. Throw the wand over the head, keeping it horizontal in the air, and catch it with the left hand as the weight is shifted from the right foot to the left. Repeat the movement with the left hand.

3. Overhead Throw *(wand vertical)*

Stand with the feet in a wide straddle, arms extended to the side and the wand held vertical in the right hand, palm facing forward. Throw the wand over the head, keeping the wand vertical in the air, and catch it with the left hand as the weight is shifted from the right foot to the left. Repeat the movement with the left hand.

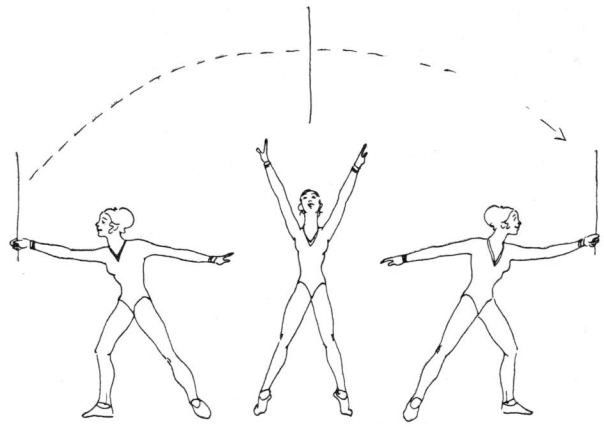

4. Overhead Throw *(wand rotating)*

Stand with the feet in a wide straddle, arms extended to the sides and the wand held horizontal in the right hand, palm facing upward. Throw the wand over the head so that it will rotate 360° in the air. Catch it with the left hand, palm facing down. Repeat the movement with the left hand.

Variation:
Walk forward while tossing the wand over the head alternately with the right and left hand.

5. Throw with a Spin
Stand with left arm in side extension and the right arm extended forward, holding the wand horizontal in front of the body. The right hand holds the wand in the middle with the palm of the hand facing down. Turn the outside of the wand down and after a half-turn release the wand. It should rotate at least once in the air parallel with the body, before you catch it in the right hand (with the palm of the hand facing down). Practice this with the left hand also.

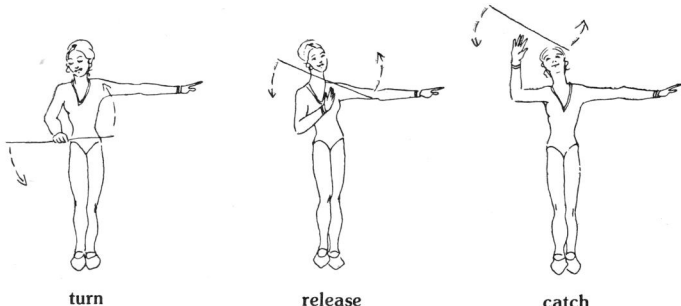

turn   release   catch

Variations:
a) Throw the wand high so it will rotate two or three times in the air.

b) After the wand is caught continue to rotate it in the hand. (See "Turning movements" on page 315.

c) Do the same movement but catch the wand with the left hand. Then throw the wand from the left hand back to the right. Establish a time pattern of throws with alternating hands.

d) Do the same toss with walking or dancing steps.

6. Partner Tossing
Partners stand facing each other, holding the wand in front of their bodies in both hands with the palms of their hands facing down. Each throws her wand in an arc to her partner, one tossing the wand high, the other low. Each catches her partner's wand in both hands with the

palms of the hands facing down. Repeat the movement several times. Try to increase the distance between partners to fifteen feet.

315

Wands, Flags, and Scarves

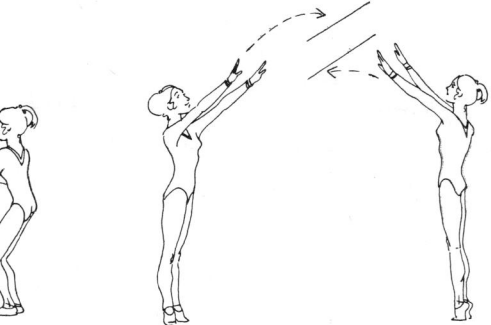

Variation:
Practice throwing and catching with both hands holding the palms of the hands up.

TURNING MOVEMENTS

The wand may be turned around its horizontal or vertical axis by spinning it with the thumb and fingers or by turning it through the use of arm movements.

1. Turning in Frontal Plane

Stand with arms extended over the head, both hands holding the wand horizontal and the palms of the hands facing forward. Turn the wand downward into a side bend to the left as the arms move into fourth position (right arm above the head and left arm in front of the body). Then reverse the movement to return to the starting position. Repeat to the opposite side.

Variation:
Perform a balancé from side to side as you do a sidebend on each balancé.

2. Turning in Horizontal Plane

Stand with arms extended over the head, wand held horizontally with both hands, palms facing forward. Turn wand by swinging the right arm in front of the head to the left as the left arm swings to the right behind the head. Then reverse the movement to return to the starting position. Repeat to the opposite side.

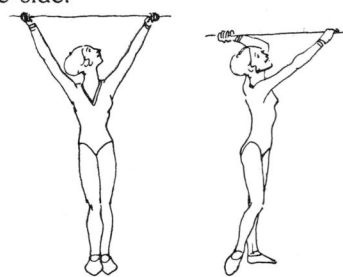

Variation:
Combine the exercise with dancing steps.

3. Horizontal Spin

Stand holding the wand horizontally in the middle in front of the body with the right hand, palm facing down. Spin the wand horizontally with three fingers—thumb, index and middle fingers.

Variations:

a) Change the spinning wand in front of the body from one hand to the other without interrupting the rotation of the wand.

b) Twirl the horizontal wand over the head with palm facing up.

c) Combine the horizontal spin with different kinds of walking and dancing steps.

4. Horizontal Twirl Above and Below the Arm

Stand with arms extended to the side, wand held in the middle with the right hand, palm facing up. Twirl the wand horizontally above the arm, then make a circle below the arm. To be able to do this exercise smooth-

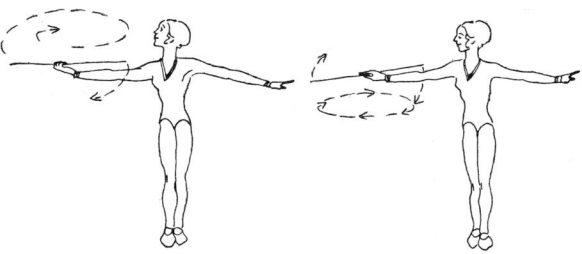

ly the hand must rotate downward and upward in a continuous successive motion. Repeat several times, then practice it with the left hand also. Practice twirling the wand in the opposite direction also.

5. Twirl in Front and in Back of the Arm
Stand holding the wand with the right hand in the middle, palm facing down. Twirl the wand clockwise in front of the arm and end the circle in a reverse grip (palm facing up). Then twirl it clockwise in back of the arm and end the movement in a regular grip. Repeat several times, then practice with the left hand also. To be able to do this movement smoothly the hand must rotate downward and upward in a continuous successive motion.

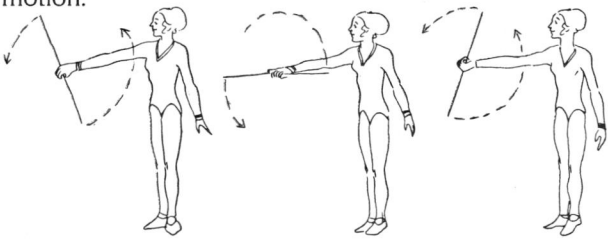

Variations:

a) Do the same movement but circle the wand counterclockwise.

b) Do the same movement while moving sideward, forward or backward with either walking or dancing steps.

6. Twirl in Front and in Back of the Head
Stand with right arm extended over the head, left arm in side extension. Hold the horizontal wand in the middle with the right hand, palm facing down. Circle the wand in front of the head, then in back of the head as described in number 5. Repeat the exercise several times in a smooth continuous manner. Practice with the left hand also.

Variation:
Do the same variations as number 5.

7. Two-Handed Twirl

Stand holding the wand in the middle, in front of the body with the right hand, palm facing down. Do a half-turn with the wand clockwise, until the palm faces upward, then bring the left hand *over* the right (palm of the hand facing up) and rotate the wand another half turn clockwise so it falls into the left hand (palm up) between the thumb and index finger. Immediately let go with the right hand and continue turning the wand with the left hand clockwise. When the left hand faces downward regrasp the wand with the right hand (palm facing down) near to the left hand. At this point the left hand is released and you are ready to repeat the movement. Twirl the wand smoothly.

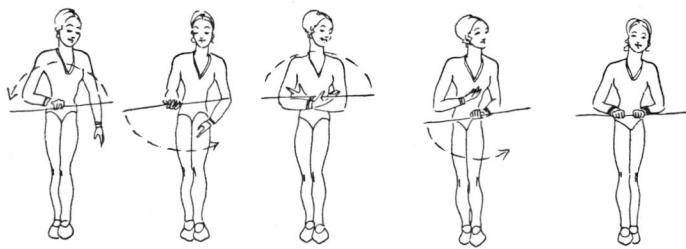

Variation:
Do the same movement with walking or dancing steps.

JUMPING MOVEMENTS

Jumping movements over the wand are difficult but are very spectacular.

1. Tuck Jump *(over horizontal wand)*

Stand holding the wand in front of you in an over grip. Jump twice in place and on the third one perform a tuck jump over the wand. This exercise is very challenging and can be achieved by few students only because great speed, flexibility and timing are required to perform it. Before attempting to jump over it practice the following skill:

Holding the wand at both ends, step over the wand with one foot and then the other, ending with the wand held in back of the buttocks. Reverse the movement by stepping over the wand backward, ending with the wand in front of the body in the starting position. Repeat this a few times and gradually bring hands closer together. Only attempt to jump over the wand if you can do this exercise with ease.

Variations:
a) Jump once in place and on the second jump tuck jump over the wand forward.

b) Tuck jump backward over the wand.

c) Tuck jump forward over the wand and immediately jump over it backward, returning to the starting position.

front view

2. Scissor Jump *(over vertical wand)*
Stand, placing the end of the vertical wand on the floor and holding the top with the right hand. Release the wand, scissor jump over it and catch it with the other hand. A good preliminary exercise for learning this movement is the following: stand and place the wand in a vertical balance position on the floor. Let go of the wand and lift one then the other leg over it and try to catch it before it falls.

3. Jumps *(over diagonal wand)*
Stand, resting the end of the wand on the floor so it is on a diagonal with the floor and holding the top of the wand with the left hand. Place all your weight on your left hand and jump over the diagonal wand sideways, ending with the wand at the right side of the body. Reverse the movement and end in the starting position.

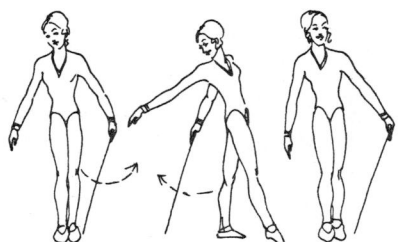

COMBINATION

Since the possible combinations are infinite you should attempt to create your own. The following is a simple example of what can be done.

1. Pose, run and hop while turning the wand in the frontal plane.
2. Pass the wand under the leg from the left hand to the right, then swing it under the leg while you perform a cat leap over it.
3. Circle the wand in back and in front of the body, as one would circle a club; then transfer it to the left hand behind the body.
4. Twirl the wand in front and in back of the left arm and then change hands in front of the body.
5. Twirl the wand horizontally in front of the body, then twirl it over the head while changing hands and turning around.
6. Twirl the wand over the right arm horizontally then toss it up in front of the body and catch it with both hands in kneeling position.

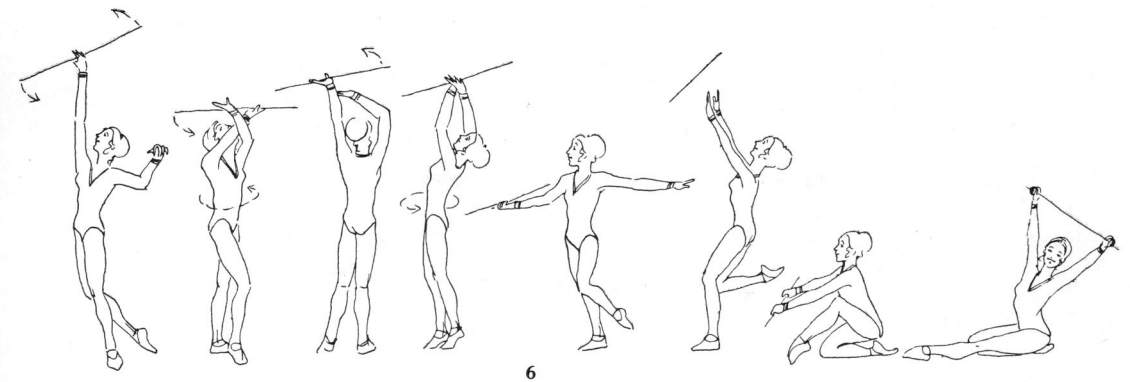

6

FLAGS

The length and width of the flags can vary. The longer the flags the greater the amount of skill that is required to work with them. The shape of the flag can vary also: it can be rectangular, square, or triangular. Whatever its shape, the flag is a very decorative hand apparatus for demonstrations and one that can be easily constructed by the gymnast or the teacher.

The *fabric* of a flag should have a flowing, light character. Silk or satin is the best but light nylon or other synthetic fabrics work just as well.

The *length of the flag* should be from 80 to 100 cm (31½″–39⅜″) for juniors and from 130 to 150 cm (51⅛″–59″) for adults.

The *width of the flag* should be from 35 to 60 cm (13¾″–23⅝″).

The *stick* to which the flag is attached should be wood. The part of the stick held in the hand may be covered by a thin anti-slip material such as tape, or it may end in a little knob like the club. It may also have a rotating handle of about 10 to 12 cm (3⅞″–4¾″) long.

The *length of the stick* should be 50 to 90 cm (19⅝″–35⅜″) and the *diameter* should be from 1 to 1½ cm (⅜″–⅝″).

Attachment of the Material to the Stick

It is not advisable to staple, nail, or tape the material onto the stick because the flag gets easily tangled around the stick. The material may be stapled to the stick, however, if the wood stick has a rotating handle which prevents the flag from getting tangled around it. If you do not have a stick with a rotating handle, sew or tape a thin wire to the width of the flag that is to be attached to the stick. It is advisable to have a ½" wide stiffening material affixed where the wire is attached to the flag to protect the fabric. Connect the two ends of the wire to the stick.

Flag routines are usually performed with two flags. The flags may both be held in one hand or one may be held in each hand. This lends great variety to a routine and allows very interesting compositions to be created.

Not all music is suitable for flag routines. The music should have a flowing quality and a medium tempo. The speed of the movements with the flag must be fast enough so that the flag always follows the stick. Lively marches or other 2/4 and 4/4 meter music are most appropriate for flag routines. If the flag hangs downward the movements are too slow. If the music is too fast the gymnast will not have time to perform the movements to their fullest possible range.

The flag can be used in a manner similar to the club. Many teachers prefer to introduce the use of the flag before the club because they are easier to work with and the fast, intricate club techniques can be mastered more readily if they are first attempted with flags. For these movements refer to chapter 7, "Clubs." This chapter deals only with movements characteristic of the flag.

SWINGING MOVEMENTS

The flag is a typical swinging hand apparatus. While swinging the flag, waves may be performed. These exercises are executed in a manner similar to that for serpentine movements with the ribbon. The waves should be the result of wrist action and the wave-like pattern should continue out to the end of the flag. When using two flags the waves can run parallel to each other or in opposite directions.

1. Swing Across the Body

Stand in a wide straddle with weight on the right foot, the arms extended to the right side and the flags held in a regular grip. Swing the flags in front of the body to the left then back to the right side. Move the hands evenly and continuously down and up from side to side in order to sketch perfect parallel waves. Transfer weight from side to side while swinging the flags.

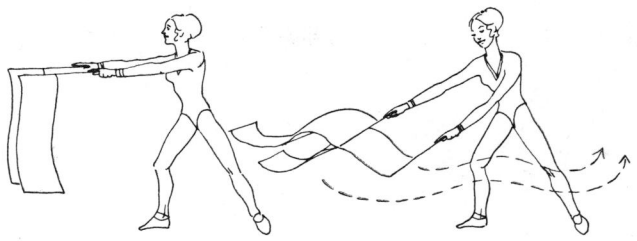

Variation:
Do the same exercise with walking or dancing steps.

2. Swing Forward and Backward
Stand with the arms extended horizontally forward and the flags held in a regular grip. Swing both flags backward at the side of the body; then swing them forward back to the starting position. Move the hands simultaneously inward and outward opposite to each other in order to sketch opposite waves.

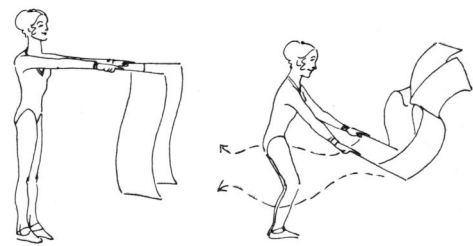

Variation:
Do the same movement with forward or backward walking steps.

3. Swing Overhead
Stand with the arms extended sideward, the flags held in a regular grip. Swing the flags downward, forward, upward over the head to the rear, then perform parallel waves over the head with a small left to right or right to left action of the hands.

Variations:
a) Do the same movement while moving forward with either walking or dancing steps.

b) Perform the same swing with various jumps.

c) Do all the above movements while performing opposite waves over the head.

4. Swing Under the Leg
Stand holding two flags in the right hand, out to the right side. Swing the flags horizontally slightly above floor level, passing over them with a jump. Also practice swinging the two flags with the left hand.

Variation:
Do a few running steps and then perform different jumps or leaps while swinging the flags under the legs.

5. Swing and Catch
Stand holding two flags in the right hand, out to the right side. Swing the flags upward, over the head toward the left side, then back toward

the right side and catch the ends of the flags with the left hand. Then turn around while holding the flags with two hands.

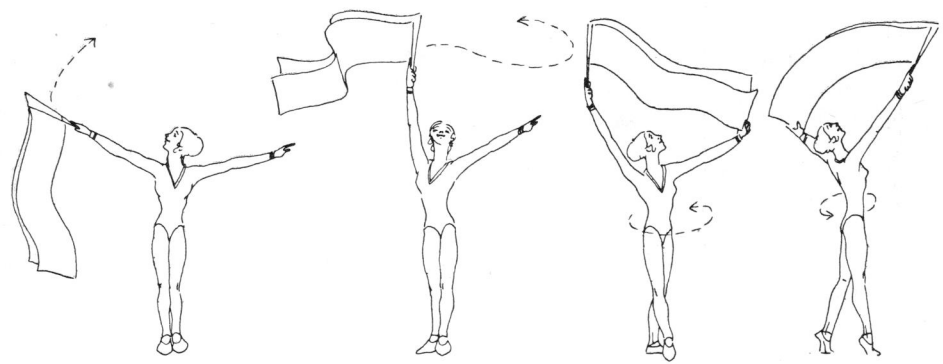

CIRCLING MOVEMENTS

Most of the circling movements and figure eights described for clubs can be performed with the flags. Some of the movements cannot be executed however because: 1) sometimes the stick of the flag is longer than the club, and 2) the flag would touch the body. The flags may be circled in the frontal, sagittal, and horizontal planes. Here only one example for each plane will be given, for more exercises see the chapter 7 "Clubs."

1. Circle in the Frontal Plane
Stand holding the flags in a regular grip with the arms extended diagonally upward. Circle the right flag downward to the right and simultaneously circle the left flag downward to the left. The flags will cross in front of the head. Practice crossing with the right flag in front, then with the left flag in front.

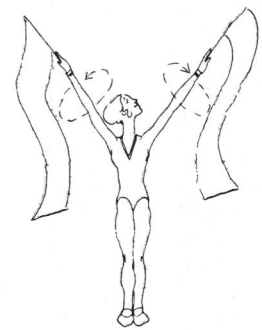

Variations:
a) Circle the flags in the opposite directions.
b) Do the above movements while moving sideward, forward or backward with walking or dancing steps.

2. Circle in the Sagittal Plane
Stand with the arms extended horizontally forward, flags held loosely in a reverse grip. Circle the flags downward outside of the arms with slightly bent elbows. Repeat several times.

Variations:

a) Circle the flags in the opposite direction.

b) Do the same movement with walking or dancing steps.

3. Horizontal Circles

Stand with the arms extended to the sides, holding two flags in the left hand. Perform horizontal circles inward overhead. Repeat with the right hand.

Variations:

a) Perform horizontal circles outward overhead.

b) Do the same movement while moving forward or backward with either walking or dancing steps.

c) Do the same movement while performing different kinds of turns, jumps or leaps.

THROWING AND CATCHING MOVEMENTS

Throwing and catching are the most difficult movements to perform with the flags. They can be performed in both the frontal and sagittal planes. Throwing and catching skills are usually combined with swinging and circling movements.

The flags must be tossed high with a good follow through so they will not collapse in flight. They must be caught at the end of the stick. Only one example will be given for each plane. See throwing and catching movements in chapters 6 "Ribbons" and 7 "Clubs" for additional exercises.

1. Throw in the Frontal Plane

Stand with arms extended to the side, flags held in a reverse grip. Swing the flags upward and toss them high over the head, one slightly in front of the other to avoid collision. Catch them with the opposite hands, palms facing upward.

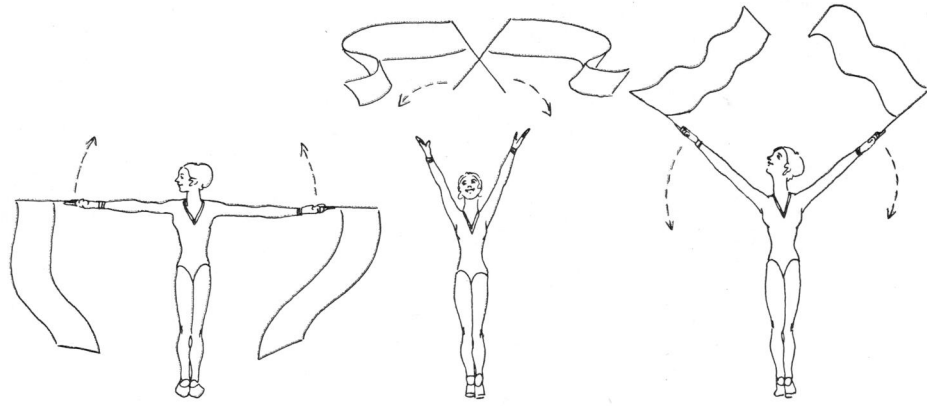

2. Throw in the Sagittal Plane

Stand with the left arm extended forward, flag held in a regular grip and the right arm extended backward, flag held in a reverse grip. Swing the left arm downward and backward, simultaneously swing the right arm upward in back of you and throw the right flag over the head, catching it in front with the right hand. Then swing the right arm downward and backward as you swing the left arm upward in back of you, and throw the left flag over the head in the sagittal plane. Repeat several times.

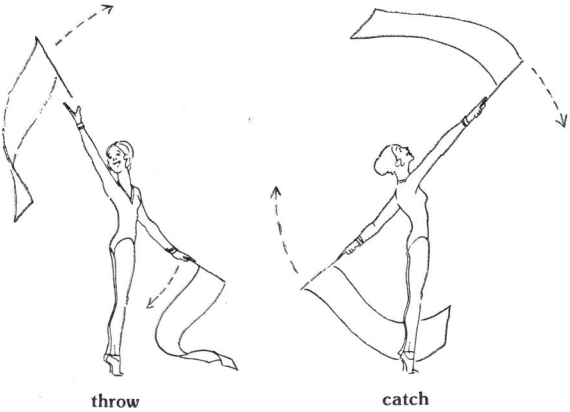

throw   catch

COMBINATION

The possible combinations of flag movements are limitless. One can have one flag in each hand, two flags in one hand, and an endless passing of one or two flags from one hand to the other. Try to combine movements into short combinations. Be sure that one movement allows a smooth transition to the next one. The following is an example of a short combination.

1. Pose, holding flags in the left hand.
2. Do a quarter turn to the right while swinging the flags over the head and passing one flag to the right hand.
3. Separate the arms and swing the flags over the head. Holding the arms diagonally upward, circle the flags downward in front of the head.
4. Swing left flag downward, then the right one. As soon as the right flag is down with the left one, continue to swing both flags upward and toss them over the head in the frontal plane while walking forward.
5. Swing the right flag downward, to the left, and upward, then swing both flags over the head as you pass the left flag to the right hand.
6. Perform a horizontal circle over the head with the flags as you turn around. Then pass one flag to the left hand and perform a body wave while swinging the flags forward, backward, and over the head, making a large circle with the flag at the sides of the body.
7. Run and leap while waving the flags over the head.
8. Swing the left flag low in front of the body, as the right flag swings over the head. Then swing them to a side extension.
9. Swing both flags downward and pass left flag to right hand in front of the body.
10. Swing the flags with the right hand over the head to the left, then back to the right and catch the ends of the flags with the left hand while you step forward to a finishing pose.

SCARVES

The use of the scarf in rhythmic gymnastics has become very popular. The scarf, which must be made of a very fine, soft fabric, is rectangular in form. The fabric must be light enough so that the scarf will not collapse. If the wrong kind of fabric is used the gymnast cannot perform some of the typical scarf exercises in her combinations because the scarf will tangle.

It is very easy to make a scarf. When you buy your fabric buy enough so that when you cut out the scarf, you can leave ¼″ on each side for a hem. When you hem each side, fold the material over ⅛″ and then ⅛″ again, and stitch up the hem.

Fabric: silk, satin, or nylon or other light synthetic fabric.

Length of scarf: from 150 to 200 cm (59″–78¾″)

Width of scarf: from 85 to 100 cm (33½″–39⅜″)

Movements with the scarf should be light, floating, and smooth. The scarf should never touch the floor or the body because this interrupts the flow of movements. Avoid sharp, fast movements, otherwise the flight of the scarf will not be smooth, since the material does not allow changing the speed of movements.

Use the scarf as an extension of the body so that when the body moves, the scarf moves, and vise versa. The whole body should be involved in every exercise. The focus should be on the scarf so that the movement of the body follows the scarf. The scarf, like all the other hand apparatus, must be in motion at all times.

The exercises should be performed with music. Select music that has a flowing quality and a medium tempo—that can be harmonized with the movement of the body and the scarf.

The scarf may be held in one hand or both hands, either along its length or along its width at the corners. When the scarf is held with one hand it can be moved in much the same way as one moves ribbons or clubs. For this reason, only movements peculiar to the scarf will be described here.

SWINGING MOVEMENTS

All scarf-swinging movements must be accompanied by body waves. There should be a total flow in the sense that every part of the body is coordinated with the swinging motion of the scarf.

1. Swing Across the Body

Stand with the arms extended to the right and the scarf held in both hands on the corners of the narrower side. Swing the scarf across the body to the left, then back across the body to the right side. Repeat several times. Keep the scarf stretched in the air.

Variations:

a) Do the same movement while walking forward or backward.

b) Do the same movement with a balancé from side to side.

2. Swing Around the Body

Stand holding the scarf with both hands, on the narrower side, left arm extended overhead and right arm to the side. Swing the right arm overhead toward the left, simultaneously bend the left arm and swing it across the body. Continue swinging the scarf in a circle around the body to the left, with the trunk arching backward and finish in the original position. Do this exercise continuously a couple of times then repeat it in the opposite direction.

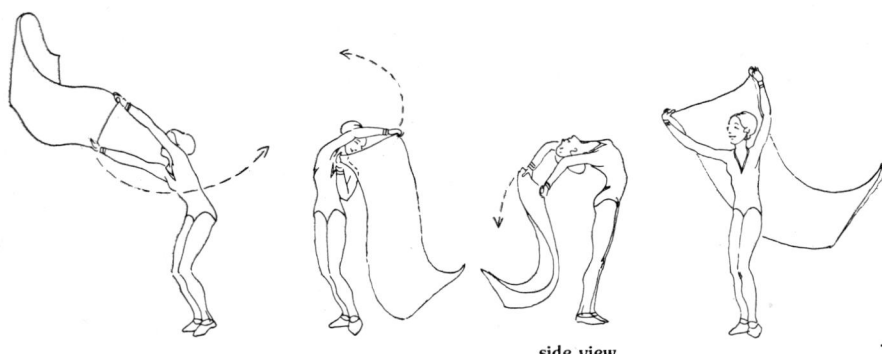

side view

3. Swing and Catch

Stand with the arms extended to the right side and the scarf held with both hands on the narrower side. Swing the scarf across the body, right arm above the left. Let go of the scarf with the right hand and with that hand catch the scarf at the opposite corner. Stretch the arms to the sides, holding the scarf in front of the body. Continue swinging the scarf around the body as described in no. 2 above.

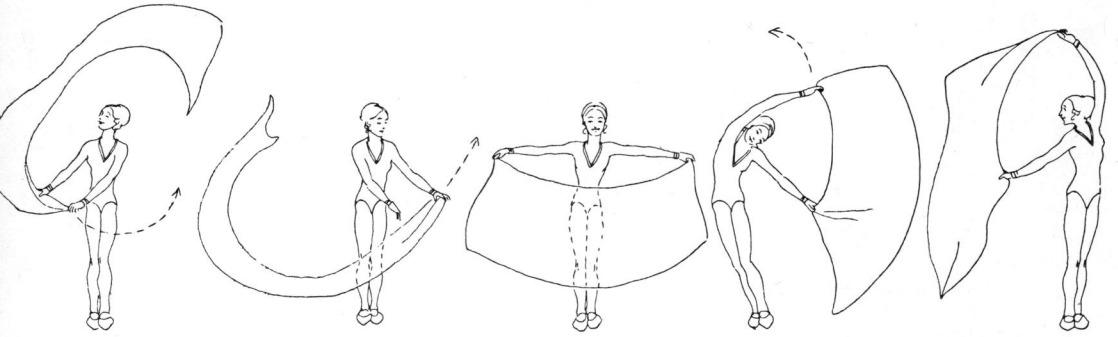

Variation:
Combine this movement with walking or dancing steps.

4. Swing Overhead

Holding the scarf with both hands on the narrow side, stand with the arms extended overhead and the scarf behind the body. Swing the scarf overhead to the front as you execute a body wave forward. Then swing the scarf upward overhead to the rear while you perform a body wave backward. Repeat this several times to get the feeling of the continuous flow of movement.

5. Figure Eight

Stand with arms extended to the right side and the scarf held in both hands on the wider side. Sketch a figure eight from the right to the left in front of the body with the right hand only. Keep the left arm in place in front of the body while the right hand sketches a figure eight. Rotate the right arm and hand in and out in a continuous successive motion.

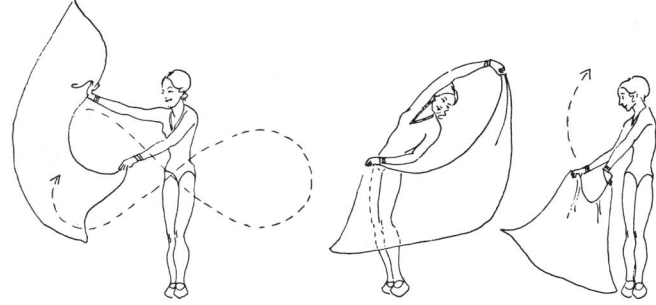

Variations:

a) Perform the same movement with the left hand.

b) Sketch a frontal figure eight using both hands simultaneously.

c) Perform figure eights in the sagittal plane with one or both hands.

d) Combine the above movements with walking or dancing steps.

SERPENTINE MOVEMENTS

These exercises are executed in much the same manner as the serpentine movements with the ribbon. Serpentines should be the result of fast wrist action and the wave-like pattern should continue to the end of the scarf. The waves may be performed on various levels both vertically and horizontally. Here only one example for each kind will be given; for more exercises see chapter 6, "Ribbons."

1. Vertical Serpentines

Stand with arms extended forward and the scarf held with both hands on the narrower end. Perform vertical waves in front of the body while

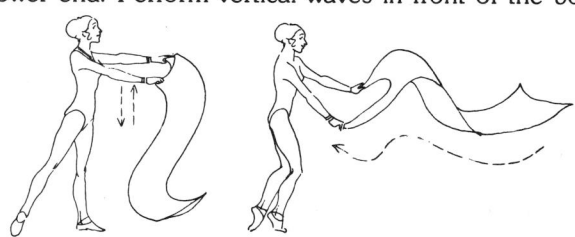

walking backwards. Move the arms and hands evenly up and down in order to form perfect vertical waves.

Variations:
a) Perform vertical serpents by holding the scarf with one hand only or holding it with two hands on the wider side.
b) Perform vertical waves either on the left or right side of the body.
c) Do vertical waves from left to right or right to left in front of the body.
d) Do vertical waves at different levels (i.e., at chest height or above the head).

2. Horizontal Serpentines
Horizontal serpentines may move either downward or upward. They may be performed in place or with walking or dancing steps. Hold the scarf with one hand by an end corner. Move the hand evenly from side to side in order to sketch a horizontal wave.

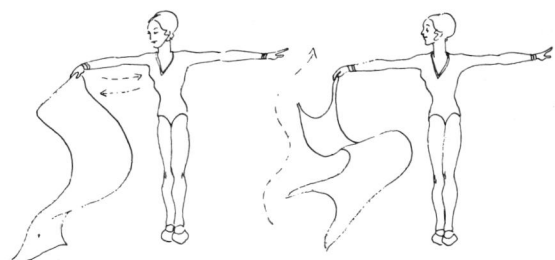

THROWING AND CATCHING MOVEMENTS

Throwing movements can be performed in the frontal and sagittal planes. The scarf may be tossed by one hand and caught with the same hand, the other hand, or both hands. It can also be tossed with both hands and caught with one or both hands. Throwing and catching movements are difficult with a scarf but they are great fun to perform. Throw the scarf with a good follow through so that it will be stretched and will not collapse in the air.

1. One-Handed Throw *(in the frontal plane)*
Stand with the arms extended to the side and the scarf held in the right hand by the corner. Swing the scarf downward across the body to the

left, back to the right and toss it high overhead. Catch it by a corner with the left hand. Repeat with the left hand.

Variations:

a) Do the same movement while walking forward or backward.

b) Do the same movement with a balancé from side to side.

c) Do the same movement but catch the scarf at the top end.

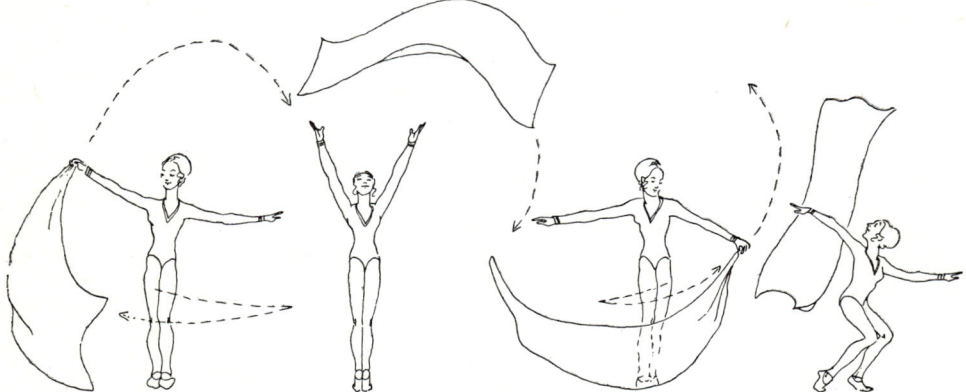

2. One-Handed Throw *(in the sagittal plane)*
Stand holding the scarf by its corner in the right hand. Swing the right arm forward and upward and toss the scarf overhead. Catch the other end of the scarf above the head with the right hand.

Variations:

a) Catch the scarf with the left hand.

b) Do the same movement with walking or dancing steps.

3. Overhead Throw *(backward)*

Stand with arms extended forward and the scarf held in both hands on the narrower side. Swing the arms downward, then upward and toss the scarf overhead. The scarf will sail backward overhead. Catch it with both hands at the opposite side.

Variations:
a) Do the same movement in a lunge position.

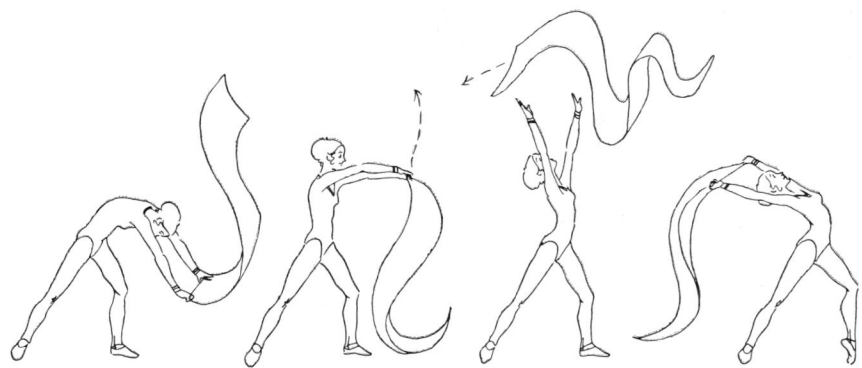

b) Do the same movement with walking or dancing steps.

4. Overhead Throw *(forward)*

Hold the scarf in both hands on the narrower side. Stand with arms extended overhead and the scarf behind the body. Swing the scarf upward and let it flow downward behind the body, then toss it forward overhead while you are walking forward. Catch the opposite end in front of the body with both hands.

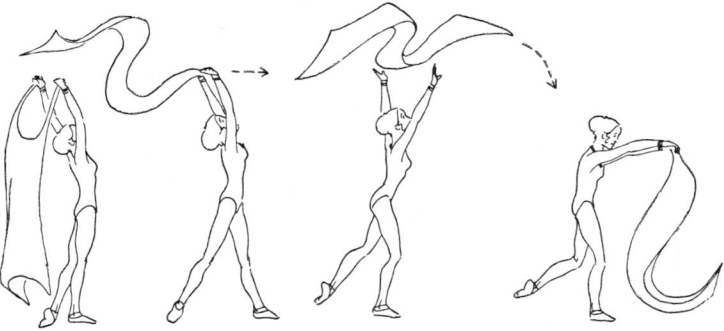

5. Throw and Turn

Stand in a wide straddle with weight on the right foot. Hold the scarf with both hands on the narrower side, in front of the body. Turn the body to the right, swing the scarf upward, and toss it overhead. Immediately do a half-turn and catch the scarf with both hands at the left side.

COMBINATION

Combine swinging, tossing, and waving movements. Be sure that one movement flows into another without interruption of the rhythm. The following is an example of a simple combination.

1. Starting pose with both hands holding the scarf by the narrower side and the scarf hanging behind the body.
2. Step forward into a moderate arabesque; then run forward while the scarf flows behind the head.
3. Swing the scarf over the head to the front while you execute a body wave forward.
4. Step into a lunge position and do a body wave backward as you swing the scarf upward and throw it overhead toward the back. Catch the scarf at the opposite end with both hands.
5. Release the scarf with the right hand and swing it with the left arm across the body to the right, back to the left, and to the rear. Change hands behind the body and swing the scarf forward with the right hand.
6. Do a moderate arabesque turn as you perform an inward horizontal circle with the scarf above the head.
7. Pass the scarf from the right hand to the left, in front of the body.
8. Run and leap while you do a sagittal circle with the scarf beside the left side of the body. Swing the scarf forward and catch it with the right hand again.
9. Run backward as you do vertical waves in front of you.
10. Step-hop while swinging the scarf over the head to the rear. Then kneel down and swing the scarf forward and overhead again to the finishing pose.

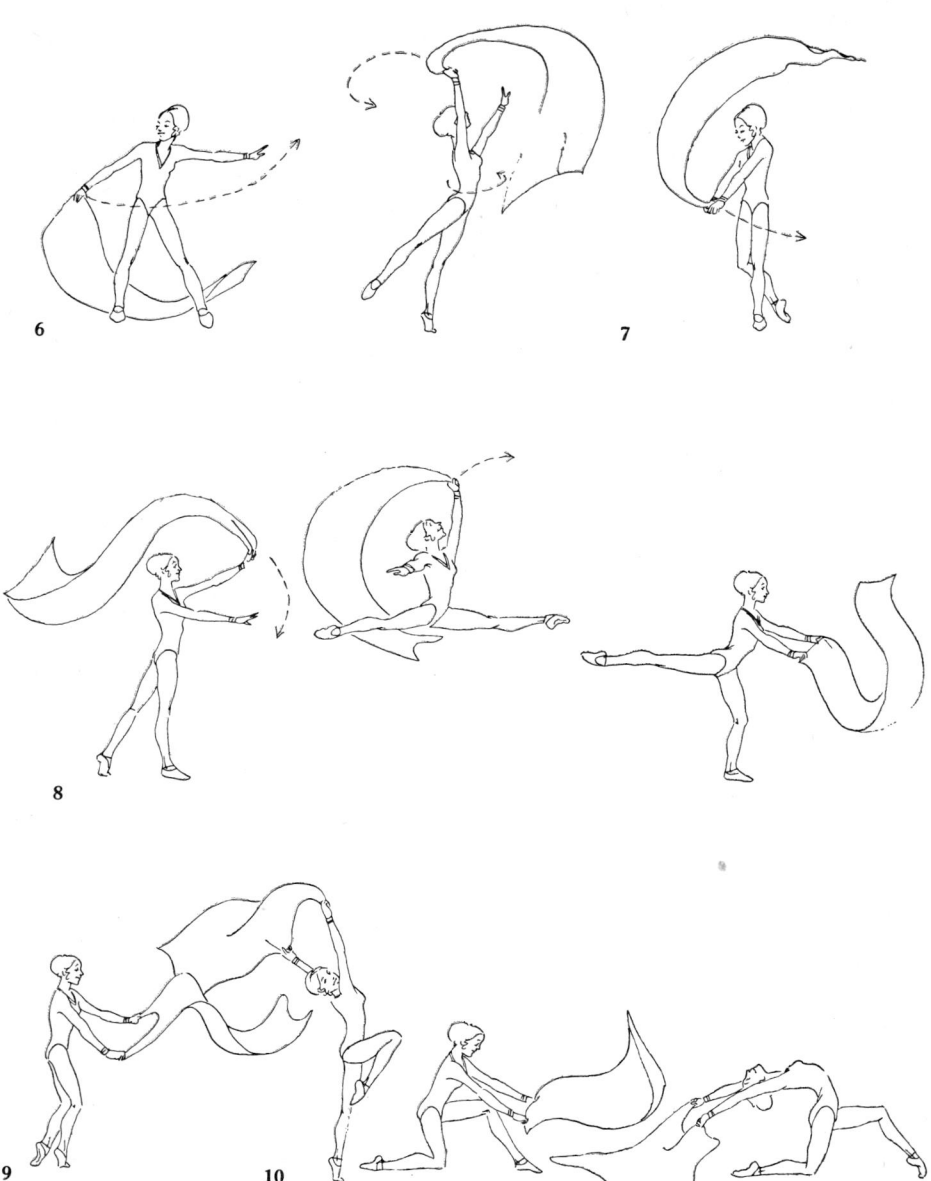

SUGGESTED GROUP ASSIGNMENT FOR SCARVES

After several individual improvisational activities with wands, flags, and scarves the teacher should set up a problem to be solved by small groups of students. Working in a group will help to develop group responsibility. Students will also learn how to synchronize their movements with others. Group assignments will also promote a feeling of team effort. As a rule students become completely involved with their problem-solving project and work twice as hard as usual.

Presented below is a problem-solving assignment for small groups working with scarves. The problem-solving method should also be utilized with wands and flags.

Problem: There are four formations illustrated below. Be inventive in the transitions from one formation to another.

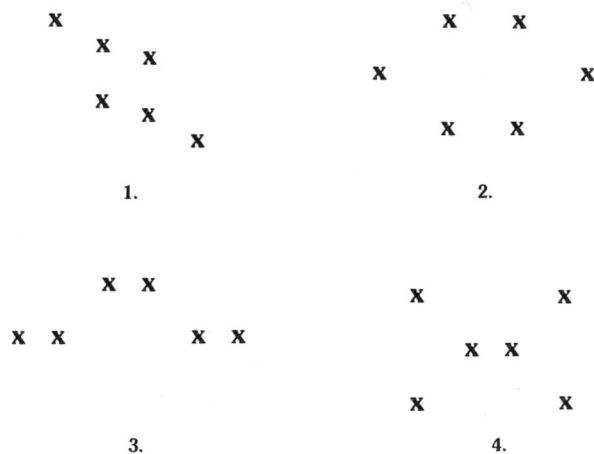

A. Use smooth, flowing movements.

B. Use your whole body to follow the movement of the scarf.

C. Try to make the various movements flow in perfect harmony with the music.

Music—Borodin "Dance of the Young Maidens" from the opera "Prince Igor"—Arrangement for scarves by H. Jones.

This music has a smooth, flowing quality which is very suitable for scarf compositions.

Music for Scarf Group Assignment

Guidelines for Planning an MRG Unit

Chapter 9

Modern rhythmic gymnastics constitutes a valuable addition to any physical education curriculum because it contributes to almost every objective of a good physical education program. A well planned, modern rhythmic gymnastics program contributes to neuromuscular coordination, balance, endurance, flexibility, agility, poise, rhythmic and kinesthetic sense and bilateral development of the body. The use of hand apparatuses helps the performer to develop manipulative skills, while at the same time, concentration on the hand apparatus helps her overcome self consciousness, allowing her movements to become less inhibited and more natural. In addition, modern rhythmic gymnastics may provide opportunities for creative expression.

Another advantage of including modern rhythmic gymnastics in a school gymnastics program is that each student can be active during the whole class period. No one has to wait for her turn to perform on an apparatus since each student has her own hand apparatus to work with.

FACTORS TO CONSIDER WHEN PLANNING A UNIT

A number of factors such as facilities and equipment available, age and ability of students, and amount of time available must be considered when planning a modern rhythmic gymnastic unit. Because all of these factors are interrelated, each teaching situation needs a custom-made unit.

FACILITIES AND EQUIPMENT

Guidelines for Planning an MRG Unit

The unit must be planned according to the space and equipment available. The facility must be large enough so that the entire class can be active at the same time and each student can move freely. The area should have a hardwood floor; a floor exercise mat is not necessary. The ceiling must be at least twenty feet high.

Most likely your school will not have all hand apparatus available so you must plan accordingly. When you have a limited budget buy balls and ropes first and then hoops, ribbons, and clubs. Before ordering your equipment, study the catalogues of major companies that supply gymnastic equipment. The author, at the present, knows of only one company in the United States that carries all hand apparatus that meet F.I.G. regulations. It is:

> Gymnastic Supply Company
> 247 West 6th Street
> San Pedro, CA 90733
> (213) 831-0131

A record player, tape recorder, hand drum, tapes, and records will also be needed for musical accompaniment. There are a few records that have been made especially for modern rhythmic gymnastics. These records are available at some local stores, as well as through the manufacturer.

Some records to consider when planning your unit are:

From *Hoctor Records,* Waldwick, New Jersey—

HLP/4010/Vol. I. Rhythmic Gymnastics, Balls and Ropes (Drury-Schmid)
HLP/4010/Vol. II. Rhythmic Gymnastics, Clubs and Hoops (Drury-Schmid)
HLP/4109 Body Waves in Modern Gymnastics (Bakos)
HLP/4110 Dance Combinations in Modern Gymnastics (Bakos)
HLP/4129 Music for Streamer Routines (Bakos)
HLP/4154 Basic Ballet for the Gymnast (Bakos)
HLP/4158 Music for Teaching Rhythmic Gymnastics (Kjeldsen)

From *Kimbo Educational Records,* Deal, New Jersey—

KLP/4000 Rhythmic Rope Jumping (Hoyman)
KLP/4030 Ball Gymnastics (Hoyman)
KLP/5040 Rhythmic Gymnastics, Hoops and Indian Clubs (Hoyman)

Composers to consider for music to accompany modern rhythmic gymnastics are: Bartok, Brahms, Chopin, Gershwin, Kodaly, Prokofiev, Ravel, Satie, Shostakovich, Sibelius, Stravinsky, and Tchaikovsky. You may listen to these composers' works in the school or city record libraries before you decide what music to buy. Try folk dance records such as schottisches, czardas, and polkas. Popular music may also be used if the rhythm is right. Popular music will interest students especially if they are creating their own combinations.

AGE

Developmental level, interests and needs of different age groups must be considered in unit planning. For example, at a higher maturity level more self evaluation and self directed activities are included.

SKILL LEVEL

The skill level of a group will determine what should be taught in a unit. At the beginning level, emphasis must be on techniques essential to modern rhythmic gymnastics such as getting the feel of continuous, flowing body movements. The unit should provide a movement experience that develops flexibility, agility, endurance, balance, and good posture. Since at the beginning level the average student is hesitant about performing in front of anyone, even her peers, students should not be asked to perform alone but rather in small groups. At higher levels students may attempt more complex rhythmic and movement patterns and should be encouraged to perform with expression and to begin creating their own patterns to music. A unit should be planned to meet the needs of all skill levels within the class.

LENGTH OF THE UNIT

The length of the unit has an effect upon what is to be taught and what should be expected from the students at the end of the unit. One cannot hope for the same progress at the conclusion of a three week unit as at the conclusion of a six week unit.

LENGTH OF INSTRUCTIONAL PERIOD

The length of class periods will influence what should be included in each class and what needs to be accomplished in a lesson. The class period might follow an outline such as this:

a) Roll call and information given to the whole group. (3–5 minutes)

b) Warm-up (5–10 minutes). The whole group works together and engages in running, limbering, stretching, and other exercises to warm up the body and prepare it for the day's lesson.

c) Review of previously learned material. (The progress of the students will determine how much time is needed here.)

d) Day's lesson (dependent upon available class time). Much can be accomplished if the class is divided into ability groups and a different activity is planned for each one.

e) Conclusion (5–10 minutes). Finish the lesson with discussion, demonstration, or some other such activity to reaffirm what has been learned during the lesson.

TEACHING METHODS

Teaching method refers to the way a teacher presents the material to be learned. Methods of teaching depend upon the age of the student and the level of skill to be taught. Each teacher must judge which methods she can use most effectively with a particular class.

THE DIRECT APPROACH

The traditional approach of teaching an activity is the direct approach. In this method the teacher explains and demonstrates how a skill is performed. The students see and hear the explanation; then they try to copy or imitate the skill. However, because learning through imitation does not produce good results with all students, other methods should also be utilized.

THE INDIRECT APPROACH

a) *Movement Exploration,* or the discovery method, is used mostly with elementary school children. This method allows each child to progress at her own rate in a learning situation that permits individual experimentation. "Who can . . . ?", "Can you . . . ?", "How do you . . . ?", "What can . . . ?" are the types of questions often asked. For example: "Who can throw the ball and catch it while she's running?" "Can you roll your hoop and keep it from falling over?"

b) The *Task Method* is particularly advantageous when a class has varied skill levels. A series of tasks is ranged according to difficulty so that both beginners and advanced students may be challenged. The specific tasks may be posted or explained and demonstrated to the whole class. Then each student proceeds to master each task at her own rate. For example, rope jumping could be divided into tasks and presented to a class in the following way.

Perform each task six times with good form and without getting tangled in the rope before moving on to the next task.

Task 1—Basic forward jump, one jump for each swing.
Task 2—Basic backward jump, one jump for each swing.
Task 3—Step-hop in place turning the rope forward.
Task 4—Step-hop across the gymnasium.
Task 5—Step-hop in place turning the rope backward.
Task 6—Step-hop backward across the gymnasium.
Task 7—Run in place, turning the rope forward, one swing for each step.
Task 8—Run across the gymnasium, one swing for each running step.
Task 9—Run backward turning rope backward.
Task 10—Run forward but swing the rope backward.
And so on.

c) The *movement analysis* method provides a technical, analytical approach that many gymnasts need in order to master skills. Knowledge and application of mechanical principles can make crucial differences to them in learning a skill well. Also, when a student understands the basic principles of movements to be mastered she is ready to analyze performances. In this method the instructor teaches the principles of movement as they apply to the skills in modern rhythmic gymnastics.

d) With the *problem solving* method students are asked to find solutions to a problem. In seeking solution to the problem, the student is encouraged to analyze, synthesize and interrelate ideas and to be innovative.

Every teacher will combine some elements of all of the above-mentioned methods, thus using an eclectic approach in teaching. Most students learn best through a mixture of imitation, exploration, analysis, and conceptualization.

Specific teaching suggestions for each hand apparatus are given following the description of the exercises in each chapter.

GENERAL OBJECTIVES OF TEACHING MODERN RHYTHMIC GYMNASTICS

The objectives listed below are general; more specific ones should be planned by the teacher for the specific unit to be taught. This list, which serves to indicate the purposes of modern rhythmic gymnastics in general and does not attempt to spell out particular learning objectives, should help the teacher to consider specific objectives for her unit.

1. To develop strength, endurance, agility, flexibility, and balance.
2. To develop poise and grace through use of natural movements.
3. To develop elegance and flow of body movement.
4. To develop good posture.
5. To develop kinesthetic sense.
6. To develop movement skills using each hand apparatus.
7. To develop coordination, rhythm, and a sense of timing by combining movement with music.
8. To stimulate enjoyment of participation.
9. To learn the carryover values of one hand apparatus exercise into all other modern rhythmic gymnastics activities.
10. To provide an opportunity to work with partners and with a group.
11. To provide an opportunity for self evaluation and evaluation of others.
12. To develop better understanding of movement skills through creative experience.
13. To learn the components of a good modern rhythmic gymnastics routine.
14. To develop self confidence.
15. To develop a sense of creating through composing a routine.
16. To provide opportunities to perform in front of classmates and schoolmates, in a demonstration or competition.
17. To develop appreciation of esthetic, graceful, and harmonious movements.

A SIX-WEEK RESOURCE UNIT

This unit is planned for beginning secondary school students. Activities included are: exercises without hand apparatus and exercises with balls, ropes, hoops, and clubs. The teacher should make adjustments to fit her situation.

Unit Objectives

The following objectives are designed to serve as a guide in the selection of skills and experiences for the students and to describe the desired outcomes of the unit. Objectives should be made clear to the students early in the unit so they will strive to achieve them.

Physical Objectives

By the end of the unit the student will be able to:

1. Demonstrate fundamental locomotor and nonlocomotor movements. gymnastics.
2. Perform dance steps such as the step-hop, schottische, polka, and waltz in rhythm to music.
3. Execute the basic skills with the ball, rope, hoop, and clubs.
4. Combine movements with hand apparatus to music.
5. Perform the basic movements efficiently and gracefully.

Psychological and Social Objectives

By the end of the unit the student will be able to:

1. Enjoy rhythmic use of her body.
2. Appreciate the fundamentals of music as they relate to movement.
3. Appreciate good performance in modern rhythmic gymnastics.
4. Work with each other in a creative way.
5. Assume leadership and followship roles when working in a group.
6. Create movement sequences.
7. Perform in front of classmates and schoolmates.
8. Release tension.

Intellectual Objectives

By the end of the unit the student will be able to:

1. Tell about the history and current status of modern rhythmic gymnastics.
2. Describe the general judging rules of the sport.
3. Identify the phrases and recognize the variations in style, mood, tempo and dynamics of the music.

4. Analyze basic movements through knowledge of the mechanical principles involved.
5. Analyze routines on the basis of compositional principles such as totality, fluidity, variety, climax, and rhythm.

UNIT CONTENT

Skills and the *progression* from one exercise or group of exercises to another used for the unit will differ in each situation. It is likely that even for a beginning class each teacher will select varied skills and different sequences, combinations, and progressions. Therefore here only the activity is listed. The instructor should refer back to the respective chapters and choose skills according to the needs of her students.

During the *introduction* to the unit, explain the purposes, and desired outcomes of the unit, and the methods of instruction, evaluation, dress, and the like. Give a short lecture about the history of modern rhythmic gymnastics and, if possible, show a short movie.

The *warm-ups* before each lesson should include stretching and limbering exercises; body waves and balances; runs, skips, and slides; and small jumps. Special emphasis should be placed on good posture and proper use of the legs and feet in all exercises.

For *group assignments* divide the class into groups and hand out the problem of routine to be demonstrated. Have small groups work independently on the problem.

During the *sixth week* give the student an opportunity either to create a solo routine or to work with a group. Each group and individual may choose the equipment to use: hoop, ball, rope, or clubs. Both groups and individuals will present their routines to the rest of their class on Thursday and to the other classes on Friday of that week. All physical education classes of that period may be invited to attend the demonstration. This will give the students an opportunity to perform in front of an audience and will also educate the other students about modern rhythmic gymnastics. Demonstration to other classes should be encouraged only if your class is ready for it.

The six-week sample unit block on page 352 shows how the activities may be arranged.

Unit Block-Out

Week	Monday	Tuesday	Wednesday	Thursday	Friday
1	Introduction History Brief demonstration or movie	Basic locomotor and nonlocomotor movements	Dance steps Music analyzation: rhythm, accent, tempo, meter, etc.	Dance movements	Short sequences of dance movements
2	Introduction to ball exercises	Ball exercises	Ball exercises (short combinations)	Group assignment Group practice with ball	Ball group demonstration Class discussion-evaluation
3	Introduction to rope exercises	Rope exercises	Rope exercises (short combinations)	Group assignment Group practice with rope	Rope group demonstration Class discussion-evaluation
4	Introduction to hoop exercises	Hoop exercises	Hoop exercises (short combinations)	Group assignment Group practice with hoop	Hoop group demonstration Class discussion-evaluation
5	Introduction to club exercises	Club exercises	Club exercises (short combinations)	Group assignment Group practice with clubs	Club group demonstration Class discussion-evaluation
6	Written quiz Groups and individuals work according to preference	Individuals and groups practice their routines	Individuals and groups practice their routines	Individuals and groups demonstrate their routines to classmates Evaluation of routines	Individuals and groups demonstrate their routines to schoolmates

METHODS OF EVALUATION

Evaluation of students may be based on intellectual development (knowledge of techniques, rules, history, principles, etc.) and on everyday participation and performances. Intellectual development is usually tested by a written test or quiz. An example of questions which may be employed in a written quiz are given below:

Written Test
True or False

_(F)_ 1. The proper way to hold the ball is by grasping it with the fingers.

_(F)_ 2. When jumping with the rope you should jump very high so that the rope will have plenty of room to pass under your feet.

_(T)_ 3. The hoop should be constantly in motion and never held in the hand as a decoration.

_(F)_ 4. The weight of a club is about two pounds.

_(F)_ 5. When performing a routine the focus should always be toward the audience.

_(F)_ 6. When tossing the ball the motion should begin from the shoulders.

1. The first World Championships in modern gymnastics were held in _(1963)_ in _(Budapest, Hungary)_.

2. Rope jumping is an excellent means of developing _(endurance)_.

3. The gymnast must always use the entire _(body)_ and move in _(harmony)_ with the motion of the hand apparatus.

4. Hoop movements are swinging, circling, throwing and catching, _(turning)_, _(rolling)_, and _(passing through the hoop)_.

5. In an international competition the following hand apparatus can be used:
   a) _(ball)_   b) _(rope)_   c) _(hoop)_
   d) _(ribbon)_   e) _(clubs)_

6. The time limit of an individual competitive routine is from _(60)_ to _(90)_ seconds.

Short Answer Questions

1. What factors should be stressed in the rope jumping technique?
2. Describe the difference between a skip and a step-hop.
3. When watching a modern rhythmic gymnastic group routine, what factors should one look for in the performance?

Practical Test

Evaluation of demonstrations should be done not only by the instructor but also by the girls who should evaluate each other's routines after the performance. The following are suggestions on how to evaluate group and individual performances.

Group Routines (problem-solving)

Each routine will be worth twenty points and will be evaluated in four areas, each area worth 5 points. The four areas are:

1. Precision of solving problems (handed out in class)
2. Technical execution
3. Originality of composition
4. General harmony of the exercise.

They will be rated excellent (E), good (G), average (A), fair (F), or poor (P) in each area. Poor is worth 1 point, fair 2, average 3, good 4, and excellent 5.

Each student will be evaluated on her technical skills and the group as a whole will be evaluated in the other areas. In this way each girl's individual skills will be evaluated as well as the whole group project. On the facing page is a sample of a score sheet that might be used.

Mary Smith received a "good" technical execution (4 pts.) and her group's routine received a "good" in both precision and harmony (8 pts.) and an "average" in originality (3 pts.). Therefore, Mary's total number of points (final score) will be 15 points.

Group Routines (optional)

These routines will also be evaluated on a twenty point scale. The four areas are: 1) Value of difficulty (5 points); 2) Originality of combinations (5 points); 3) General harmony of the exercise (5 points); and 4) Execution (5 points).

Individual Routines

Individual routines will also be evaluated on a twenty point scale. The

Event: BALL												
Individual Performance								Group Performance				
Name	Final Score	E 5	G 4	A 3	F 2	P 1			E 5	G 4	A 3	F 2	P 1
1. Mary Smith	15	X					Precision	X			
2.							Originality		X		
3.							Harmony	X			
4.											
5.							Total: 11 points				
6.											

four areas are: 1) value of difficulty (5 points); 2) originality of combinations (5 points); 3) execution (5 points); and 4) general impression (5 points).

Some of the main points to look for when evaluating the routines are:

Difficulty—difficulty of movements and difficulty of exchanges of hand apparatus.
Composition—originality, variety of movements, variety of formations, use of area, smoothness of transition.
Harmony—harmony of movements with music, preciseness and beauty of the formations, good rhythm.
Execution—good form, lightness of execution, total body movement, good posture.
General impression—sureness, fluency, grace, and elegance in movements, expression.

The students may also evaluate their own group members and themselves on their performance and attitude. A sample of a group and self rating form follows on page 356.

Group and Self Evaluation Form

Group # _____

Hand apparatus _____

Evaluator's name _____

Use the following scale for evaluation:

poor—1
fair—2
average—3
good—4
excellent—5

Group Members

group interest						
cooperation						
democratic						
constructive member						
contributed ideas						
participation						
spirit						
leadership						
Total points						

Modern Rhythmic Gymnastic Competition

Chapter 10

RULES FOR COMPETITION

A brief summary of the general competitive rules will be given here. For more details consult the F.I.G. Code of Points—Modern Rhythmic Gymnastics which is available from the United States Gymnastic Federation, P.O. Box 4699, Tucson, Arizona 85717.

All exercises, whether compulsory or optional, are judged on a ten point scale by tenths of a point by a jury of four judges and one superior judge. The four judges give their scores independently and each score is given to the superior judge for verification. From the four scores obtained from the judges the lowest and highest are scratched and the middle two scores are averaged. The superior judge's score is not counted but the average must be in line with the score of the superior judge according to the F.I.G. point differences:

0.30 point for scores from 9.50 to 10
0.50 point for scores from 8.50 to 9.45
1.00 point in all other cases

In the finals in each event, the point differences between the scores shall not be greater than:

0.20 point for scores from 9.50 to 10
0.30 point for scores from 9.00 to 9.45
0.50 point for scores from 8.00 to 8.95
1.00 point in all other cases

If the middle scores are out of range the superior judge calls a conference and communicates her score. The middle score furthest from the score of the superior judge must adjust so that the scores fall within the accepted range. Except in finals, the judges also consult after the first exercise of each event in order to find a base score to use as a common starting point.

The six best gymnasts in the preliminary meet in each event compete in the finals. The final score is obtained by totaling the preliminary meet score with the final performance mark.

JUDGING COMPULSORY EXERCISES

A compulsory exercise may be reversed, but only in its entirety. The routines have an established list of general faults with corresponding penalties in order to be judged correctly. The ten points are divided as follows:

Four points for Composition
> 2 points for exactness and correctness of all parts of the exercise.
> 0.5 point for exactness of the orientation and the changes of place.
> 1.5 points for exactness of rhythm of the exercise.

Six points for Execution
> 1 point for elegance of the gymnast
> 1.5 points for sureness of execution
> 1.5 points for amplitude of the movements
> 1 point for coordination of the movements
> 1 point for harmony with the music

JUDGING OPTIONAL EXERCISES

The judging of the optional exercises is based on the following:

Seven points for Composition
> 5 points for difficulty
> 1 point for originality and value of combination
> 1 point for the relation between the musical accompaniment and the exercise.

Three points for Execution
> 1.5 points for execution
> 1.5 points for general impression

Difficulty—5 points
In order to receive the full five points for difficulty, a routine must

contain two superior and six medium difficulties. Each superior difficulty is worth 1.0 point and each medium receives 0.5 of a point. From these eight difficulties at least three must be performed with the left hand. Medium moves do not make up for superior difficulties.

Originality and Value of Combinations—1 point

To earn full credit for originality and value of the combinations, an exercise must contain all the recommended techniques and elements of that particular event and show original or unique combinations. Faulty combinations are: monotonous design, insufficiently used space, illogical connection of particular elements, insufficient use of hand apparatus, and the like.

Relation to Musical Accompaniment—1 point

All exercises must have musical accompaniment of one instrument. The quality of music should blend with the movement and personality of the gymnast. There is a penalty if the musical accompaniment is not one instrument, if there is no harmony between movement and music, and so on.

Execution—1.5 points

Movements performed with poor technique are penalized. Common execution errors are: rhythm breaks, unpointed toes, bent legs, loss of balance, low and heavy jumps or leaps, loss of apparatus, etc.

General Impression—1.5 points

This refers to the overall presentation of the routine. Under this area the judges look for lightness, grace, expressiveness, and ease of execution.

Duration of the Exercise

The length of the routine is one minute to one minute-thirty seconds. If the exercise is too short 0.05 point is deducted for each second it is short, if it is too long 0.3 point is deducted. This penalty is deducted from the total score.

Competition Area

The performing area is always 12 meters by 12 meters (approximately 40 feet by 40 feet). The gymnast(s) must perform within this area. In national and international meets two floor areas are provided for the competitors. They have a choice of a mat-covered area or a hardwood floor area which is marked with a border. If the gymnast steps over the boundary line she is penalized. Such a penalty is deducted by the superior judge from the average score.

Broken Hand Apparatus

If hand apparatus breaks during the course of competition the coach is authorized to supply a replacement for the damaged equipment. The penalty for this will be in proportion to the loss of rhythmic measures and to the general impression given. This rule applies to both the individual and team competition.

TEAM COMPETITION

A team must consist of six gymnasts doing an optional routine with the hand apparatus selected for competition. Length of time for team competition is from two minutes-thirty seconds to three minutes. Penalty for being over or under this time is the same as in the individual competition. In team competition, however, the team has an additional thirty seconds during which to enter the floor area. The entrance can be made with or without music. The entrance and the routine must be separate. The composition must start on the floor area. (NOTE: individual competitors cannot use music for entrance to the floor area.)

Technique and difficulty requirements in a group routine are the same as those imposed for individual exercises with the same hand apparatus. But in a group exercise four of the eight difficulties performed must involve the exchange of hand apparatus between group members. In addition, a group routine must have at least six different formations or pattern changes.

Judging Team Competition

Team competition is judged by two groups of judges. Each group of four judges has its own superior judge. One group judges the composition (5 points) and the technical value (5 points), while the other group evaluates the execution (5 points) and general harmony (5 points) of the routine. Thus, the group routine is scored from 0.0 to 20.0 points. The first group of judges looks for *what* the gymnasts do: the number of difficulties, the number and difficulty of exchanges, the number of patterns, the area covered, originality, and the like. The second group of judges looks for *how* the gymnasts perform the routine: rhythmical faults, lightness of execution, preciseness of patterns, individual and group faults, etc.

SUGGESTIONS FOR LOCAL MEETS

Because it is difficult to obtain qualified judges for local or nonchampionship meets, the number of judges may be less than the required five used for championships meets. In most school or local meets there are two judges. In this case the judges' scores are averaged, and the average becomes the official score. One of the two judges should be designated as the superior judge. It is her duty to see that the two scores are within range and she makes the final decision in all cases of disagreement.

Another approach has also been used very successfully for school dual meets. This method is called the *Flag Meet*. In a Flag Meet judging is not based on a ten point scale but rather on the fact that one gymnast is better than the other. Two team members are ranked for each event: the number six girl on team A competes against the number six girl on team B, the number five girl of team A against the number five girl of team B, and so on. Three judges make a decision as to which gymnast is better after both competitors have performed their routines. Each judge has two flags, an A and a B. Upon the signal from the superior judge, they flash their choice simultaneously. Since there are three judges there are no ties. With this system, one can use as judges people who have limited backgrounds in modern rhythmic gymnastics. These people do not have to know the F.I.G. point system of evaluation for modern rhythmic gymnastics, they need only appreciate the form, harmony of composition, feminine grace, and the difficulty of the exercise and then make a decision as to which of the two performers is better.

Sometimes it is hard for people with limited backgrounds in modern rhythmic gymnastics to recognize the difficulties in a routine. A solution to this problem is to ask the coach or the gymnast to list the difficulties in the routines prior to the meet. This can make judging a much easier task. The form on which to list difficulties should be sent out with the invitation letter and entry form. See page 367 for a sample form.

This system of listing difficulties also can be used very successfully with traditional scoring when you must use relatively inexperienced judges who still have difficulty recognizing the many different medium and superior movements. However, it should be remembered that only moves which are completed or almost completed should receive credit.

ORGANIZING AN MRG MEET

Organizing and running a good and efficient modern rhythmic gymnastic meet is not easy. The host school or club must be responsible for many details if the meet is to run smoothly. There is much organization necessary prior to the meet, at the meet, and following the meet. Each of these will be discussed separately to help you if you are directing a modern rhythmic gymnastic meet at your school or club.

PLANNING THE MEET

1. Plan the time, place, program and budget for all expenses well in advance.

   Place: The gymnasium where the meet is to be held must be large enough to accommodate two competitive floor areas and to allow ample room for judges and scorers. The height of the gymnasium must be at least six meters (19.7 feet). For dual or local meets the use of one area on which the girls are accustomed to work is sufficient. The gymnasium should be reserved months in advance and publicity sent out at least one month before the meet.

   Budget: The entry fee should cover all expenses of the meet. Usual expenses are judges fees, ribbons or medals for the winners, janitorial services, and miscellaneous expenses such as paper and postage.

2. *Invitations* should be sent out at least a month in advance, preferably earlier. The notice should state date, time, place, type of meet (compulsory or optional), entry fee, deadlines for entries, name and address of the meet director, and any other special information required. An entry blank should accompany the invitational letter. See the sample invitation letter on page 368 and the sample entry blank on page 369.

3. *Meet Personnel*

   1 meet director: Assumes responsibility for the overall organization of the meet. Decides upon the place and time; arrangement of floor space, chairs, etc.; notifies schools and clubs of time and place and sends them entry blanks; orders awards; organizes the sequence of events and order of the contestants; procures officials; and so on.

   1 meet referee: Sees that all the rules and regulations are enforced; meets with the judges prior to the meet to discuss the common basis from which to rate the performances; checks all hand apparatus used in the meet to be sure they meet requirements; rules on all protests. In a small meet, the duties of the referee may be assumed by the superior judge in addition to her own assignments.

   1 or 2 superior judges: This will depend on the number of events run at one time. Gives signal to gymnast to begin her exercise, calls a conference after the first routine to help the other judges arrive at a common basis for scoring; checks to see that the two middle scores fall within the proper range indicated by her own score; supervises the

timers; deducts from the average score, if necessary, for time infractions and stepping out of boundary lines; may also take on the duties of meet referee in a small meet.

2 to 8 judges: Depending on the number of events run at one time and whether the superior judge is also used as one of the judges. Score each performance conscientiously and impartially.

2 to 4 line judges: Depending on the number of floor areas. Raises flag to notify the head judge any time a gymnast steps over the boundary line; keeps the flag raised until the head judge signals that she has made note of it.

3 scorers (1 chief scorer and 2 assistants): Record all scores; average the scores; calculate the results; total the scores for the all-around event.

1 to 4 timers: Time the routines to make sure they are within the time limit; give warning signal at one minute and twenty-five seconds and a second signal at one minute and thirty seconds in individual competition. In team competition, give a signal during the entrance at the twenty-fifth and at the thirtieth second, and during the routine at two minutes and fifty-five seconds and a final signal at three minutes.

1 to 2 flashers: Flash the official or average score.

2 to 9 runners: Depending on the number of judges. Take judges' score to the superior judge after each performance, then to the head table.

1 announcer: Keeps the meet moving by informing the competitors of the line-up, explains what the sport is about to the audience and keeps them interested in the meet.

Other personnel: Depending on the type of meet:

    locker room attendant
    nurse or doctor on call in case of emergency
    music monitor
    photographer
    people to organize performers
    program seller or distributor
    ticket seller
    ticket checkers at the doors

4. *Score sheets* should be prepared before the meet after names have been drawn to determine the order of the performers. Score sheets, such as those shown on pages 370 and 371, should be available to the judges, the scorers, and the coaches of the participating teams. The score sheets illustrated are based upon the premise that the superior judge is also used as one of the judges.

5. *Judge's worksheets* should also be prepared prior to the meet. It is helpful to have different colored worksheets for different events. For example, you might use white for ball, yellow for rope, green for ribbon, and pink for hoop. A sample judge's worksheet is shown on page 371.

6. *Items to check a few days before the meet:*

   1. Confirm your reservation for the gymnasium.
   2. Write to the judges reminding them of the time, place, and giving any special instructions necessary.
   3. Send reminders to the scorers, flashers, etc.
   4. Prepare checks for the judges, nurse, and other paid personnel.
   5. Prepare duty lists for personnel—this will prevent confusion during the meet.
   6. Make copies of the final order of the competition.
   7. Make copies of the judge's worksheets.
   8. The announcer's sheet should be completed.
   9. Prepare programs for spectators.
   10. Arrange for parking.
   11. Appoint a jury of appeal to handle protests. This usually includes the meet director, the referee, and the superior judge for the apparatus concerned.
   12. Prepare a floor plan showing the way in which the gymnasium is to be set up. The following example floor plan is based upon the premise that there are:
       a) Two areas, one with a mat and one without, available to the gymnasts.
       b) Two groups of four judges, each with a head judge, one referee and a meet director.
       c) Three line judges.
       d) Five runners.

e) Two timers.
f) Three scorers.
g) One flasher.
h) One announcer.

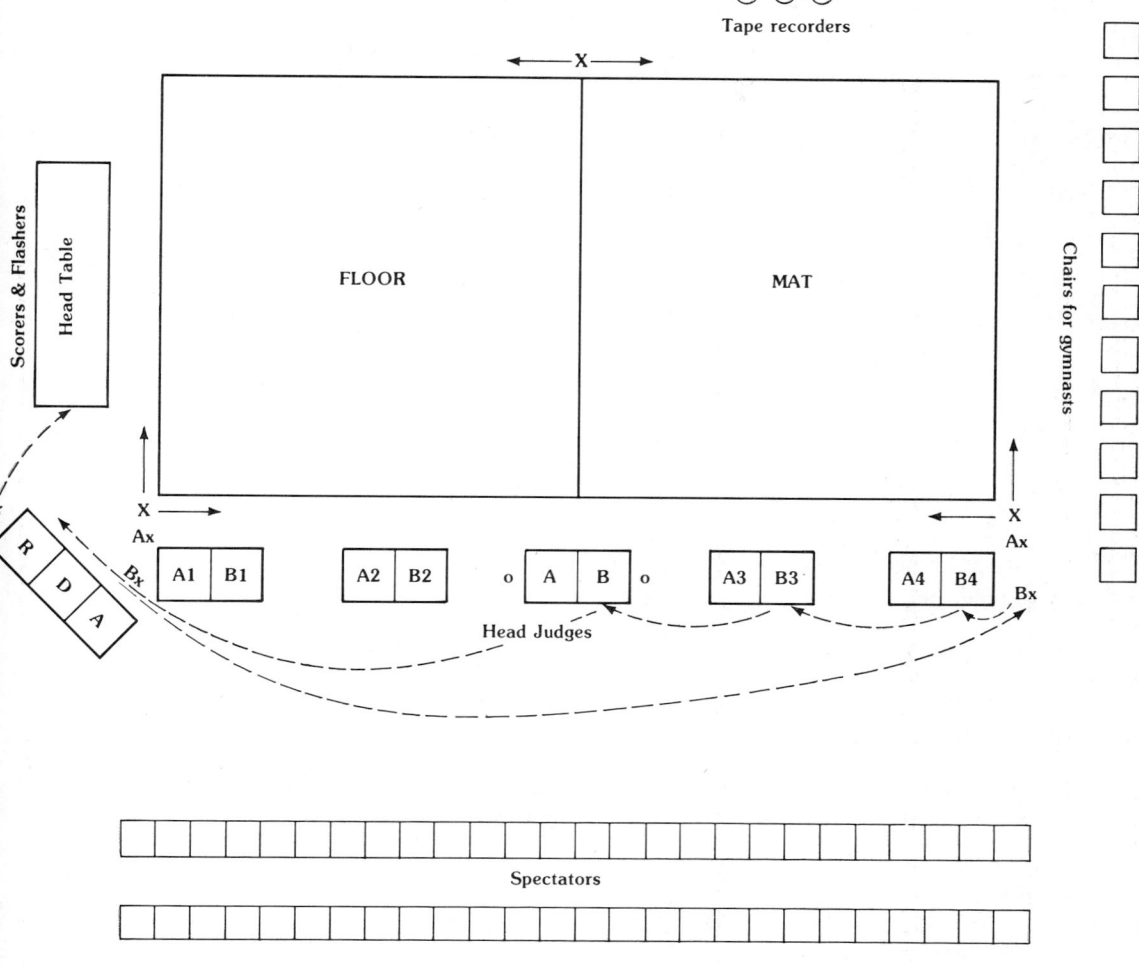

A: group A judges
B: group B judges
o: timers
x: line judges
Ax: runners for A judges

Bx: runners for B judges
Rx: runner for referee
R: referee
D: meet director
A: announcer

In this arrangement, group A judges evaluate the ball routines and group B judges evaluate the rope exercises. Gymnasts alternate: one performs ball, the next rope, and so on. This is a very efficient way to run a meet because it allows one group of judges to evaluate the performed ball routine while the other group judges the next gymnast's rope routine. This way the competition can run smoothly with no stops which makes it more enjoyable for both participants and spectators.

PREPARATION ON THE DAY OF THE MEET

1. Set up the gymnasium as shown on the floor plan and make final check of all preparations.
2. Mark the boundaries of the floor areas.
3. Place the judges' worksheets, pencils, and paychecks on their chairs.
4. Place the stop watches on the timers' chairs.
5. Place the flash card on the flasher's chair.
6. Place a score sheet on judges', scorers', referees', meet director's, and announcer's chairs.
7. Present all helpers with a list of their duties.
8. Distribute the order of competition to the coaches and participants.
9. Check the hand apparatus (weighing and measuring) of each contestant one hour prior to the competition.
10. Meet with the judges and coaches a half hour before the meet to answer any questions.

PROCEDURES IN THE ACTUAL MEET

1. Start the meet promptly.
2. The meet should start with a march of all the contestants, led by flag bearers. A suitable march should be played. This should be followed by a salute to the flag and the National Anthem.
3. The meet director welcomes the audience and the participants.
4. The announcer then makes a statement regarding the procedures for the meet—i.e., where the warm-up area is, which events are to be called and in what sequence. All pertinent information should be announced, including intermission.

5. Awarding of ribbons or medals at the completion of the meet. speaker.
6. At the conclusion of the award ceremony the meet director should thank the judges and all the other assistants for making the meet successful and thank the spectators and gymnasts for coming.

POST-MEET DUTIES

1. After the meet run off the results and send the participating schools or clubs a copy.
2. Publicize the meet by giving the final results, photographs, and a general statement regarding the meet to school papers, local papers, and gymnastic magazines.

Sample Form

Moves of Difficulty to be Included in the Routine

Name _____ No. _____ Event _____

Fill out before arriving at meet. Should be handed in to the head table by the coach upon arrival.

Refer to the current edition of the F.I.G. Code of Points for a listing of medium and superior difficulties.

Medium Moves

1. _____
2. _____
3. _____
4. _____
5. _____
6. _____
_____
_____

Superior Moves

1. _____
2. _____
_____

367
Modern Rhythmic Gymnastic Competition

Sample Invitational Letter

MODERN RHYTHMIC GYMNASTIC COMPETITION
Sponsored by the
United States Gymnastic Federation

Date: Saturday, May 11, 1974

Time: 10:00 a.m. (warm-up 9:00 a.m.)

Place: San Francisco State University
1600 Holloway Avenue
San Francisco, California 94132

Gymnasium in Physical Education Building

Eligibility: Girls 14 years or over

Entry fee: $2.00 per gymnast for each event

Events: Individual Optional Routines with:

1. Ball   3. Ribbon
2. Jump Rope   4. Hoop

Gymnasts may enter from 2 to 4 of the above events. The all-around award will be based on scores earned in all four events.

Requirements: 2 superior difficulties
6 medium difficulties
At least 3 difficulties must be performed with the left hand.

Musical accompaniment: Only taped *piano* recordings may be used. One tape for each gymnast and for each exercise. The speed of the tape, the name of the gymnast and the event must be printed on the tape. Tape recorder will be provided.

For further information on rules see Code of Points for Modern Rhythmic Gymnastics. It can be purchased from USGF, P.O. Box 4699, Tucson, Arizona 85717 for $2.50.

Registration deadline is *April 30, 1974*

Send registration and entry fee to:

Prof. Andrea B. Schmid
Women's Physical Education Dept.
1600 Holloway Ave.
San Francisco, Calif. 94132

Please bring your own locks and towels.

Sample Entry Blank

MODERN RHYTHMIC GYMNASTIC MEET
Saturday, May 11, 1974

School or club affiliation _____

Address _____
        Street   City   State   Zip Code

Teacher or coach name _____

Entry deadline: April 30, 1974

Enclose entry fee of $2.00 per gymnast for each event.

Name	Age	Ball	Rope	Ribbon	Hoop	Fee
Sue Perkins	15		X	X		*$4.00*
Nancy Smith	18	X	X	X	X	*$8.00*

                                                Total remittance   *$12.00*

Mail to: Prof. Andrea B. Schmid
         Women's Physical Education Dept.
         San Francisco State University
         San Francisco, Calif. 94132

Sample Score Sheet—Single Event

MODERN RHYTHMIC GYMNASTIC MEET
San Francisco State University
May 11, 1974

Event: *BALL*

Judges:

Superior: *Karen Moore*

2: *Marie Perkins*

3: *Edith Miller*

4: *Kathy Johnson*

Name	Number	Judges score 1	2	3	4	Official Score	Place
1. Janice Green	20	~~5.8~~	~~6.1~~	5.9	6.5	6.2	2
2. Nancy Smith	7	5.6	5.4	~~5.3~~	~~5.6~~	5.5	3
3. Julie Ng	14	7.0	~~6.1~~	6.8	~~7.1~~	6.9	1
4.							

Sample Score Sheet—All-Around Events

MODERN RHYTHMIC GYMNASTIC MEET
San Francisco State University
May 11, 1974

Event: ALL AROUND

Name	Number	Ball	Rope	Ribbon	Hoop	Total Score	Place
Janice Green	20	6.2	7.0	6.5	6.4	26.1	2
Nancy Smith	7	5.5	7.0	6.8	7.5	26.8	1
Julie Ng	14	6.9	5.9	6.5	6.7	26.0	3

Sample Judge's Worksheet—Optional Exercise

Scratch Area

Event _____

Gymnast _____

COMPOSITION—7 pts.:

Elements of difficulty (5) _____

Originality & tech. value (1) _____

Relation to accompaniment (1) _____

EXECUTION—3 pts.:

Execution (1.5) _____

General impression (1.5) _____

_____
Judge's signature

FINAL SCORE _____

Glossary

Alternate circles One arm circles in the opposite direction from the other arm.

Amplitude The ability to perform a movement with the fullest range of extension of all parts of the body.

Arabesque A position in which one leg is extended back; position of arms varies.

Asymmetrical circles Performing one type of circle with one arm, and at the same time executing another type of circle with the other arm.

Attitude A position in which one leg is raised with knee bent, either in back or front of the body.

Axis An imaginary straight line around which the hand apparatus or body rotates.

Balance Ability to keep the center of gravity over the base of support and to maintain equilibrium.

Balancé A rocking step usually in 3/4 time.

Body wave Wave-like movement going through the entire body. It may be performed in the forward, backward, or sideward direction.

Cabriolé A jump in which the legs beat together in the air.

Cat leap Also called *pas de chat;* a traveling jump in which first one bent leg and then the other is raised. The bent legs pass each other in the air.

Chaînés A series of half turns on the balls of the feet.

Changement Changing of the feet in the air by jumping from fifth position to fifth position.

Chassé A step in which one foot chases the other.

Code of points The international book of rules for judging of gymnastics competitions.

Composition A planned continuous series of movements.

Compulsory exercise A prescribed set of exercises required of all competitors in a given event.

Curled arm From a front or side arm extension, turning the palm downward, inward, and upward.

Diagonal plane Also called *oblique plane;* imaginary division of the body diagonally from one shoulder to opposite hip. Movements "in diagonal plane" are performed parallel to this plane.

Difficulty The rating of a skill or series of skills by the International Gymnastic Federation (F.I.G.).

Double-folded rope A quadrupled rope.

Doubled rope Rope folded once.

F.I.G. Federation of International Gymnastics.

Frontal plane Imaginary division of the body into front and rear halves. Movements "in frontal plane" are performed parallel to this plane either in front of or in back of the body.

Front stride A position in which one leg is extended forward and the other leg backward. Legs are separated about a length of a large step.

Gallop An exaggerated series of slides.

Glissade A gliding step usually done in preparation for a jump or leap.

Grip The hand-hold that the gymnast has on the hand apparatus. It varies with the type of movement being performed. *See:* Regular Grip and Reverse Grip.

Horizontal plane Parallel to the floor.

Inward circle Start the circling exercises either downward or forward, depending on type of movement.

Inward turn Turning in the direction of the supporting leg.

I.O.C. International Olympic Committee.
Jump A spring into the air from two feet.
Lateral Side, sideways.
Lateral plane *See:* Sagittal Plane.
Leap A jump from one foot onto the other foot.
Long axis An imaginary line running vertically through the center of the body.
Lunge A standing, front stride position in which the forward knee is bent and the other leg is straight.
Medium difficulty An intermediate skill which in competition receives 0.5 point for its completion.
Mill circles Arms "chase" each other in a windmill fashion. The arms are 180° apart.
M.R.G. Modern rhythmic gymnastics.
Oblique plane *See:* Diagonal Plane.
Optional exercise A routine composed by the individual from movements of her own choice.
Outward circle Start the circling exercises either upward or backward, depending upon the type of movement.
Outward turn Turning in the direction of the raised leg.
Over grip *See:* Regular Grip.
Pirouette A complete turn on one leg.
Plane Imaginary, two-dimensional surface in which movements are performed. There are the sagittal, frontal, horizontal, and diagonal planes.
Plié Bending of the knee or knees.
Polka A dance step performed in uneven rhythm with hop-step, close-step pattern.
Pose Esthetically pleasing momentarily held position.
Positions of the feet There are five basic ballet positions of the feet: first, second, third, fourth and fifth position.
Pronation Position of the hand or lower arm is toward the body with the palm down.
Quadrupled rope A double folded rope.
Regular grip Also called *overgrip;* palm of the hand faces downward
Reverse grip Also called *undergrip;* palm of hand faces upward.
Routine An arrangement of movements, combined according to the

ability of the gymnast and the competitive rules, that a gymnast performs in a competition.

Sagittal plane   Also called *lateral plane;* imaginary division of the body into right and left halves. Movements "in sagittal plane" are performed parallel to this plane on either side of the body.

Scale   A balanced position on one leg with the other leg raised backward and the upper body lowered slightly forward; position of arms varies.

Scissor kick   Also called *hitchkick* or *pas de ciseaux;* a jump, in which both straight legs pass each other in the air.

Schottische   A dance step performed in even rhythm with step-step-step-hop pattern.

Skip   A series of fast step-hops taken with alternate feet. The rhythm is uneven.

Slide   Usually in gymnastics is referred to as a *glissade* or *chassé;* ordinarily it is done sideward.

Split   A position in which one leg is extended forward, the other leg is extended backward at right angles to the trunk.

Squat   A position in which the knees are bent and the heels are close to the buttocks.

Stag leap   Front leg bent and the other leg extended backward in the air.

Step-hop   A step followed by a hop on the same foot. The rhythm is even.

Straddle   A position in which the legs are separated sideways.

Superior difficulty   An advanced skill which in competition receives 1.0 point for its completion.

Supination   Position of the hand or lower arm is away from the body with the palm up.

Tour jeté   A jump with a half turn in which weight is transferred from one foot to the other.

Tuck   A position in which the knees are bent and are close to the chest.

Under grip   *See:* Reverse Grip.

U.S.G.F.   United States Gymnastics Federation.

Vertical   Perpendicular to the floor.

Waltz walk   Walking steps in a 3/4 rhythm emphasizing the first count.

Bibliography

Books

Balazs, Eva. *Gymnastique Moderne I—Rhythmic Rope Jumping.* Waldwick, N.J.: Hoctor Publications, 1970

———. *Gymnastique Moderne II—Rhythmic Gymnastics with Hoops.* Waldwick, N.J.: Hoctor Publications, 1971.

———. *Gymnastique Moderne III—Rhythmic Gymnastics with Balls.* Waldwick, N.J.: Hoctor Publications, 1971.

———. *Gymnastique Moderne IV—Rhythmic Gymnastics with Indian Club Streamers, Shawls and Pennants.* Waldwick, N.J.: Hoctor Publications, 1971.

Bode, Rudolf. *Rhythmische Gymnastik.* Frankfurt am Main: Wilhelm Limpert—Verlag, 1957. (Written in German.)

Bowers, Carolyn O. (ed.). *DGWS Selected Gymnastics Articles.* Washington, D.C.: American Association for Health, Physical Education and Recreation, 1971.

Brown, Margaret C., Sommer, Betty K. *Movement Education: Its Evolution and a Modern Approach.* Reading, Mass.: Addison-Wesley Publishing Co., 1969.

Carlquist, Maja. *Rhythmical Gymnastics.* Trans. by Roper, Reginald E. and others. London: Methuen Co. Ltd., 1955.

Chamberlin, Vesper. *How to Twirl a Baton.* New York: Statler Records, Inc., 1963.

Cochrane, Tuovi S. *International Gymnastics for Girls and Women.* Reading, Mass.: Addison-Wesley Publishing Co., 1969.

Drury, Blanche J., Schmid, Andrea B. *Gymnastics for Women.* Third Edition. Palo Alto, Calif.: Mayfield Publishing Company, 1970.

Exercise avec deux massues, imposé, pour le Ve Championat du Monde de Gymnastique rhythmique moderne 1973 (Compulsory Exercise with Clubs for 1973 World's Championships). Fédération Internationale de Gymnastique, 1973. (Written in French.)

F.I.G. Code of Points—Modern Gymnastics. Women's Technical Committee—Committee for Modern Gymnastics, 1970.

F.I.G. Liste des résultats (since 1948). Fédération Internationale de Gymnastique. (Written in French.)

Fourth Championships of the World Gymnastique Moderne, Varna, Bulgaria, 1969. Tucson, Arizona: United States Gymnastics Federation, 1969.

Grant, Gail. Technical Manual and Dictionary of Classical Ballet. Second Edition. New York: Dover Publications, Inc., 1967.

Hammond, Sandra N. *Ballet Basics.* Palo Alto, Ca.: Mayfield Publishing Company, 1974.

Heinss, Melitta. *Künstlerische Gymnastik für Kinder* (Artistic Gymnastics for Children). Berlin: Sportverlag, 1970. (Written in German.)

Hendershott, Renée. *Fundamental Aspects of Control and Placement and Progressive Ballet Barre for the Gymnast.* Lakewood, Ohio: Hendershott, 1969.

Herold, Wolfram, Fluch, Dorle. *Turn Sprache Deutsch* (German Gymnastic Language). Celle, Germany: Pohl-Druckerei und Velagsanstalt, 1972. (Written in German.)

Jacquot, Andrée. *Gymnastique Moderne.* Second Edition. Paris: Éditions Amphora, 1971. (Written in French.)

Keleti, Ágnes, Kovács, Éva F. *Müvészitorna* (Artistic Gymnastics). Budapest: Sport Lap és Könyvkiadó, 1953. (Written in Hungarian.)

Kerezsi, Endre. *Gymnasztika.* Third Edition. Budapest: Sport, 1968. (Written in Hungarian.)

Medau, Hinrich. *Moderne Gymnastik Lehrweise Medau.* Celle, Germany: Verlag Pohl-Druckerei und Verlagsanstalt, 1967. (Written in German.)

Prchal, Mildred (compiler). *Modern Rhythmic Gymnastics Competitive Exercises for III, II, I Classes.* Tucson, Arizona: United States Gymnastics Federation, 1974.

Réglements de III e Championat du Monde de Gymnastique Moderne. (Rules for the Third World's Championships) Copenhagen: Kristensen, 1967. (Written in French.)

Rice, Emmett A., Hutchinson, John L. and Lee, Mabel. *A Brief History of Physical Education.* Fifth Edition. New York: The Ronald Press Company, 1969.

Schmid, Andrea B. (ed.). *DGWS Gymnastics Guide.* Washington, D.C.: American Association for Health, Physical Education and Recreation, 1971.

Shanet, Howard. *Learn to Read Music.* New York: Simon and Schuster, 1962.

Sherbon, Elizabeth. *On the Count of One.* Second Edition. Palo Alto, Ca.: Mayfield Publishing Company, 1975.

Van Dalen, Deobold B., Mitchell, Elmer D. and Bennett, Bruce L. *A World History of Physical Education.* Englewood Cliffs, N.J.: Prentice-Hall, Inc., 1961.

Wallace, Lu (ed.). *DGWS Gymnastics Guide.* Washington, D.C.: American Association for Health, Physical Education and Recreation, 1973.

Wendt, Hildegard, Hess, Ruth. *Künstlerische Gymnastik mit Handgeräten.* (Artistic Gymnastics with Hand Apparatus.) Berlin: Sportverlag, 1971. (Written in German.)

Zabka, Norma B. (ed.). *DGWS Gymnastic Guide.* Washington, D.C.: American Association for Health, Physical Education and Recreation, 1965.

Periodicals

Federation Internationale de Gymnastique Bulletin. (Written in French and English.) USGF, P.O. Box 4699, Tucson, Arizona 85717.

Gymnast. Sundby Publications, P.O. Box 110, Santa Monica, Ca. 90406.

Mademoiselle Gymnast. Sunby Publications, P.O. Box 777, Santa Monica, Ca. 90406.

Olympische Turnkunst. Pohl-Druckerei und Verlagsanstalt Otto Pohl, 31 Celle, Postfach 103, Germany. (Written in German, English and French.)

Other Sources

Cerna, Kveta. Member of the F.I.G. Modern Rhythmic Gymnastic Commission. Personal notes from Judging Clinic directed by Mme. Cerna at Northeastern University, Chicago, Illinois, May 21–May 23, 1974.

Foerster, Irmgard. Member of the F.I.G. Modern Rhythmic Gymnastic Commission. Personal Interviews, Düsseldorf, Germany, May 28–June 1, 1972.

Nagy, Valérie H. President of the F.I.G. Women's Technical Committee. Personal letters.

Personal notes from Intercontinental Modern Rhythmic Gymnastics Judging Course, Madrid, Spain, February 20–26, 1975.

1547-6
22-66